Vossische Zeitung
Amerikas neuer Präsident
Abrüstung
B.Z. am Mittag
Der Reise-Rekord des englischen Thronfolgers
Die größte Auto-Schau am Kaiserdamm eröffnet
Tempo
Präsident Hoovers erste Rede: „Rüstet endlich ab!"
Berliner Morgenpost
Macht Platz für Stresemann!
Berliner Montagspost
Mit ausführlichen Sportberichten
Begeisterter Flieger-Empfang in New York.
Die Grüne Post
Sonntagszeitung für Stadt und Land
Norddeutsche Allgemeine Zeitung
Thronverzicht Kaiser Wilhelms II.
Aufruf zur Nationalversammlung.
Die Internationale
Arbeiter! Soldaten! Genossen! Brüder!
Ebert Reichskanzler.

BY WOLF VON ECKARDT

Mid-Century Architecture in America
(editor)

The Challenge of Megalopolis

Eric Mendelsohn
(Masters of World Architecture series)

Life for Dead Spaces
(with Charles M. Goodman)

A Place to Live: The Crisis of the Cities

BY SANDER L. GILMAN

Johannes Agricola von Eisleben, Die Sprichwörtersammlungen (editor)

Form und Funktion: Eine strukturelle Untersuchung der Romane Klabunds

NS-Literaturtheorie (editor)

The Parodic Sermon in European Perspective: Aspects of Liturgical Parody from the Middle Ages to the Twentieth Century

BERTOLT BRECHT'S BERLIN

WOLF VON ECKARDT
& SANDER L. GILMAN

BERTOLT BRECHT'S BERLIN *A Scrapbook of the Twenties*

1975

Anchor Press/Doubleday Garden City, New York

Grateful acknowledgment is made to the following for permission to reprint copyrighted material: selections from the works of Bertolt Brecht, reprinted with the permission of Pantheon Books, a division of Random House; selections from the diaries of Harry Kessler, Holt, Rinehart and Winston; selections from the essays of Heinrich Mann, Aufbau Verlag; selections from the works of Erich Kästner, Atrium Verlag; selections from the poetry of Gottfried Benn, Limes Verlag; selections from the works of Alfred Döblin, Walter Verlag; selections from the essays of Carl von Ossietzsky, Aufbau Verlag; selections from E. Kurt Fischer, *Dokumente zur Geschichte des deutschen Rundfunks und Fernschens,* Musterschmidt Verlag; selections from the diaries of Käthe Kollwitz, Gebr. Mann Verlag; selections from the letters of Max Reinhardt, Georg Prachner Verlag; selections from the essays of Alfred Kerr, Kiepenheuer & Witsch Verlag; selections from the letters of Alban Berg, Albert Langen-Georg Müller Verlag; selections from the works of Ernst Krenek, Albert Langen-Georg Müller Verlag; selections from the writings of "tusk," Südmarkverlag Fritsch; quotations from the writings of Werner Hensel, Bärenreiter Verlag; quotations from Werner Helwig, *Die blaue des Wandervögels,* Sigbert Mohn Verlag; quotations from Werner Kindt, *Grundschriften der deutschen Jugendbewegung,* Eugen Diedrichs Verlag; selections from Hermann Kesten's letters, Kurt Desch Verlag. In addition, we wish to acknowledge the use of all other copyrighted material noted in the documentation. Through the confusion of war and the division of Germany, it was impossible to trace the owners of some of the material used. We hereby thank those authors whom we were otherwise unable to find.

Library of Congress Cataloging in Publication Data
Von Eckardt, Wolf.
Bertolt Brecht's Berlin.
Includes bibliographical references.
1. Berlin—Social conditions. 2. Berlin—Popular culture. I. Gilman, Sander L., joint author. II. Title.
HN458.B4V65 309.1'43'155
ISBN 0-385-05501-3
Library of Congress Catalog Card Number 73-9153

PRINTED IN THE UNITED STATES OF AMERICA
FIRST EDITION

For Wolf's mother and Sander's wife

We are deeply grateful to Michael Morley, Senior Lecturer in German, University of Auckland, New Zealand, for his help at the Brecht Archive in East Berlin; to Marilyn Fries, for her aid in the search of West Berlin archives; to Heinz Politzer, Professor of German at the University of California at Berkeley, for his aid and comfort; to Ernst Offermanns, for the use of materials from his collection of Berlin memorabilia; to the John Simon Guggenheim Memorial Foundation for helping finance a study year during which much of the research for this book was undertaken; to all the personnel at the various archives and libraries in Germany, East and West, as well as in the United States, for their aid; to Dorothy Sutton for the cheerful and attentive accuracy with which she prepared the manuscript; and to Judith Martin for her sharp pencil and even sharper mind with which she improved and encouraged this effort.

W.V.E. *and* S.L.G.

CONTENTS

	INTRODUCTION: *"Thank You, Hitler"*—by Wolf Von Eckardt	xiii
1	REVOLUTION: *"Workers! Soldiers! Comrades! Brothers!"*	1
2	INFLATION: *The Revolution of Values*	13
3	AFTER HOURS: *Bright Lights and Dark Magnets*	21
4	THE UNDERWORLD: *Whores, Dope, and "Wrestling Clubs"*	33
5	THE INTELLECTUALS: *Soft Eggs, Satire, and Forebodings*	41
6	NEWSPAPERS AND RADIO: *Much Heat and Little Light*	49
7	ART: *Manifestoes at the Crossroad*	61
8	THEATER: *Poesy, Stairs, and Morality Suspended*	77
9	FILM: *Magic, Mountains, and Mirrors*	91
10	MUSIC AND DANCE: *. . . And All That Jazz*	107
11	ARCHITECTURE: *"The Crystal Palace of a New Faith"*	117
12	SPORTS: *Mens Politica in Corpore Sano, and Horses, too*	129
13	YOUTH: *The Greening That Turned Brown*	139
14	COLLAPSE: *No Jobs but a Storm of Heils*	147
	NOTES	157
	BIBLIOGRAPHY	161
	INDEX	163

INTRODUCTION: *"Thank You, Hitler"*

Bertolt Brecht, about 1930 [*Brecht Archiv, East Berlin*]

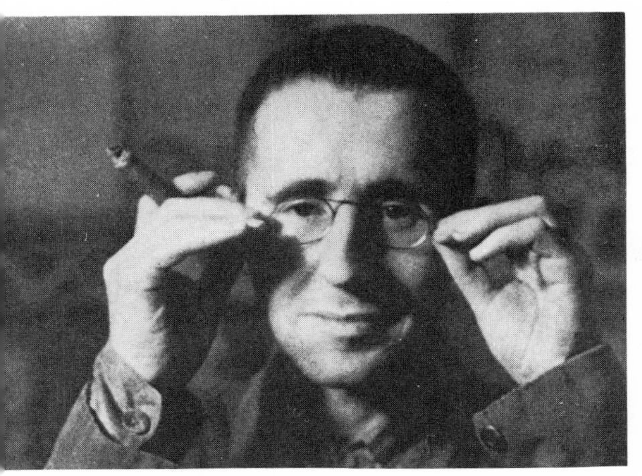

By the time I arrived, the party was over. Some people had already left or, worse, disappeared. Others we knew were looking for the exit.

But the trappings were still there and so were some staling leftovers. The famous cafés were still famous—though you didn't ask where the prominent guests had gone. The old cabarets were still playing—though the political jokes were veiled or whispered. The theaters were still bright—though they performed mostly safe classics. The concert halls had lost some of their best performers. The best books had been burned. In the art galleries were empty spots where the "degenerate" paintings had been removed.

It was 1934. I was sixteen. Berlin was still Berlin.

I could still get an idea of what that great binge had been like. It wasn't really busted. There was a new government. Stormtroopers marched through the streets, shouting, "Germany, wake up!" Their noisy brass bands drowned out the old tunes. The party sort of petered out, dazed and hung over, in that awful dawn of Hitler's Third Reich.

It wasn't our Reich. I didn't know any Nazis, except Helene, my mother's red-haired Pomeranian maid. It was as though we were occupied by a foreign power. There was still life under that occupation. My father and I played our *Threepenny Opera*

Flower vendor at Leipziger Platz [*Landesbildstelle, West Berlin*]

records over and over again. But we would first carefully close the windows and turn the record player down.

Pirate Jenny and Mack the Knife came out of London, of course. But the airs of their songs and their antics, their enthusiastic cynicism, reflected—to me, at least—the airs and the antics and the enthusiastic cynicism of Berlin between the Kaiser and Hitler. Kurt Weill's music and Bertolt Brecht's lyrics, I dare say, could only have been written at that time and place. That explains the title of this printed documentary. This book is not about Bert Brecht. It is not about the playwright, but his stage. It is about Bert Brecht's *Berlin*.

I was born in Berlin just before the 1918 revolution. But I was brought up in Heidelberg, where my father was a professor, as well as in a boarding school near the Lake of Constance. I had visited Berlin on occasional vacations, but these excursions, though they had their memorable moments, gave me only a child's perspective of the place. The zoo and that sort of thing. I experienced the city only after my father had the distinction of being one of the first university professors to be dismissed by the Nazis. Some of the brownshirts who repeatedly searched our Heidelberg home at dawn and burned his books late at night had been his students. He moved to Berlin because the capital promised relative anonymity. I was taken out of that expensive boarding school because we were suddenly poor. You see so much more when you are poor.

We lived on Wichmannstrasse in what was later called "inner exile." My father worked for a clock manufacturer who had the guts to hire him. Our apartment was in a slightly ramshackle middle-class Berlin tenement. Most of Berlin's middle-class apartment houses were tenements. They were designed not by architects but by the Imperial Prussian Police Department. You had to go through the bedroom to get through a long, narrow corridor into the kitchen. That's why I seldom had breakfast in those days. I had to punch the time clock at my job before seven and I did not want to wake up my father and Marianne, his second wife. Sometimes, God forgive me, on my way down that dark staircase I sneaked a roll or even a bottle of milk that had been delivered to one of the apartments below. It seemed part of the *Threepenny Opera* ethic.

I bicycled to my job with Pass & Garleb, a large printing firm on Bülowstrasse. To get there I passed the movie palaces that had played *The Blue Angel* and *Girls in Uniform* and were now playing *Hitlerjunge Quex*, a tearjerker about a Hitler Youth. The Femina, the big night club, which had displayed pictures of smiling, near-naked girls on its billboards, now featured tense-looking Italian jugglers. The new Reich Chancellor did not approve of decadent burlesque, you see. But he liked Mussolini.

Pass & Garleb, where I served as an apprentice, paid me seven marks fifty a week the first year and twelve marks the second. It was enough for cigarettes and lunch, flowers for an occasional girl, and pickled cucumbers at the Wannsee beach on Sundays. At Wannsee everyone ate cucumbers pickled in a place called Lübbenau.

Bicycling is the best way to be one with the pulse of the city, particularly early, when the city, too, is getting itself into motion. The shopkeepers pulled up their iron shutters. The girls dashed out of the entrance halls, very rushed and earnest until they would suddenly smile to themselves over

Gossip in front of a bakery [*Staatsbibliothek, West Berlin*]

some memory of the night before. The streetcar bells had a more poignant ring than they did in the day's later din.

Walking into the Pass & Garleb composing room was like walking back into the Weimar Republic. The typesetters were mostly old and all of them were socialist labor union men. They would send me out for rolls and milk—that was part of the apprenticeship. Sometimes they were gruff. "Turn around when you talk to me," old Mr. Keesbeck would yell at me, "or is that your face?" Berliners have that kind of humor. I soon learned not to be afraid of them because they all had socialist hearts and were never unfair. More importantly, under the circumstances, *they* soon learned not to be afraid of *me*, that whippersnapper with the aristocratic "von" in his name. I couldn't tell them, of course, that my mother was Jewish and had gone to America, that my father's second wife was half-Jewish, and that his books had been burned. Mr. Garleb had taken me on reluctantly enough. But Mr. Keesbeck learned to trust me after a while. I guess he noticed that I, too, rushed to the men's room when I saw the Nazi shop steward come strutting through the composing room so I wouldn't have to say "Heil Hitler." We smoked in the men's room and, cautiously, Keesbeck would feel increasingly free to reminisce for me about the old days that suddenly seemed good, now that everything was bad. He talked about the inflation and the street battles with the Commies and Stormtroopers. We would exchange the latest anti-Nazi jokes, like the one about Karl Valentin, the Munich comedian, who, even while the big Nazi rally was going on in Nuremberg, rushed in front of the curtain, raised his right arm and yelled: "*Heil* . . . dammit, now I forgot his name!"

But not for a minute could anyone really forget that name. All too often, one of the old typesetters failed to show up in the morning. We all knew what happened, though no one ever mentioned it. The place was called Oranienburg and was the first concentration camp, not far from Berlin. Some men came back after a couple of weeks or so, terribly thin and terribly silent. We tried to pretend that we had not even noticed their absence.

A few times I went out on weekend hiking excursions into the woods with a youth group. It had been part of the Eberhard Köbel's Jungenschaft, the most progressive wing of the youth movement, and had somehow managed to stay together although, or perhaps because, it had nominally joined the Hitler Youth. We pitched tents in a secluded forest, lit a campfire, cooked, or rather burned, rice, drank tea, and sang all the old songs—Red Army Cossack songs about the Volga, labor union songs, American folk songs. Someone would recite poetry, the kind that was printed in all lowercase letters, and we would talk about revolution—any old revolution—and get high on the heat of the fire and our singing and swinging. None of us had heard of pot or grass. But I think I got a whiff of Woodstock.

One night I bicycled way out into the workers' district beyond Alexanderplatz and in some very dark basement room had a talk with Bill, the secret leader of this underground youth group, now that Eberhard Köbel had fled. Bill talked and talked very earnestly about Marx and Lenin and the brotherhood of man and said that the Nazis were just the necessary prelude to the true revolution that a chap like me

should be working for. I liked his revolution. My only objection, I said, was that it was directed by Moscow. Of course it was, Bill replied. "Well, not by Moscow but *from* Moscow. Moscow happens to be the headquarters of the Third International, the world socialist movement, of which the Soviets were only one member, with no more of a voice on the Comintern than Germans or any one else."

I was perhaps even more deeply impressed by my visit with Melchior Lechter, the graphic artist of the Stefan George circle. George was the poet and prophet of an esoteric, intellectual aristocracy to come. He called it "The Third Reich." The Nazis stole the term from him. The work of the George circle, including new translations of Dante and Baudelaire, was printed in uncial letters which Lechter designed and decorated in sensuous Art Nouveau style, reminiscent of Aubrey Beardsley. I had grown up with these books and the somber, measured, melodious poetry they contained. My father would often recite it while shaving. It clung like verbal incense.

Melchior Lechter's apartment smelled of real incense and was dark, very darkly curtained in purple velvet. What light there was, was stained by colored glass of Lechter's design, naked youth lifting torches out of limpid vegetation, I suppose. The master wore a velvet, medieval gown and cap and seated himself on a carved oak throne as soon as he had opened the door. I had the feeling that I was expected to kneel before him, but I don't think I did. I was just awed as he gave me a kind of benediction, though I don't know what he said. I heard only that verbal incense. Its sanctimonious mysticism made me uncomfortable. I never felt the same about Stefan George after that, although I acknowledge his great art and enormous influence on the German intellect of his time. My visit to Taliesin West, Frank Lloyd Wright's abode, some thirty-three years later, gave me the same eerie feeling as my short visit with Melchior Lechter. Frank Lloyd Wright was the Stefan George of architecture.

At about five in the afternoon I was sure to find some friends of my parents with a little cash to spare at Café Zuntz on Tauentzienstrasse. Zuntz served as a sort of exile for intellectuals who no longer wanted to be seen at the Romanische Café down the block. The Romanische was by now full of Nazis with intellectual pretensions. The loan at Zuntz usually came with good pastry.

One day I managed to borrow enough money from Paul Zucker, the architect and art historian, to have some left over after the most urgent bills were paid. I called my friend Reginald and we went out on the town and ended up at the Taverne, a place that still had some real atmosphere.

It still had so much atmosphere that, having bribed the pianist with a carafe of Moselle, we could persuade him to play *Threepenny Opera* songs. Suddenly everyone started singing along. Berlin, as I said, was still Berlin. We sang quite a lot before the head-waiter bounced us. "I don't want the Gestapo down my neck," he fumed.

In the fall of 1936 my mother returned from America to fetch my sister and me. Helene, the red-haired maid, cried as we left for New York. God knows how she got to be a Nazi. I never asked her. She was a very decent woman and, I am sure, did what she could, quietly, to protect my mother. She apparently had some clout, too, for she had joined the Nazi Party early and old party comrades counted a lot more than the opportunists who joined only after Hitler's assumption of power. One of the movers who came to pack was a hefty woman named Igel. Before Hitler, Igel had run a famous lesbian bar on Kurfürstendamm.

We left Berlin from Bahnhof Zoo and Carola, my last German flame, who studied drama and who could make herself cry real tears, ran alongside the departing train to the end of the platform. I kept waving my handkerchief halfway to Hamburg. For two years, two exciting and, as educators say, "formative" years, I had lived in the dim decay of Bert Brecht's Berlin—a time and place that seeded much of our culture.

Opposite page: Alexanderplatz, Friedrichstrasse, Potsdamer Strasse, Kaiser Wilhelm Gedächtniskirche. Right and below: The unemployed as well as war veterans took to the streets. [*Landesbildstelle, West Berlin*]

Most of it germinated, grew, and flourished on American soil.

By the time I arrived in New York, in fact, many important Berliners were already there. Others we knew were waiting for their entry permits at various American consulates. Part of the party had moved to the New World.

Alvin Johnson had launched the "University in Exile" at the New School for Social Research, and my mother's second husband, the economist Emil Lederer, was its first dean. Among the university's many notables were that pillar of the Weimar Republic Arnold Brecht, as well as Hans Staudinger and Frieda Wunderlich and Gerhard Colm. Karen Horney, who became my mother-in-law, was also teaching at the New School. So was Erwin Piscator. Max Reinhardt was producing his *The Eternal Road* on Broadway.

Paul Tillich was uptown at the Union Theological Seminary. Albert Einstein was at Princeton. Marlene Dietrich was in Hollywood, as was Thomas Mann.

Heinrich Brüning, the former Reich Chancellor, taught at Harvard.

Bertolt Brecht had arrived, and so had Kurt Weill and Lotte Lenya and George Grosz. Kurt Valentin's gallery on New York's Fifty-seventh Street introduced the work of Paul Klee, Wassily Kandinsky, Max Beckmann, and the others. Laszlo Moholy-Nagy launched a new Bauhaus at Chicago. Mies van der Rohe launched the architecture school at the Illinois Institute of Technology. Walter Gropius and Marcel Breuer taught the new architecture at Harvard.

Paul Hindemith was here and so was Otto Klemperer. But enough. Everyone was "an American."

"So it happens that to America . . . there have come a group of immigrants," wrote Bruce Bliven in *The New Republic* of November 10, 1937, "unlike any the world has seen before—individuals of such distinction that never, under ordinary circumstances, would they dream of transplanting themselves. These men and women are scientists, creative artists, musicians, philosophers. Theirs is a culture as high as can be found anywhere in the world. Already, they have contributed notably to the enhancement of our civilization; but what they have done thus far is certainly unimportant compared with the great promise that stretches forward through the years. I feel that we Americans owe a profound debt of gratitude to Hitler for making possible this enrichment of our collective life. Thank you, Hitler."

I was drafted into the U. S. Army to pay my debt to Hitler by joining the effort to defeat him. By the time I returned to Berlin as a member of the first United States contingent to enter the smoldering city in July 1945, *that* party was over, too—thoroughly over. Our apartment house on

Above: Playgrounds were scarce and flags plentiful. [*Landesbildstelle, West Berlin*]
Opposite page: Book stalls, unhappy students, anxious tenants [*Landesbildstelle, West Berlin*]

Wichmannstrasse was gone. In fact, all of Wichmannstrasse was gone. I could not even get through the rubble on Bülowstrasse where Pass & Garleb had been.

A day or two after we entered the city, I saw a crudely lettered poster pinned to a tree announcing a performance of *The Threepenny Opera*. It was, I believe, the first theater performance in Berlin since the fighting had stopped and was given, if I remember correctly, at the Theater am Schiffbauerdamm, where, seventeen years earlier, the opera's premiere had been held. It was, at any rate, in the Soviet sector. I got leave and a jeep and went. I did not find the theater—only more ruins. Then I saw people climbing those ruins and followed them through a tunnel-like entrance. It led into the auditorium which had red, upholstered seats but no roof. Despite the open air, there was that peculiar smell, that smell of Germany's defeat—part soapless humanity, part cold ashes, and part . . . there were still bodies under that rubble. The audience was mainly Soviet soldiers. I think I was the only American there. I was a little nervous.

Then Kurt Weill's familiar music struck up. It had never moved me so much. The beggars on the stage needed no grease paint to look haggard. They were haggard, starved, in genuine rags. Many of the actors, I learned backstage during intermission, had only just been released from concentration camp. They sang not well, but free.

"We got together and we all agreed," one of the actors told me. "The first play we wanted to do was *The Threepenny Opera*. The first thing we wanted to do," he repeated. "I suppose we all felt that doing Brecht again was like pinching your ear. If you could do *that*, it is true. The nightmare is over."

Driving back to my unit, I hummed Polly's farewell song: "There was a time and now it's all gone by . . ." Driving through the ruined city, I thought: It can be remembered, but not recaptured. It's all gone by.

But more than a quarter century later Sander Gilman and I talked about that. Sander is my son-in-law as well as a professor of German literature at Cornell. He spent a summer in Berlin, both East and West, and at various other places in Germany, combing about two dozen libraries plus a dozen film and photographic collections. "The Germans aren't as methodical as the world gives them credit for," he reported. Luckily, Sander Gilman, American born and bred, *is* methodical. He found quite a bit for us to work over.

Sander would go to the librarian, explain his purposes, and the same dialogue would inevitably ensue:

"What do you have?"

"What do you want?"

"How can I know what I want if I don't know what you have?"

Sander got some of the best pictures in this book from a junkman who picked old photo albums out of Berlin's trash and junk piles.

Long live junkmen with a sense of history.

Wolf Von Eckardt

BERTOLT BRECHT'S BERLIN

1

REVOLUTION: *"Workers! Soldiers! Comrades! Brothers!"*

I came to the cities in a time of unrest,
When hunger reigned.
I came to the people in a time of uprising,
And I rebelled with them.
(So the time passed away
Which on earth was given me.)
BERTOLT BRECHT

In Berlin the unrest came to a climax on Saturday, November 9, 1918.

It had started to rain before dawn, but by morning the rain had turned to drizzle. The city awoke to its dreary routine and its factories filled with workers.

World War I had dragged on for one thousand five hundred and sixty-three days.

There would never be a revolution in Germany, Lenin had predicted, because Germans would storm a railroad station only after they had purchased tickets.

Yet, with a cease-fire in sight, the sailors had mutinied the week before at Kiel, the Imperial Navy base. The sailors knew (though the Kaiser and his civilian cabinet didn't), that the High Command had decided to end the war, Wagnerian style, with one last blast of a naval battle. "Don't worry," one of the sailors wrote his father. "We are not going to let them kill us on the last day."

So the Kiel mutiny of November 3 triggered revolution, after all. The sailors moved south, helping to organize "workers' and soldiers' councils" along the way. When their train approached Cologne, the mayor, Konrad Adenauer, asked the railroad officials to stop it, so he could have the rebels arrested. The officials refused. It was a regularly scheduled train.

On that drizzly morning of the ninth, when the revolution reached Berlin, the generals confronted their chain-smoking, vacillating commander in chief. As one of his adjutants, Lieutenant Colonel Alfred Niemannn, remembered it, the Kaiser explained that *he* would lead his troops home as soon as the armistice was signed.

One of the generals replied:

"The armed forces will return home in peace and order under their generals, but not under the leadership of Your Majesty."

The Kaiser's eyes lit up in anger. He stretched himself to his full height. He moved toward General Gröner, the Quartermaster General, and spoke with a sharp vibrato: "Sir, I demand that you put that statement in writing. I want the statements of all my commanding generals in black and white that the armed forces no longer stand behind their supreme commander. Has not every soldier sworn me an oath of allegiance?"

[*Landesarchiv, West Berlin*]

Right: "The great, long yearned-for day has arrived." Loyalty to the Kaiser had become a fiction and revolutionary soldiers took up battle stations on the roof of the Brandenburg Gate. [*Landesbildstelle, West Berlin*]
Below: Kaiser Wilhelm II, after much vacillating, left for Holland and mailed his official abdication three weeks later. [*Landesbildstelle, West Berlin*]

"It is now only a fiction," replied the General.

The Field Marshal, Paul von Hindenburg, attempted to mollify the Emperor: "As a result of the news from both the battlefield and the home front, neither General Gröner nor I can guarantee the dependability of the military services."

The Kaiser's face froze. In all the inner struggles of the past few days, in all the conflicts with the war cabinet and overheated public opinion, his single guiding light had always been his firm, proud belief in the loyalty of the man in uniform. Was this an illusion, a mirage?

In the meantime a series of phone calls had come in from the Reich Chancellery in Berlin.

The Chancellor seemed to be besieging the Kaiser. The situation in Berlin could not be put off. Masses of extremist workers had left their factories. The troops had joined them. Bloody street fighting was in sight. Only the Emperor's immediate abdication could prevent a potential civil war and secure a continuity of government.[1]

The rebelling workers and soldiers meanwhile moved from the industrial suburbs to the center of the capital. Reich Chancellor Prince Max von Baden, capitulating to the inevitable, urged the Kaiser to abdicate. The Kaiser refused.

By noon, hundreds of thousands of people had stormed Berlin's government center. On his own authority, the Chancellor informed Wolff's Telegraph Bureau, the quasi-official news agency, that the Emperor had decided to resign.

So that day, November 9, the evening edition of the *Norddeutsche Allgemeine Zeitung* carried the banner headline: KAISER WILHELM II RENOUNCES THRONE. The Crown Prince would take over, the story said, and appoint Friedrich Ebert, the leader of the Social Democratic party, as the new Chancellor of the Reich.

As it turned out, the Crown Prince fled Germany along with his father, who mailed his official abdication nineteen days later from Amerongen, Holland.

But "Fritz" Ebert, less than fifty at the time, was indeed appointed by Prince Max. Ebert, an artisan, trade unionist, journalist, member of the Reichstag and finally party chairman, later became the first President of the Weimar Republic. He died in office in 1925. He was an able politician and would much rather have established a mildly socialist and strongly democratic government under the monarchy. But now he hastily formed a "provisionary workers' and soldiers' council," which issued a proclamation:

Workers! Soldiers! Comrades! Brothers!

The great, long yearned-for day has arrived. As of November 9, the German people have taken the power in their own hands.

As of November 9, Germany is a Republic—a socialist republic of workers and soldiers.

Our hearts are filled with pride . . .

The first provisional government of the new German Republic, hands in laps, poses for its first photo. From left to right are Dr. Otto Landsberg, Philipp Scheidemann, Gustav Noske, Friedrich Ebert, and Rudolf Wissell. [*Landesbildstelle, West Berlin*] Below, right: Between headlining the Kaiser's abdication and the proclamation of the workers' and soldiers' councils, the *Norddeutsche Allgemeine Zeitung* changed its name to *Die Internationale*. [*Landesarchiv, West Berlin*]

Norddeutsche Allgemeine Zeitung

Thronverzicht Kaiser Wilhelms II.

Aufruf zur Nationalversammlung.

Die Internationale

früher: Norddeutsche Allgemeine Zeitung

Arbeiter! Soldaten! Genossen! Brüder!

Ebert Reichskanzler

The *Norddeutsche Allgemeine Zeitung* printed the proclamation in its morning edition the next day. Only by then the name of this newspaper had changed to *Die Internationale*.

If their hearts were filled, the bellies of Berlin's workers and soldiers—along with those of everyone else—were empty.

At the Invalidenstrasse, according to one

In these days of turmoil and turnips, horses accidentally killed in the street fighting (above) often provided precious protein for starving Berliners. Many of them, particularly the children (right), ventured far out into the Brandenburg woods to gather brushwood for cooking and heating. [*Landesbildstelle, West Berlin*]

account of that time, lay two reasonably well-fed horses, which had just been shot in the street fighting:

The bystanders viewed the cadavers with sympathy. An off-duty streetcar conductress held a sort of funeral sermon: "You didn't deserve this . . . But at least you didn't starve to death."

"Nor do I intend to starve," said a boy, pulling out his pocketknife. "These nags aren't made of paper!"

He was about ready to dig in when his friend stopped him. The friend had not yet been totally demoralized by the war and life in Berlin.

"You don't know if they're dead. You should at least wait until the vet gets here."

"A vet? You can see in their eyes they're dead. They don't move when I touch 'em. Let's get to work," he said softly so that the bystanders would not hear.

During this debate, a group of women had vanished in the direction of a neighborhood bar. They soon returned with glistening objects in their hands or partially hidden under their aprons.

Malnutrition was etched on their faces. Flat-chested and sunken-cheeked, eyes like darkened caverns, they worked their way through the crowd which had continued to gather.

They were no longer the first. A taxi driver began by cutting a piece from one of the haunches with his pocketknife. A street sweeper and the boy had begun to work on the other carcass. Even his sympathetic friend had dug in.

The women went at it systematically. They carefully removed the hide, then they butchered the flesh beneath it. Many hands were at work, but everyone got something for his effort.

"Meat at last," one of the women cried out. "I'm fed up with eating only turnips . . ."[2]

Turnips had turned a good many upright German workers into radicals. The Spartakusbund—the "Spartacists"—the extreme left wing, led by Karl Liebknecht, had gained from the turmoil. They hysterically cried for "the dictatorship of the proletariat." Guns could be bought on the streets for less than a dollar apiece. Ebert, a lukewarm socialist, and his Social Democrats

were utterly unprepared to assume power. They detested the collapse of authority, disobedience, rabble-rousing, and hysteria. They had talked revolution for more than half a century. But they were no revolutionaries, certainly not if it meant anything like what had just happened in Russia.

While crowds milled in the streets, the new government tried to face political reality. It was not so sure it really wanted the "socialist republic of workers and soldiers" it had just proclaimed. Philipp Scheidemann, a Social Democrat and Reichstag deputy, recorded the next step in his memoirs:

. . . The Reichstag looked like a giant military base. Workers and soldiers came and went. Many were armed. Hungrily, I sat in the dining room with some friends, including Ebert, who had just come to the Reichstag from the Reich Chancellery. We were served only a thin, watery soup . . . Then a mass of workers and soldiers stormed into the room, approaching our table.

Fifty people all crying at the same time: "Scheidemann, come with us! Philipp, you must come out and speak. Yes, Scheidemann, come quickly, Liebknecht is speaking from the balcony of the Palace."

"So what?"

"No, no, come! Speak!" Dozens of people attempted to persuade me until I finally left with them.

The great entry hall presented a dramatic picture. Rifles were stacked in pyramids. From the courtyard, one could hear the stamping and neighing of horses. In the hall itself, thousands of milling people seemed to be talking or screaming simultaneously. We hurriedly entered the reading room. I wanted to speak to the masses from a window of this room. On my left and right those who had accompanied me attempted to explain what had occurred on the streets. . . .

Someone shouted: "Liebknecht wants to announce the formation of a worker's republic."

Now I saw the situation clearly. I knew his demands: "All power to the workers' and soldiers' councils."

Germany a Russian province, a branch of the international Soviet? Never!

A father and his son join the effort to restore order. [*Staatsbibliothek, West Berlin*]

Friedrich Ebert, an artisan, trade-unionist, journalist, member of the Reichstag, leader of the Social Democratic party, able politician, became the first President of the Weimar Republic. [*Landesbildstelle, West Berlin*]

There was no doubt: Whoever could bring the masses into motion, whether "Bolshevistically" from the Palace or "Social Democratically" from the Reichstag, would have won. I saw the Russian madness before me, the replacement of the Czarist terror by the Bolshevist one. "No! Not in Germany."

At this moment I stood at the window.

Thousands of arms extended, waving hats and caps. The cries of the crowd echoed loudly. Then everything became still.

I spoke a few words, which were enthusiastically received.

"Workers and soldiers!

"We have come through four terrible years of war. The sacrifice in goods and blood was horrible. The war is over! The murdering is past. The result of the war, its distress and misery, will be with us for many years. The defeat, which we tried to avoid at any price, has not been spared us. All our attempts at rapprochement were sabotaged. We were mocked and slandered.

"The Emperor has abdicated. He and his friends have disappeared. The people have conquered them all, up and down the line . . .

"Workers and soldiers! Be conscious of your historical missions today. The inconceivable has occurred. Great and unfathomable work stands before us.

"Be united, faithful, and conscious of your duty. The rotten old monarchy has collapsed. Long live the new! Long live the German Republic!"

Seemingly infinite rejoicing followed. Finally the crowd began to move to the Palace. The Bolshevist threat to the Fatherland was crushed. The German Republic was alive in the minds and hearts of the masses.

I quickly returned to the Reichstag dining room to finish my soup.[3]

At four o'clock that afternoon, Karl Liebknecht spoke to the crowds in front of the Palace. He proclaimed a German Soviet Republic. But he was too late. Hesitantly, to be sure, a new and tenuous German democracy—to be ratified and given a constitution at Weimar the following year—was born.

The dynamic and fanatic Communist leader of the second revolution was Karl Liebknecht, shown here (grasping a chair) as he addresses a demonstration from the Prussian Parliament Building. [*Landesbildstelle, West Berlin*]

Fritz Rück, a young socialist poet, captured the excitement in a poem:

Workers, parading in celebration,
indolent and self-conscious.
Ripping with crude force
—but with hidden respect—
the final flashy rags from the body
of the imperial whore Berlin
so that she stands
stripped, bare
in the November light.

A melody sprang up in
the gray slums.
They sang,
day in, night out.
Revolution!
The little shop girls,
tinier than usual,
and yet there was a new pride
growing in them,
suddenly, overnight,
like Jack's beanstalk.
The red flags waved
over the Königgratzer Strasse,
radiating revolution
in the city,
showing the way.
And they came,
the graceful girls
women, aged and careworn,
men and boys
tired of war, ready to fight . . .[4]

There was still much fighting ahead.

The Spartacists had not given up. In Russia, too, they reasoned, the moderate Kerensky had been followed by the radical Lenin. By December the Spartacists had joined with other radical Socialists to form the German Communist party and get on with socialism and revolution.

The Ebert government responded by coming to terms with the generals, but the generals had lost control of what remained of their defeated troops. Volunteers were recruited, to form the Freikorps. Most of them were free-wheeling mercenaries, led by disgruntled, ultranationalistic officers, who would go to any lengths to establish law and order. Communist violence was bad. The white terror proved worse.

Broadsides began to appear throughout Berlin:

> *Workers! Citizens!*
> *Our Fatherland is in danger of collapse.*
> *Save it!*
> *It is threatened, not from without, but from within!*
> *By the Spartacus Group!*
> *Kill their leaders!*
> *Kill Liebknecht!*
> *Then you will have peace, work, and bread.*
>
> *The Front Soldiers*[5]

But Liebknecht was not yet dead. He launched a second revolution on January 6, 1919. It was provoked by the appointment of a new chief of police, who was less sympathetic to the radicals than his predecessor, Emil Eichhorn. The Communists seized not only Berlin's police headquarters on Alexanderplatz, but several newspaper offices and public buildings.

Count Harry Kessler, a poet and diplomat as well as the indefatigable diarist of the Weimar Republic, kept track of the turmoil:

Monday, 6 January 1919

Eleven o'clock, corner of Siegesallee and Viktoriastrasse. Two processions meet, the one is going in the direction of Siegesallee, the other in that of Wilhelmstrasse. They are made up of the same sort of people, artisans and factory girls, dressed in the

[*Landesbildstelle, West Berlin*]

The upright, idealistic, and utterly unprepared Social Democrats (center) were instantly attacked by Communists from the left and nationalists from the right. [*Landesbildstelle, West Berlin*] "KILL LIEBKNECHT!" says the Freikorps broadside (below), which mysteriously appeared all over the city. The command was soon obeyed.

Arbeiter, Bürger!

Das Vaterland ist dem Untergang nahe.
Rettet es!
Es wird nicht bedroht von außen, sondern von innen:
Von der Spartakusgruppe.

Schlagt ihre Führer tot!
Tötet Liebknecht!

Dann werdet ihr Frieden, Arbeit und Brot haben!

Die Frontsoldaten

same sort of clothes, waving the same red flags, and moving in the same sort of shambling step. But they carry slogans, jeer at each other as they pass, and perhaps will be shooting one another down before the day is out. At this hour the Sparticists are still fairly thin on the ground in Siegesallee. Ten minutes later, when I reach Brandenburger Tor, vast masses of them are coming down Unter den Linden from the east. At Wilhelmstrasse they encounter just as immense a throng of Social Democrats. For the moment everything is peaceful.

Suddenly, shortly after one, a tremendous uproar: 'Liebknecht, Liebknecht! Liebknecht is here!' I see a slender, fair-haired youth running away from a mob. They catch up with him, strike at him. He keeps on running. I can see the fair-haired head, with the breathless, flushed boy's face, amidst the fists and brandished sticks. From all sides there are shouts of 'The young Liebknecht! Liebknecht's son!' He stumbles, disappears under the seething mob. I feel sure that they will beat him to death. But suddenly he is visible again, his face mangled and blood-stained, exhausted but supported by Spartacists who have rushed in and now drag him away.

Friday, 10 January 1919

During the night a proper skirmish developed for possession of the Mosse publishing-house and printing-works. So far it has been in the hands of the Spartacists.

Saturday, 11 January 1919

The impression made by the shelled Leipziger Strasse was eerie. The lightless façades of the houses towered even more hugely in the darkness. At street-corners people could be seen taking cover because uncertain what to do. At every crossing a small, murky, shapeless throng dithered before the empty but fire-raked side-streets as on the edge of a

[*Staatsbibliothek, West Berlin*]

Count Harry Kessler, a diplomat and the Republic's most ardent diarist, as painted by Edvard Munch in 1906. [*Nationalgalerie, West Berlin*]

Rosa Luxemburg, murdered along with Liebknecht, was a widely admired Communist theoretician. [*Landesarchiv, West Berlin*]

chasm. Trams still ran, without lights, but throwing off electric sparks which crackled like fireworks and were briefly reflected in the wet, glistening roadway. Patrols encouraged the frightened groups to use the trams as being comparatively the safest means of conveyance. Many however were not prepared to take the risk and stayed stuck in doorways. This dumb panic in a tangle of streets turned into a battlefield was one of the most weird scenes these revolutionary days have presented.

Monday, 13 January 1919

. . . At twenty to eleven at night there was an outbreak of violent fighting, with rifle-fire and the pounding and chatter of heavy and light machine-guns. Right outside my door, it seemed. Sometimes it sounded as though the door was being stove in by rifle-butts. The uproar lasted twenty minutes, followed by sudden complete quiet. The Spartacists, their major effort having failed, are conducting a guerrilla war, by day from the roof-tops, by night from out-of-the-way streets. Liebknecht has disappeared.[6]

By the time the Ebert government had brought in some three thousand Freikorps volunteers, the second revolution had been fairly well crushed by the Berlin police with the help of the few troops stationed in the city.

To many Berliners, however, the Freikorps appeared as the savior of the new democracy it was soon to help destroy. One volunteer, Artur Iger, who viewed the events from the right wing of the political stage, vented his emotions in purple prose:

"They're coming! They're coming!" An unforgettable procession . . . Man after man, faces as if cast in bronze, shoulder to shoulder, these magnificent figures, the liberators of Berlin, return from their task, rifles at rest. And behind them a column of the prisoners—disgraces to their uniforms, the three hundred Spartacists, some of them women, seem ready for the rope . . .

A single thought enlivens the crowd, a single feeling envelops the throng of happy women and men and seizes the youths who have survived the terror: The criminals have not won their criminal game, the beautiful metropolis on the Spree has not become the spoil of this human dross.[7]

A few days later, on January 15, a band of "these magnificent figures," these "liberators," raided an apartment in Berlin's Wilmersdorf district, seized the leaders of the Spartacists, Karl Liebknecht and Rosa Luxemburg, and murdered them.

The assassins escaped with cynically short sentences. The Social Democratic government, as historian Golo Mann has noted, was "extremely angry about the assassination." But it was, after all, involved in it and was unable, and to some extent unwilling, to control the Freikorps.

For a majority of Germans, Liebknecht and Luxemburg later became mythical villains—bellows to fan Nazi passions. A vocal minority considered them unforgettable martyrs. The socialist poet Oskar Kanehl wrote in 1920:

Karl Liebknecht.
You are alive.
Your proletarians live.
Your fist is present in hundreds of
clenched fists.
Your heart beats in thousands of hearts.
You call with millions of voices:
Long live the revolution![8]

The German revolution did live on—but in the end, Adolf Hitler won it.

Eugen Bertolt Brecht arrived on the scene on a cold and wet morning late in February 1920, the year after the Spartacist uprising. He had wanted to move from Munich's provincial atmosphere to the center of Germany's intellectual ferment. "You should steal five hundred marks and follow me," he wrote his young artist friend Caspar Neher. "Everything is overflowing with dreadful tastelessness. But on what a level!"

The tastelessness level, he found, was also cold and inhospitable. After three weeks of living on bean soup and "all the free bread you can eat" at Aschinger's, an inexpensive restaurant, Brecht went back to Munich.

On the day he left, the shooting had started again. An adventurous chauvinist named Wolfgang Kapp had aroused the Freikorps again to stage a putsch. He managed to occupy Berlin, force the government to flee, and establish himself as Chancellor for three days. The legitimate army, the Reichswehr, stood by to see what would happen. What happened was that Berlin's workers went on general strike. All work, all services, all trains, trams, and trucks stopped. That was the end of Kapp.

Bert Brecht, as he now called himself, did not return to Berlin for four years. He wrote *To Posterity:*

Roads, in my day, led only into morass.
Speech betrayed me to the slaughterer.
There was little I could do.
But without me
The rulers would have felt more secure.
This, at least, I hoped.
So the time passed away,
Which on earth was given me.[9]

A third revolution, was the short-lived Kapp putsch, a coup d'état staged by the nationalist radicals of the Freikorps, shown planting their flag in Unter den Linden. Kapp's grip on Berlin was broken by a general strike. [*Landesbildstelle, West Berlin*]

Eugen Bertolt Brecht at eighteen, four years before his first, brief visit to "the dreadful tastelessness" of Berlin. [*Photo: Fohrer*]

Inflation brought soup kitchens into the tenement courts and . . . [*Staatsbibliothek*, West *Berlin*]

2

INFLATION: *The Revolution of Values*

The worst was yet to come.

"WORK IS SALVATION," said one of the myriad posters that papered Berlin as the street fighting subsided.

The poster shows a grimly determined *Landsmann* in the dawn of a new day, seeding new industries, homes, and commerce on dark acres of graveyards and smoldering ruin. The exhortation must have appealed to Berlin's blue-collar workers and vast, gray middle class. For in all their political confusion, their faith in the rewarding virtue of hard labor and thrift was still unimpaired. There was much "work ethic" among this "silent majority."

But the reward for honest living was now worthless money. In the end, a worker needed a shopping bag to carry one day's miserable wages to the grocer. And thrifty middle-class Germans carted their life savings to the butcher or baker in wheel barrows.

The German inflation of 1919 to 1923 was, according to many historians, more demoralizing than the defeat of their armies and the frustration of their revolution.

It began innocuously enough. In 1919, 1920, and early 1921 the value of the mark dropped from the prewar 4.2 per dollar to 75. That was bad, but bearable. Since the German government needed foreign currency to pay reparations to the victors, the money flowed abroad in an ever bigger stream. With so much of it abroad that it lost value. The German government thereupon resorted to its old habit of simply printing more money. By November 15, 1921, you had to pay 258 marks for one dollar.

On September 16, 1922, the exchange rate for the dollar had risen to 1,460 marks. On February 1, 1923, it was 48,000 marks.

More printing presses, even those of newspapers, were pressed into service. They printed ever larger denominations. A 10,000-mark bill came to be worth next to nothing.

. . . the slogan WORK IS SALVATION became a bitter irony. [*Staatsbibliothek, West Berlin*]

There is no disease quite as bad as this . . . The sight of women, their hurriedly pulled on housecoats, their bitter passive faces. The queues always end up with the same result: the city, the great city of stone, has been bought out. Rice yesterday cost 80,000 *marks a pound, now it costs* 160,000 *marks, tomorrow it will perhaps double again, the day after tomorrow the man behind the counter is likely to shrug his shoul-*

More and more bank notes with more and more zeros were printed, until finally bundles of worthless billion (in German, *Milliard*)-mark bills became toys for the children. [*Staatsbibliothek and Archiv für Kunst und Geschichte, West Berlin*]

ders: "We're out." And noodles? "Out of them, too." So buy beans, lentils, peas, only buy, buy, buy. The piece of paper, the brand-new bill, still damp from the press, paid this morning as salary, shrinks in value on the way to the merchant. The zeros, the ever-growing zeros! "A zero is really nothing!" Hate, despair, need, grow with the value of the dollar. The daily exchange rate determines the daily temperament. All emotion goes into mockery: "Butter is cheaper! Yesterday 1,600,000 marks, today only 1,400,000 marks!" It is no longer a joke, but reality, written in pencil and hung in the shop window.

"All right, now, give me my butter," a woman shouts. Your butter—by the time your turn comes, there won't be any more butter. The answer is a shattering of glass from the dairy products case, smashed by an umbrella handle. The policeman, standing guard outside, takes the sobbing woman out of the store. He will bring charges.[1]

By September 1923 the banks refused to accept any checks under 50,000,000 marks.

On October 4, 1923, a dollar was worth 440,000,000 marks. The frenzy accelerated:

56,000,000,000 to one dollar on October 23, 1923;
143,000,000,000 to one, on November 1, 1923;
630,000,000,000 to one, on November 8, 1923;
2,500,000,000,000 to one, on November 17, 1923;
4,200,000,000,000 to one, on November 20, 1923.[2]

Wages and salaries never caught up. Even the fortunes of the rich who had invested in gold and treasures were wiped out.

In the summer of 1923 Berliners paid 600 marks to ride the trolley, 1,440 marks for a pint of milk, 100 marks to mail a letter, and 60 marks to make a phone call. You were better off with something to trade. Two eggs would buy you a shave.

But who could get two eggs? Farmers did not care much for those million- and trillion-mark bills. Some artists, like Moholy-Nagy, lacking paint or worthier objects, pasted this paper money into their collages.

The city government reported in 1923 that less than 10 per cent of Berlin's families earned enough to maintain a decent standard of living. Malnutrition spread rapidly from the proletariat to the skilled workers and pensioners to the middle class. Berlin was crowded with starving people.

The horror is the same in all of the houses in Berlin, North and East: airless, cramped conditions—little space, too many people.

Four or five adults and children live together in each room, three or more people to a bed. The furniture, the wallpaper, the walls, and the ceilings are dilapidating . . . Hardly one apartment in the city has all its windowpanes; in the poor neighborhoods, whole rows of windows are covered with paper or boards. Even bed linen is a rarity. Three or four children share one bed, with rags serving as blankets.

Even rudimentary underwear is lacking in many cases . . .

There are neither towels nor soap. Cleaniness, once the pride of low-income Berliners, must be fought for. Yet, people struggle to stay clean in spite of their abysmal poverty . . .

Without the emergency relief supplies of the Quakers, the sole sustenance for thousands of families, an entire generation of children would grow up without having eaten anything more substantial than bread, ersatz coffee, and boiled vegetables.[3]

In addition to the Quakers and the American Relief Administration, headed by Herbert Hoover, there was the Salvation Army. Its benevolent street campaign may account for the continued popularity in Berlin of Bernard Shaw's *Major Barbara.*

"Shaw is the wittiest German dramatist of the century," someone remarked. "Too bad he is English." The Salvation Army is also the subject of one of Bert Brecht's early plays, *Saint Joan of the Stockyards.*

But the beneficiaries of the Salvation Army did not always repay Christian charity with Christian kindness. Harry Domela tells about it in his autobiography, *The False Prince.* Domela became famous and immensely popular for impersonating Prussian royalty. No one seemed to mind that it was a self-serving hoax. Once he stayed in a Salvation Army shelter with a friend:

A bed of iron. A mattress of wire. Under it a wire basket for valuables and papers. Wolf and I had our beds next to each other. It was too noisy to sleep. Most men sat lethargically, spooning down their soup and listening to others speak. The speakers raved ever louder. They were ragged, frightening men, who seemed capable of anything. As Wolf took off his watch to put it in the wire basket, one of them reached over and grabbed it. Wolf, as quick as he was, was struck by one of the others so that he fell back on the bed. Then the whole band jumped us. They outnumbered us and we were badly beaten. I was hit in the mouth with something that ripped open my gum. Wolf looked dreadful. His forehead was bleeding; he had been hit with brass knuckles. His watch had vanished. I became angry. This scum! I knew how Wolf had taken

The once upright German worker (above) lost faith in a Republic where (left) fifty million marks bought no more than one turnip. [*Archiv für Kunst und Geschichte and Staatsbibliothek, West Berlin*]

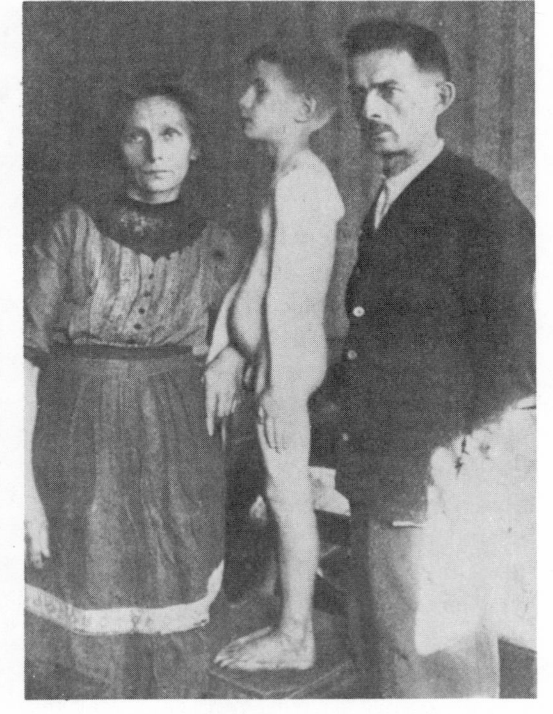

The old saw their savings gone, the young scavenged in garbage. The son of a carpenter (near left), who had to feed a family of seven on 120 marks a week, was among the thousands of children who suffered serious malnutrition. Money was carried to the banks in laundry baskets and the unemployed lined up for watery soup (below). But there were also those who got rich. Bowler-hatted Hugo Stinnes (right, above) built a huge industrial empire on the paper money. [*Staatsbibliothek, Landesbildstelle, Archiv für Kunst und Geschichte, West Berlin, and Count Harry Kessler* Die Nation, *op. cit.*]

care to keep his watch through all the bad times, sentimentally clinging to it. Wolf asked me to change the subject. Next to me lay a bum. "Well, you had luck—yup, luck —a couple of weeks ago" he stuttered, "they bashed an Arab—on the head—for his coat —anyhow, he no longer needed it the next morning."[4]

Inflation gushed on. The money presses kept rolling. No one, not even the government, quite understood what was happening.

With hindsight, historians now explain that the absence of countermeasures on the part of the government was not entirely a matter of helpless innocence about the secrets of money. The complete ruin of the German currency, after all, served a patriotic motive: it would put an end to reparation payments to the Allies.

Industry, less noble in its purposes, knew full well, furthermore, that only paper changed hands, making the rich richer and the poor poorer. No real assets were lost—no land holdings of the Junkers, or factories, or mines. They kept producing. They produced goods for wages of paper covered with lengthening rows of zeros. Products could thus be sold all the more cheaply on the world market. Even at home, for that matter, the glittering shop windows enticed a frantic urge to spend, spend, spend.

"While politicians driveled constantly about misery and lost honor," writes Golo Mann, "this 'inflation,' one must emphasize even today, was one of the instruments which industry used to regain the position it had lost for a short time after 1918."

Bloated profits were made.

In Berlin a giddy, greedy gaiety hung over the city like an intoxicating smog. There was an inflation even of drinking, dancing, and sex.

It happened in the Hundekeller, one of the few remaining beer cellars, which, for the most part, had given way to more fashionable bars. Everything was quiet. But when a skinny American ordered champagne for everyone, along with food and whiskey, the cellar quickly filled. No one found it unusual when the foreigner began to throw American small change on the floor, shouting that only naked women were allowed to pick it up.

A few girls smirked. But when an older, heavy-set woman quickly stripped off her blouse, skirt, and underwear, dropped to her knees, and began to collect the coins, many of the other girls stripped and joined her.

Most of the men laughed.

Only one complained and cursed the proprietress.

"What's wrong? These girls have to work a whole day for one American penny. Money doesn't stink, not dollars, anyway."[5]

Foreign businessmen began to pick Germany clean with their hard currency. A Dutch visitor, who had found Berlin's neckties cheap and brought four thousand of

them home to Amsterdam, remarked to a German travel companion: "It seems to me you Germans have not only lost the war, but also your business sense."

He was mistaken. There were far too many German profiteers. Sharpies who had never seen a cow managed to raise the price of butter quicker even than the value of the mark could sink. The Berliners called them *Raffkes* and told innumerable jokes about their vulgarity.

The Salvation Army fought its good fight on the streets and in the beer gardens, Berlin children sent "thank you" letters with poems and paintings to America's Hoover Commission, and the shelters overflowed. [*Landesarchiv and Landesbildstelle, West Berlin, and from Hans Ostwald,* Sittengeschichte der Inflation]

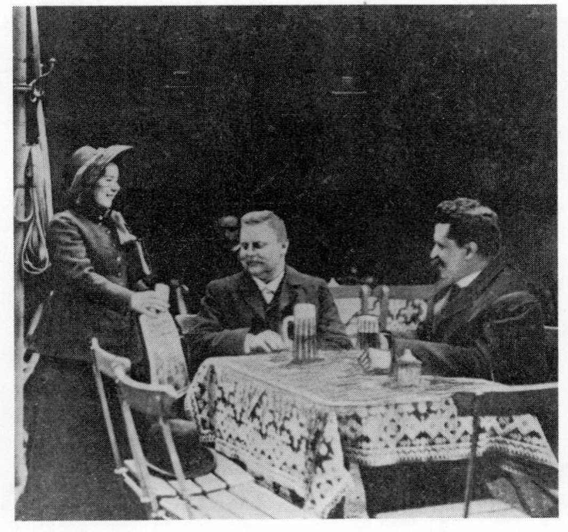

"You know, we could rent advertising space on your decolleté and make a fortune," the *Raffke* told the movie starlet he had picked up in a bar. "In fact, you'd make me a good wife—six acts and not a word spoken," he added—those being the days of the silent films. "Your bosoms and my butter—that's art."

The greatest *Raffke* of them all was Hugo Stinnes, who built out of paper money what was probably the most inflated, most far-flung industrial empire of all time—coal, iron, shipping, paper, automobiles, anything. It collapsed when he died in 1924, leaving some of his associates in debt for the rest of their lives.

If you knew how, making a fortune was easy, as Erik Jan Hanussen, the popular mind reader, fortuneteller, and vaudeville star, told it in his autobiography. He persuaded the director of Circus Busch to pay him a month in advance—in Austrian stock:

We went together to the bank and I received my stocks. When I had them under my arm, I said:

"Sir, how many Austrian shares do you still have?"

His face saddened.

"A whole mountain of them, take a look."

"Wouldn't you be interested in finding out what these shares are worth?" I asked.

"What are they worth?" he asked.

"They're worth five dollars a share."

When he found out that the actual value was now 99,000,000,000,000 marks, he had to sit down. He had made more money than he had made for the past ten years of Circus Busch.

"Sell them immediately," I said. "By noon they will again be worth no more than five dollars. Now they are worth over a hundred dollars! Sell the stocks and put the fortune in real estate, diamonds, or pins and towels, for all I care. You have about three hours. By the time the stock exchange closes, it will be too late."

"I think I leave well enough alone, Mr. Hanussen, and wait until the stocks reach two hundred dollars."

He's still waiting.

I left with my stocks and began to buy. I bought and bought, shoes and stockings, flag poles and beer mugs, porcelain and iron stoves. I bought top hats and leather spats. At eleven o'clock, I was already receiving only about half as much, but I was

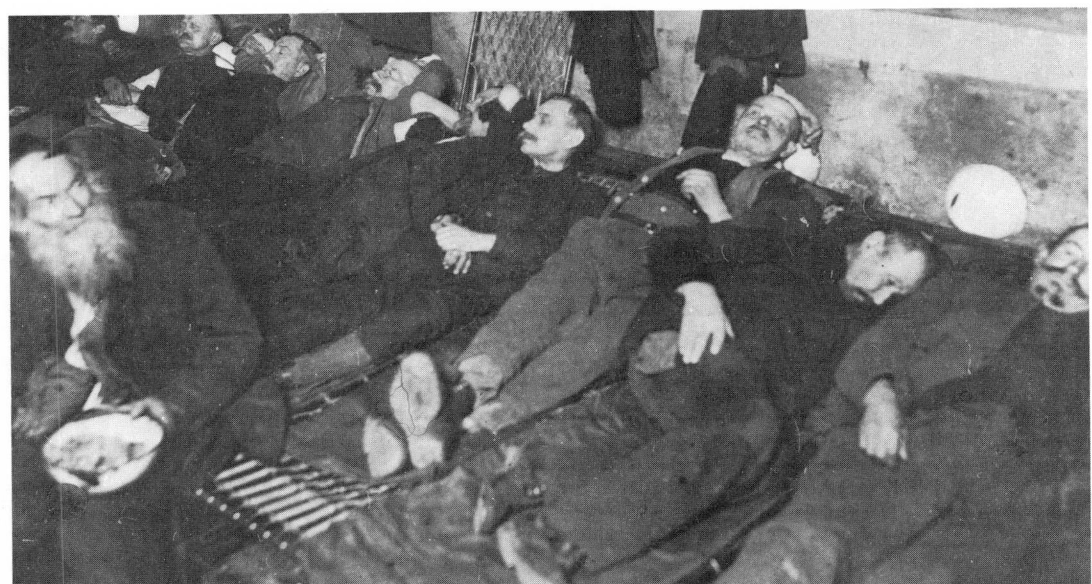

As the money presses rolled, Berliners frantically danced the Charleston and the other new American steps. [*Staatsbibliothek, West Berlin*]

On November 20, 1923, the inflation was over, but much of the giddy, greedy gaiety continued. [*From Hans Ostwald,* Sittengeschichte der Inflation]

already about three fourths through my shares.

When I had swapped the last shares in a large record store on the Friedrichstrasse for about a thousand records and forty record players, I just had time to say to the owner of the shop:

"Call the exchange and order the stocks sold. You still have five minutes."

Luckily he did. At twelve noon the stock price fell from 99,000,000,000,000 marks to four dollars.

The Rentenmark *had arrived!*

I hadn't lost a minute.[6]

The *Rentenmark* was the government's woefully belated cure of the madness. It was issued on November 23, 1923, by the new Commissioner for National Currency, Hjalmar Horace Greely Schacht, a private banker and middle-of-the-road politician who had been summoned by President Ebert when the old head of the Treasury had fortuitously died.

You could now exchange one trillion (1,000,000,000,000) of the old marks for one of Schacht's new *Rentenmark.*

Hjalmar Schacht thus managed to re-establish the value of money in Germany. But the German sense of values, the old propriety—political and moral—and faith in the new Republic were gone. Hard work and thrift no longer meant salvation.

Despite the cure, Berlin remained in a state of delirium.

[*Staatsbibliothek, West Berlin*]

3
AFTER HOURS

Bright Lights and Dark Magnets

Berliners called their delirious escapes from reality "*Amusmang.*" (They mangled a good many French words—like *amusement*—into their dialect. In the early nineteenth century, one fifth of the city's population consisted of French Huguenots—Protestants driven from home by religious persecution—who had been granted asylum as much for their skills and industry as to demonstrate Prussia's religious tolerance.)

The common man's most wholesome *Amusmang* were summer Sunday excursions to the lakes and woods—Krumme Lanke, Müggelsee, Wannsee, and the sandy forests of Grunewald or the hills east of the city. Buses, streetcars, and trains were packed with families and lovers. At the end of the line, the fun inevitably began with a cold jug or two of *Weisse mit Schuss,* light beer with—*de gustibus non est disputandum*—a shot of raspberry syrup. Berlin's popular songs abound with tales of young virtue lost in the pine-scented woods.

But most of the action was after dark. Eugen Szatmari confessed in his 1927 guide that Berlin's night life defied description. There was too much variety and excitement.

Despite all the tourists from the provinces and abroad, Berlin at night, this light-filled, sparkling, champagne-bubbling, jazz-droning, noisy, too noisy, always overflowing Berlin night, still belongs to the Berliners. In Paris and Vienna the character of the night life is determined by tourists. But the Berliner considers his night his own. He wants his fun. He wants to be amused. He is not one of those who go to sleep with the chickens. Wherever the Berlin night flickers, native Berliners are in the majority . . .

Berlin is surrounded by beautiful lakes and woods easily accessible by bus, streetcar, or rapid transit. On clear summer weekends the whole city seemed to empty out in pursuit of fresh air, nature, and solitude. But many Berliners never got further than the beer gardens, dance hall, or amusement parks at the end of the line. [*Landesbildstelle, Staatsbibliothek, and Archiv für Kunst und Geschichte, West Berlin*]

Aside from the theaters and movie houses, the concert halls and the Six-Day Bicycle Race (when held); aside from the elegant hotels, the restaurants, cafés, and confectionery shops; aside from the countless bars, dance halls, and cabarets, which only a very thick tome could list; aside from the light-flooded Friedrichstrasse, and the Kurfürstendamm, and the places on the Jäger- and Behrensstrasse, where you find a night club in every house . . . where admission is free and a thousand shapely legs are displayed . . . aside from all this, there are two kinds of places: those one talks about and those one doesn't talk about, but frequents just the same.[1]

One talked about the popular *Varieté*, or vaudeville shows in the amusement palaces, such as the Wintergarten or Scala, which entertained the multitudes:

A maharaja, complete with turban and number one wife, prepares to stretch out on a bed of nails. But his act requires that at least six people stand on his chest. He entreats volunteers from the audience to come up onto the stage. First he tempts them in suitably broken German: "Gentl'men, pleez come." When this has no effect, he forgets himself: "Come on, get going!" he shouts in a perfect Berlin accent . . .

The enormous cellar, rebuilt as a theater, contains the flower of the neighborhood youth, young lovers, and whole families. For the independent merchants there is a wine terrace. The audience enjoys everything. And why not? The tickets cost only sixty pfennig. For that you get stale air and a program which runs from half past seven to one o'clock in the morning. Not to be sneezed at . . .

Before the intermission the master of ceremonies, dressed in black and silver, recommends, in high-flown verse, the hot dogs and the cold beer. Afterward there is a first-rate sketch: "Madame Olala," starring the wife of the owner. Her ensemble includes [the popular stars] Max Hansen, Max Adelbert, Max Pallenberg, Paul Nikolaus, and Otto Gebühr. Well, not in person, that would be a bit much to demand for sixty pfennig. But each actor in this ensemble is a type, each has a knack for impersonating various well-known stage personalities . . . It really could have been him, but it wasn't—was it?[2]

What the vaudeville was for the proletarian Saturday night, the revue was for the middle class. In the Metropol, with 1,800 seats; the Admirals-Palast, with 2,200; and in Max Reinhardt's rebuilt circus, the Grosses

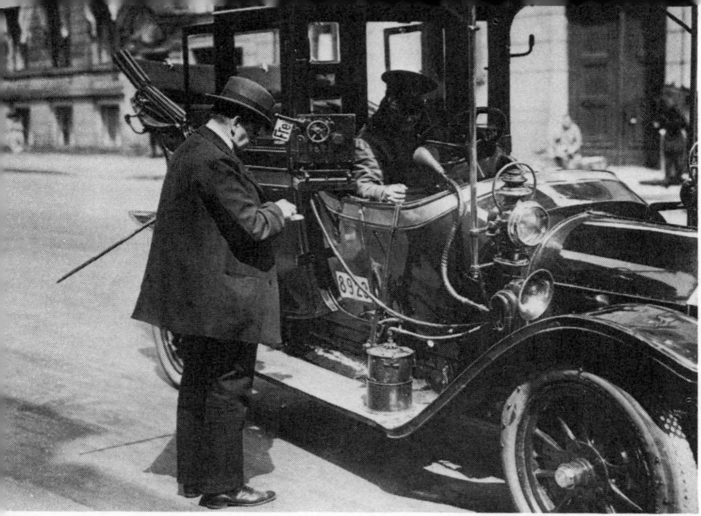

Schauspielhaus, with up to 5,000 seats, the revue held sway.

Patterned after the *Ziegfeld Follies,* the revues offered the best comics, naked girls, brilliant dance numbers, naked girls, imaginative costumes, naked girls, naked girls, naked girls . . .

Not that one had to go to a revue for a girlie show. The Münzstrasse was lined with clubs where for a small fortune and the risk of arrest, you could surreptitiously see "artistic dancing." But the revues raised the nude dance and the tableau to a kind of an art. Nudity was not the sole drawing card—and you could take your wife, if that's whom you wanted to take.

The revue was passive escape. The cabaret was more demanding. The Berlin cabaret, dating back to the 1890s, was based on the French model—short revues, usually topical, often political in nature, interlarded with songs. It was the place to go for those on the go in Berlin. It was out to startle rather than convert. Erich Kästner's *Fabian,* a novel about Berlin at the time, gives us an idea what it was like:

On the rickety stage, an inanely smiling girl leaped up and down. She seemed to be a sort of dancer. She was dressed in a bilious green, homemade dress, holding a branch of artificial flowers in her hand, and periodically threw herself and the branch in the air. At stage left, a toothless old man sat at an untuned piano playing the Hungarian Rhapsody.

Whether the girl and the piano had any relationship to each other could not be judged. The elegantly dressed public drank wine, talked loudly, and laughed.

"A telephone call for you, Miss!" catcalled a bald gentleman, who seemed to be at least a chairman of some board. The others laughed even more. The dancer refused to be disturbed and continued to smile and jump. Then the piano stopped. The Rhapsody *was finished. The girl on stage tossed a bitter look at the piano player and continued to hop—her dance was not yet finished.*

"Mama, your kid's calling," croaked a woman wearing a monocle.

"Yours too, lady!" someone shouted from a distant table.

The lady turned around. "I don't have any children."

Berlin's hectic night life was reflected by the bright lights that illuminated the many shopping and entertainment streets, such as Kurfürstendamm and Friedrichstrasse. The photo above shows the night scene at Luna Park, a downtown amusement park somewhat similar to Copenhagen's famous Tivoli. The photo below shows the corner of Unter den Linden and Friedrichstrasse. The taxi at the upper left was photographed around 1920. [*Landesbildstelle, West Berlin*]

"That's a joke on your children!" someone called from the back.

"Shut up," someone else shouted. The exchange stopped.

The girl continued to dance even though her legs must have been hurting. Finally she had enough, landed in an unsuccessful curtsy, smiled even more foolishly than before, and stretched out her arms. A fat man in a tuxedo stood up. "Excellent, really excellent! Report in the morning to beat my carpets." The public applauded and shouted. The girl curtsied again and again.

Then someone came out of the wings, pulled the reluctant dancer from the stage, and returned.

"Bravo, Caligula!" shouted a woman in the first row.

Caligula, a rotund Jew with horn-rimmed glasses, turned to the man next to her. "Is that your wife?" he asked.

The man nodded.

"Then tell your wife to keep her trap shut!" Applause. The man in the first row turned red. His wife looked flattered . . .[3]

Some years later, cabaret became, in today's jargon, politically relevant. New places included the Schwarze Kater in the Friedrichstrasse and its neighbor, the Café Zielka; the resurrected Grössenwahn in the Café des Westens on Kurfürstendamm; and the Alt-Bayern across from the Friedrichstrasse railroad station.

At Alt-Bayern, where one could find pseudo-Bavarian yodeling and folk dancing, Hellmuth Krüger, the master of ceremonies, expressed a middle-class yearning with a satirical daily prayer:

Dear God, let me become an American,
that's my greatest wish on earth.
Everything in America is larger, better,
faster than here—

Despite the growing popularity of the movies, the twenties were the years of vaudeville. Berlin had several *varieté* theaters. The largest and most famous were the Wintergarten and the Scala. Above, left: The Arthur Klein Family clowns and plays music on wheels. Above: A performer who called herself "Miss Nobody" bends iron bars without apparent effort. [*Archiv für Kunst und Geschichte, West Berlin*]

Respectable *Gemütlichkeit* prevailed at Resi, a popular night club near Alexanderplatz (above), while the more expensive cabarets, such as Die Weisse Maus (The White Mouse), featured thinly veiled tableaus (near right). Everywhere there were girls, girls, girls. The Tiller Girls at the far right are dancing on the street to advertise their show at the Scala. The actual evening performance was probably more precise. [*Staatsbibliothek, West Berlin*]

at least, I think it is.
The houses are higher and the
millionaires richer
than in the old out-of-work world.
Every beggar has his own car,
but there aren't many beggars.
They deliver newspapers when they are
kids;
that earns them their first million.
And they pray to God to deliver them from
their true selves
and give them chewing gum instead.
And give them, this day, their daily beer,
whiskey, and wine!
For Prohibition, they say, cannot be God's
will.
Dear God, let me become an American.[4]

In rhyme and song, Berlin's political cabaret critics and satirists, such as Walter Mehring, Klabund, Kurt Tucholsky, and Joachim Ringelnatz, who came from Munich and was dressed in a sailor's suit, offered their footnotes to the daily headlines, twitting and ridiculing the floundering Republic. The cabaret Schall und Rauch, which had been launched by Max Reinhardt before the war, re-opened with the songs of Paul Graetz and parodies by Hans Heinrich von Twardowski. At the Grössenwahn was Rosa Valetti; and at the Kuka, or Künstler-Café (Artists' Café), Erich Weinert held forth.

Among the wittiest of the cabaret

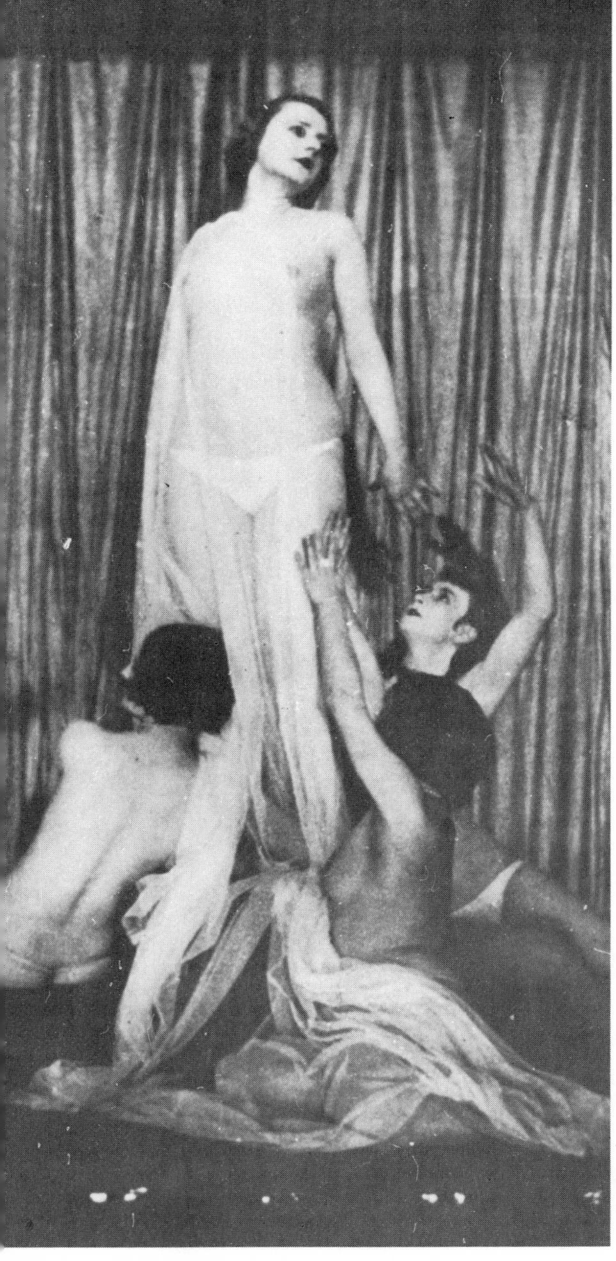

Conferenciers, as the Germans called the master of ceremonies, was Werner Finck, who opened his Katakombe in 1929. By then the National Socialist German Workers' party had gained steadily at the polls and rowdy brownshirts were increasingly evident on the streets. Finck would step in front of the curtain and tell the one about the law student sweating through his examination. His professor asked about the plea of insanity as grounds for acquittal. The student couldn't remember. "Now, come on," said the professor helpfully. "You read the papers. You know that every day defendants, whose crime has been proven, are acquitted, not because they are minors, not because they acted in self-defense, but because . . ."

The student still seemed lost. Then, suddenly, his face brightened and he said triumphantly: "Because they are Nazi, sir!"

Berlin did not have any indigenous carnival, Mardi gras, or *Fasching*. But it had its great balls. They were the zenith of the social season and there was one for just about every profession, taste, and *Weltanschauung*, from the notorious artists' ball at the Academy to the stiff reunion balls of elite-regiment officers. Everybody who was anybody came, and the nobodies came too. The decorations and costumes were often as elaborate as they were risqué.

The cabaretist "Pick Nick" relates:

One day my wife found me, after a long

Josephine Baker, the American singer and dancer whose base was the *Folies-Bergère* in Paris, also frequently visited Berlin to add sparkle to Berlin's night life. [*Landesbildstelle, West Berlin*]

search, in my study and said: "Listen, love, I've got a fabulous idea."

Since only women have fabulous ideas, that is, ideas which develop into fables, I put my pencil away, closed my typewriter, packed my papers into my briefcase, and said: "OK, shoot."

"What about going to the ball on Saturday?"

So that was the idea. I was extremely proud of my wife.

"What ball do you want to go to?"

"What about the Dance Instructors' Ball at the Philharmonic Hall?"

"How come?" I asked thoughtfully. "Will there be dancing there?"

My wife tossed me a glance of a loony-bin guard and rushed out . . .

On Saturday I tossed myself into my tuxedo, stuck a small tray and a bottle of club soda in my pocket, and was ready.

"Why are you doing that?" my wife demanded.

"You'll see," I answered with determination.

At the checkroom there was a crush like a fire sale. I sent my wife into the ballroom, threw a napkin over my arm, took the bottle on the tray in my right hand, and stormed into the room with the battle cry: "Comin' through, please, comin' through!"

I was in. But immediately someone grabbed me by the arm. "Say, didn't you just serve me? I want to pay for the two bottles immediately."

On the table stood two bottles of Bernkasteler. I didn't have the faintest idea what they cost, but even at school I was good at arithmetic.

"Two Bernkasteler at 12.40 marks makes 25.80 plus ten per cent makes 28.70," I muttered and looked piercingly at him. He gave me thirty marks. This gentleman obviously couldn't add as well as I.

After I had gotten rid of the tray and napkin, I looked around the room. It was wreathed in smoke. A joyful, illustrious society surrounded me . . . Suddenly a hefty lady aimed herself toward me, raised her lorgnette, and asked:

"You, listen, where is Victor?"

"Victor left a while ago with a young lady. I think they've gone to play ring-around-a-rosy."

"Oh," the lady sobbed.

"Don't despair," I said to her. "I know the lady well. She's the wife of a janitor."

Then the lady stared at me.

"But you're not my brother-in-law at all."

"No. I never claimed to be."

Sobbing, the much plagued woman vanished. God knows where Victor went. But God keeps his mouth shut.

Searching for my wife, I reached a table covered with the most remarkable profusion of items, objects which in earlier periods would have been given to the natives of far-off colonies to make it seem advantageous for them to be exploited by the whites. It was the raffle. I bought twelve draws and won a case of herring, which was carefully dusted. I took the herring by the tails and tossed them to the crowd. "Laugh it up!" I cried. "Laugh it up!" An enormous fellow thereupon presented me with a kidney punch. Actually, I prefer liver pâté to kidney punch.

"I'm going to call a foul," I said haughtily and collapsed into the directors' office.

There sat six extremely morose gentlemen —the ball committee. They had just divided up the gate and were in the process of deciding which one of them would get the door prize when I entered. I quickly observed that my presence was unnecessary and departed. One shouldn't pester busy people.

"Where have you been?" my wife asked when she finally located me.

"I was outside a bit."

"Outside?"

"Yep, dancing. At first the cars were somewhat bothersome, but after a while you hardly notice them."

Suddenly a trumpet sounded.

"Look, there's going to be a floor show," my wife said, drawing on her limited experience in these matters. "Hesterberg, Soneland, Massary, Claire Waldorff, Valetti, and Resi Langer have promised to show up."

"There they are, all together," I answered.

Variety shows were every bit as lavish as the *Ziegfeld Follies* in New York or the *Folies-Bergère* in Paris. This Berlin hit show, an expensive production staged in 1926 at the Admirals-Palast, includes three all-girl troupes, the Tiller Girls, the Admiral Girls, and the Paris Mannequins. [*From the program*]

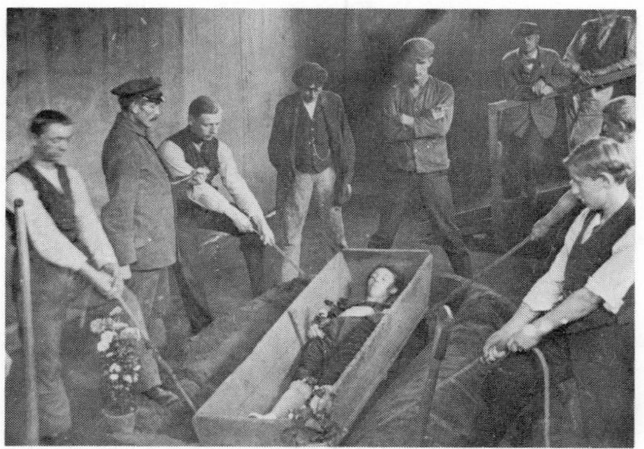

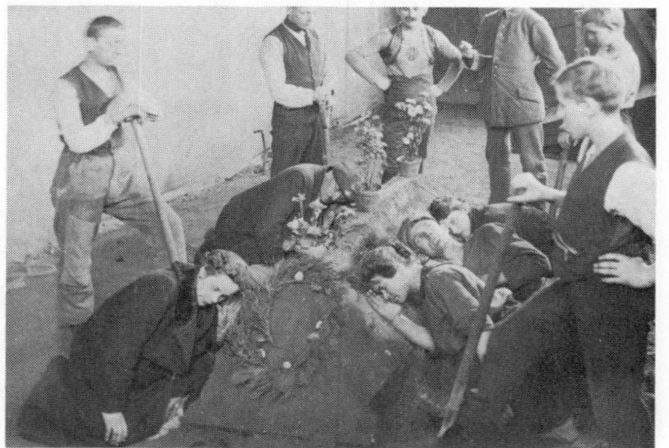

If most entertainment was sexy, some of it was macabre. Above: This amusement park show is entitled *Buried Alive*. Below: The Mexican circus performer Martini Szeny is about to unchain himself as he is dragged through the streets by a motorcycle. [*Archiv für Kunst und Geschichte, West Berlin*]

Six dolled up Tiller Girls stood on a table and did deep-knee bends.

It was a stable, prewar table.

"Fabulous," said a man behind me and applauded discreetly.

After the show the lights were dimmed. That is, they were turned down a little too late.

"Pay attention, now comes the surprise!" whispered my wife, who is an incurable optimist.

In this case, however, she was right. At that moment I began to scream at the top of my voice: "Fire! Help! Fire!"

Six dead and thirty-four walking wounded were swept out. "Only six dead?" a corpulent man asked of a thin one. "And not one prominent name among them? That won't make any headlines!" They were gentlemen of the press.[5]

The balls continued into morning. Afterward the tired dancers swept along to Aschinger's. It was *the* place to go, for everyone at any hour whether he was slumming or barely existing. Everyone got free rolls and bowls of pea soup. The recipe for the soup was created by a Nobel Prize-winning chemist. According to one account, the consumption of beer sausages at Aschinger's increased from 40,000 pairs to 65,000 pairs when Hindenburg became President of the Reich in 1925, presumably because the Field Marshal inspired new confidence in bourgeois stability.

The night clubs one did not talk about, according to Szatmari's guide, included the Residenzkasino, "Resi" for short, where every table was equipped with a telephone so one could call anyone in the place and get acquainted. Or, there was Eldorado, where you got a prize for the most original costume: first prize a live monkey, second prize a live parrot.

The band blares a Charleston, it's overcrowded, smoky, hot, crazy, and different. Tails and sports jackets, mink and pullovers, all mixed up. Paper streamers fly all over the dancing couples . . .

There is a secret about the place that belongs to the Berlin night. This place, one of Berlin's most popular, recruits its patrons mainly from circles where the arithmetic of love is not without its mistakes. Here men do not only dance with women but also with men. And women dance with women. And the nice gentleman from Saxony, who dances with the blond singer, doesn't have the slightest idea that his blond lady is a man . . . Unfortunately, even the Eldorado has lately become fashionable. It has moved to the Motzstrasse, into a more elegant environment, and has become clean and fancy. It has lost its old atmosphere.

But even the Eldorado, despite its regular clientele, does not belong to the bars that one really *doesn't talk about . . . they are known only to the initiated . . . they are the magnets of the Berlin night.*[6]

There were two kinds of night clubs. Those one talked about and those one didn't. Eldorado in the Motzstrasse was one of those discreet places "where the arithmetic of love is not without its mistakes." The only woman in this picture is the one seated at the left front. [*Staatsbibliothek, West Berlin*]

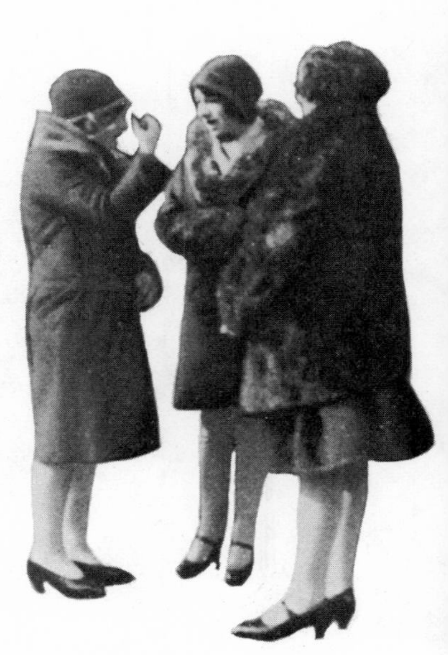

4

THE UNDERWORLD

Whores, Dope, and "Wrestling Clubs"

And some danced with death, as a poster on Berlin's ubiquitous *Litfassäulen*, or advertising pillars, warned.

The poster was put up by the government and took its slogan from a poem by Paul Zech:

The clouds blow, slamming shut,
The streets shout sound and light
And in the white sea of lights
Nothing bears a human face.
With animals' jaws and vultures' claws
They succumb to the final joy
And dance, while the thunder rolls,
To the sound of the drums and blabbing lips:
Berlin, wake up, don't be lazy.
You're dancing with gold!
Berlin is a pool of pitch,
Where the whore, Madam Waste-Your-Time,

Reclines in a golden rocking chair
Inflating the naked body,
Swallowing, skin, hair and all, the youths,
Forgotten by their fathers.
Gasping their final breaths
On the battlefield, strangled by poison gas:
Berlin, pay attention,
You're dancing with Satan!
They dance about the golden calf
From dawn to midnight black
And never know the reason why,
Raging beyond them in the war of brothers
Stupid men butchering one another.
Sometimes a flute screams
Calling them to masquerade, to parade:
Berlin, stop, and don't forget,
You're dancing with the plague.
The war ate all the men away
Ah God ain't worth a cent,
His image is tattered with blood and shit.
Where, where
Will the last storm clouds chase us?
The earth is damned
Screaming its final hour
From dawn to dawn:
Berlin, stop, wake up,
You're dancing with death.[1]

Leading the dance were touters who accosted people on the street after dark, promising all sorts of pleasures. At best, their victims were led to some basement joint where, for atrocious prices, they were treated to questionable champagne and even more questionable dance numbers. Sometimes you did not even get that much:

Alexandrinerstrasse. Midnight. We get out of our cab about three buildings from the bar. This is a security measure, so that no one notices that we have come by cab, a simple tactic but practical. When we enter the bar, I realize that the guy who touted us here really put one over on us. It is extremely dull.

At one table there is a party of overstuffed joes, singing folksongs— And at the toilet door reels a blond prostitute, who clearly has seen better days. Next to her, her "friend." Beggar and scalawag all in one.

A small beer costs ten pfennig in this "love" bar. Well, there are always places like this when you go bar hopping.

Thank God there is a subway stop almost in front of the door.[2]

Prostitution was rampant.

"Hey, buddy . . ." A youngster grabs my sleeve. He was maybe ten or twelve years old, a fresh expression on his face, a face framed by wisps of hair streaming out from under his cap. "Hey, buddy, buddy, ya got some time?" The youngster stands still and a secretive expression steals across his face. "Come here a minute into the doorway." I hardly have to fear being mugged, so we go for "a minute into the doorway." "I got a nice piece for you, if you got some time." Curious, I reply that I've got time. "I've got a sister, a real nice piece, I tell ya." "I believe you, but why did you call me in here to tell me that?" The boy grinned and twisted at his coat buttons. "Don't look at me like that; I tell ya she's really a knockout." I again professed my lack of comprehension and finally learned that I was supposed to "love" his sister. She is a real "knockout," "cheap" but no "used mattress." This was the advertising vocabulary of a twelve-year-old in a doorway in the Frankfurter Allee. I was interested in getting to know the specific circumstances of this

"'Hey, buddy . . .' A youngster grabs my sleeve. He was maybe ten or twelve years old . . ."

line of business, and so I went along. "Nifty," said my guide. "I knew right away you was a sport."

We stopped in front of a massive apartment block in the Breslauer Strasse. "OK, we live here; can ya give me somethin' for my trouble? It's usually fifty pfennig." After *I had paid his "commission," the business continued. Through the courtyard gate we entered the inner court, littered with garbage cans. Two, three flights of stairs, high above us burned a tiny kerosene lamp. My guide opened the door and we were in a kitchen, which smelled strongly of cabbage and herring. The boy asked me to wait, vanished, and reappeared with his "sister." She was about thirty-six to thirty-eight years old, and, if related at all, was the boy's mother. Otherwise she was dressed cleanly and not unattractive. The youngster disappeared and I carefully began to ask the woman about the situation, explaining that curiosity had brought me to learn a bit about this type of soliciting. She led me into the other room. Behind a curtain the bed linen glowed a bright white . . . The woman explained while chain smoking: "God, ya gotta live . . . I used to go on the street . . . but the competition was too much . . . my husband has been dead for eight years . . . and how can you get married again in all this misery . . . The boy is my stepson, my husband's kid . . . Two of my friends sent their husbands hustling . . ." On the Frankfurter Allee I see the boy again, grabbing someone by the sleeve: "Hey, buddy . . ."*[3]

More respectable and younger streetwalkers usually started on Kurfürstendamm, with its expensive shops, restaurants, and bars. Then, slowly, they had to move further downtown to Nollendorfplatz and their prices moved down, too, from fifty to twenty marks. By the time a woman had to go as far downtown as Bülowbogen, she would do it for ten marks. At Büschingplatz, one mark fifty was all she could expect.

On Büschingplatz, across from 18 Büschingstrasse, among a group of "colleagues," stands a woman. She is obviously a prostitute. She seems only a large, thin shape in a black coat. The hat is pushed far over her face . . . "Are you coming?" says the broken voice of an old woman . . .

She climbs the stairs slowly, leaning heavily on the railing. The flashlight is dim. We don't stop on the fifth floor. There is still one more flight of narrow stairs. Finally, we are in her apartment and the batteries die. A dog jumps at me in the dark. The place reeks of cats . . .

The woman takes off her coat and hat . . . She sits on the foot of the bed, looks at me, and says nothing. Only one eye looks at me. The other is blind, covered with an inflamed lid. Her hair is only a few inches long and snow white, her pinkish scalp shining through. Her face is gray, pale, and sunken. Her hands, crippled with age, try to tie a knot in her hair . . . I am ashamed, give her money, and leave.[4]

Perhaps it was that same woman Gottfried Benn, a physician and poet, saw at the morgue:

The last molar of a whore,
died without name or address,
encased a gold filling.
All her others had gone,
as if in silent agreement.
This last one was knocked out by

"... 'I've got a sister, a real nice piece.' ..." [*From Weka (Willi Pröger)*, Stätten der Berliner Prostitution]

the coroner's assistant, who pawned it to go
dancing.
For, he said,
Only earth should return to earth.[5]

Prostitution, as happened so often, led to drugs, or was it the other way around? Bert Brecht, at any rate, wrote a poem about it:

I'm a turd. From myself
I can only demand
weakness, betrayal, and ruin
but one day I notice:
It's getting better: I've wind in
my sails: my time is here, I can be
better than a turd—
I've begun.

Because I was a turd, I notice
when I am drunk, I lie down
Simply and don't know
who walks across me, now I don't
drink anymore.
I have stopped cold.
Sadly I must
do much that hurts me to keep me
alive; I've eaten poison, which would have
killed four horses, because it was
the only way to stay alive; every once in a while
I sniffed cocaine, until I looked
like a sheet without bones.
Then I looked in a mirror—
And stopped.
They tried to give me syphilis
but they didn't succeed,
They could only poison me
with arsenic: I had tubes in my side
from which, day and night, pus flowed.
Who would have thought that men would
ever again excite me?
I immediately began again.
I never took a man along who didn't
do something for me, and I needed everyone.
I'm almost without feeling,
No longer moist
But
I still feel it going in and out, but mostly in.
I still notice that I call my enemy "old whore"
and recognize her as an enemy when a man looks at her.
But in a year
I will have shaken even this—
I've begun.
I am a turd, but everything is
for the best. I'm coming.

Left: The more attractive streetwalkers usually started on Kurfürstendamm. In time they moved to the less fashionable Nollendorfplatz and Friedrichstrasse (where this picture was taken) and charged less for their services. Above: The typical lodging of a Berlin prostitute. [*From* Weka (Willi Pröger), Stätten der Berliner Prostitution]

I am the sex of tomorrow
Already not a turd, but
the hard mortar from which
cities are made.
(*I heard a woman say that*)[6]

Dope—morphine, heroin, and cocaine—was not hard to find, according to police reports of the time. You could get it even at hot dog stands, and Berlin had its "coke" (short for cocaine) cafés, much as Peking had its opium dens. You could get the stuff from the owner, the waiters, or some steady patrons. The pushers were all over.

If the police got tough, the pushers got more careful; they would resort to coded advertising. The addict would, for instance, find some numbers scribbled on the day's latest *Litfassäule* poster. On one of them, on Wittenbergplatz, the numbers read:

12
9
14
11
—
31
—
4
6

The first set of numbers stood for the number of a letter in the alphabet—12=L, and so on. The set spelled "Link" and meant "Linkstrasse." Then came the house number, and next the time, from four to six, when you could get the "cement" or "cocoa," as cocaine was also called. On occasion, there would be a police raid, though police officials complained that it was hard to take effective action.

There was no clearly defined gangster district in Berlin, nothing like London's Whitechapel. But there was no dearth of gangs. They would gather anywhere in the city, like the clustering streetwalkers—even in the fashionable West.

Most of them, however, would hang out in the workers' districts, in Wedding or Moabit, or around Alexanderplatz, which was dominated by the big, red "Alex," the police headquarters building. Stepping into a bar in one of these neighborhoods, you might find a big sign to inform you that you have entered the home of the "Savings Club 'German Oak.' "

A savings club in this part of Berlin?

Other criminal gangs had other camouflaging names, such as "Evergreen," "Forget-Me-Not," "Black Bear," or " 'Tween Us." The disguise of these "social clubs" was only superficial. The police knew most of these groups of second-story men, bank robbers, strongarm men, and their hangers on.

Each of the clubs had its dive, full of dark characters and brightly painted hussies, that must have inspired Brecht's *Threepenny Opera*.

Eugen Szatmari advised the readers of his aforementioned guidebook not to visit these

Drugs were not hard to find. Pushers were everywhere. This photo, from the collection of a police detective, illustrates how cocaine was sold in perfume bottles. [*From Ernst Engelbrecht,* 15 Jahre Kriminalkommissar]

places alone. But some adventurous thrill seekers did go slumming in gangster bars. The regulars would recognize strangers at once and pay no attention. The patrons never minded respectable cash.

It was, of course, a risky kind of *Amusmang*, and not everyone was as brave—or lucky?—as the fellow Szatmari tells about:

It once happened that the late actor Lambertz-Paulsen, who was as strong as he was fearless, was beaten up, robbed, and thrown out on the street by two criminals in a gangster dive near the Schlesischer Bahnhof. He

Criminal gangs were camouflaged as social clubs. This "wrestling club," which had its picture (above) taken with a police mascot, called itself "The Harmless Thirteen." Right: A typical bar. The sign means "Last Resort." [*Staatsbibliothek, West Berlin*]

returned to his club, where, by chance, he ran into a friend who was a professional boxer. Actor, boxer, and two others drove back to the dive, where they still found the offenders. Lambertz-Paulsen, beaten up and bloody as he was, took revenge. Plenty.[7]

Another observer, the journalist Leo Heller, described another underworld scene in 1927:

In a dive in the Münzstrasse we walk past a door marked with a large chalk zero. Behind it sits a man at a table, staring at the ground as if deep in thought. Even so, he is paying close attention to the goings on at the neighboring table. Suddenly he whistles softly. Someone just walking past hears the whistle and stops.

Evenin', Max.
Sit down, Erich.
I ain't got no dough.
I'll pay . . . You wanna——
Wanna what?
Pull somethin' off? A slick piece! Completely safe.
What do I do? Look out?
No, a bit of safe work. Not difficult. An old bucket.
Nothing else? Seems easy . . .
Don't worry! Got your tools?
A few, but enough.
Good, then we leave at four! Meetcha at the Alex. But don't come stoned! And don't tell Trude anything.
Goddam, the broad is OK.

All broads are alike, Max! They'll turn ya in sooner or later. OK, deal closed . . .

Waiter, two schnapps . . .[8]

In 1929 Alfred Döblin wrote a novel called *Berlin—Alexanderplatz*. Here is a passage about a night out with a *Ringverein*, or "wrestling club":

Saturday night Franz is along for the first time. Franz Biberkopf, he's sitting in the car, they all know what to do, he's got his role down just like the others. Everything follows quite businesslike . . . At ten they opened the building for the others, no one in it was the wiser, there are only offices and businesses. Then they start peacefully to work, one at the window, looking out, one staring into the courtyard, then cutting through the floor, half a meter square. The plumber does it with a blowtorch, wearing safety glasses, when they've gotten through the wood of the ceiling below, a banging, a scraping—it's nothing, only bits of heavy plaster falling through; the ceiling is collapsing from the heat, they stick a fine silk umbrella through the first opening, most of the pieces fall in, most, one can't catch all of them. Nothing happens; beneath them everything is dead quiet.

About eleven they break in, first the elegant Waldemar, because he knows the layout. He goes down the rope ladder like a cat. He is doing it for the first time, no trace of fear, these are the pure-bred greyhounds, they have the most luck, until something goes wrong, of course. And then another one must go down. The steel ladder is only two and a half meters long, not long enough to reach the ceiling. They push some tables together, then the others let the ladder down slowly, and there we are. Franz stays on top, lying on his stomach above the hole, hauling up, like a fisherman, the bales of cloth they send up, pushing them behind him where someone else is already standing. Franz is strong. Reinhold, who is below with the plumber, is amazed. Neat thing, what a one-armed man can do. His arm works like a crane, it is fantastic, an unbelievable piston. Afterwards, they drag the baskets downstairs. Even though someone is guarding the courtyard entrance, Reinhold patrols. Two hours more and everything will be all right, the night watchman comes through the building, don't start anything, he's not goin' to notice anything, he'd be stupid for the couple of marks he gets to get himself shot. No. See, there he goes, a good man, we'll leave a hundred marks for him. Now it's 2:00, at 2:30 the car is coming. In the meantime, those above are eating breakfast, not too much schnapps, someone'll make a noise, and now it's 2:30. Two men had pulled their first job tonight, Franz and the elegant Waldemar. They quickly flip a coin, Waldemar wins, he's got to put the final seal on today's job, he's gotta go down the ladder once more, into the dark, plundered warehouse, and there he bends down, pulls his pants down, and empties the contents of his bowels on the floor.[9]

The authorities did their best to respond to such insults. One summer day, one of these gangster "clubs" went on a lakeside picnic and had a great time—planning the next bank robbery. As the boys were talking, a launch with a *Gesangverein*, a singing club, landed nearby, lustily singing "*Ach, Du lieber Augustin.*"

The singers turned out to be cops.

A police riot squad in 1921. Berlin's police was as efficient as any. [*Landesbildstelle, West Berlin*]

The Romanische Café. [*Drawing by Rudolf Grossmann*]

5

INTELLECTUALS: *Soft Eggs, Satire, and Forebodings*

Berlin's intellectuals, and those who wished to be known as such, gathered in the cafés.

Elsewhere, one might look for the intellectual elite behind desks and classroom lecterns. In Germany, intellectuals had rarely held office, rank, or title, which meant that they did not count for much among their countrymen. Those who had authority were rarely intellectual.

But in the Berlin of the twenties it seemed different. Intellectuals gained some prominence. And one way of showing they had made it was to be seen at the Romanische Café, which was comparable to the Café du Dôme in Paris and the Café Central in Vienna at the time.

The shabbily splendid Romanische was located across from the Kaiser Wilhelm Gedächtniskirche. It was filled, almost around the clock, with painters and art dealers, writers and publishers, journalists and editors, radio entertainers and broadcasting officials, musicians and conductors, actors and producers, dancers and choreographers, psychiatrists and divorce lawyers, bohemians of all kinds, who seemed to be lost, girls of all ages who hoped to be found, and a lot of cigarette smoke and stale air.

The air, contrary to frequent assertions, was not all these *Luftmenschen*, or "air people," lived on. They also sustained themselves—often with money they borrowed, table hopping, from one other—on coffee and a fashionable soft-boiled egg, served in a glass.

As one wit rhymed:

Once man was like God,
But that has been spoiled.
Now man rules alone
On an egg, soft-boiled.[1]

In the first flush of excitement, Berlin's intellectuals eagerly rallied to the banners of the revolution. But disillusionment was swift and all but a few either withdrew into a haughty, apolitical stance or changed from passionate partisanship to passionate polemics. The left-wing polemicists enjoyed the new democracy mainly as an object of ridicule. And they all talked and talked and talked.

Much of the talk found its way into print and broadcast and sparked a burst of new literature: out of the Romanische came many a novel that is now considered classic; many a play that is still performed; movie scripts that still move us; a surfeit of articles in Berlin's surfeit of magazines (literary and otherwise); and reams of *Feuilletons* (as the Germans call cultural feature stories and critical reviews) that filled the city's newspapers (which, by 1930, numbered no less than 147).

The artists at the Romanische Café—among them were George Grosz, Emil

Samuel Fischer, at right, Germany's foremost publisher, in 1927 with Hermann Stehr, Gerhart Hauptmann, and Mrs. Hauptmann. [*Archiv für Kunst und Geschichte, West Berlin*]

Orlik, and Max Slevogt—tended to gather mainly in the smaller room, "the swimming pool." The literary people preferred the larger room, "the non-swimming pool." In it you could find Bert Brecht, Heinrich Mann, Billy Wilder, Joseph Roth, Carl Zuckmayer, and such visitors from abroad as Thomas Wolfe or Sinclair Lewis and his wife, Dorothy Thompson.

Almost every prominent writer in the Western world came to Berlin at one time or another during the twenties, though, except for Christopher Isherwood, they never stayed as long there as they did in Paris. The Romanische Café was their point of contact.

The gossip columnist "Rumpelstilzchen" (Adolf Stein) complained that the regulars at the Romanische were cliquish. You had to come steadily for some time and become part of the general crowd before you could join one of the various exclusive groups. Casual droppers-in were nuisances. Rumpelstilzchen once saw Else Lasker-Schüler, Germany's leading woman poet at the time, at the Romanische, in an emotional outburst:

One of the Mosse papers published a slimy, sentimental piece about Lasker-Schüler. It says that she is in financial trouble and down to painting picture postcards . . . And what do you know! One of those nouveau-riche droppers-in runs up and buys one from her.

There she stands in a telephone booth and yells at the feature editor to print a retraction at once. "You don't know what you've done to me! Now the shitheads from Kurfürstendamm are coming here and offering me five marks! . . . I could shoot you . . ."[2]

Rumpelstilzchen wryly observed that Kurfürstendamm would have served the poet better by buying her books rather than her postcards.

A most controversial topic of high-brow talk—a topic which soon had a subliminal influence on the art and literature of the time—was the intellectual revolution Sigmund Freud had set off in Vienna. In its early days of almost religious faith and fervor, psychoanalysis was doubtlessly more talked about in Berlin than in any other metropolis, including Vienna itself. The world's first public psychoanalytical clinic and training school was founded in Berlin in 1921. Its teachers and students spread the gospel according to Sandor Rado, Franz Alexander, Karen Horney, Otto Fenichel, Melanie Klein, Wilhelm Reich, Karl Abraham, and Hanns Sachs, the chief analyst at the Berlin school. Freud himself attended Berlin's psychoanalytic congress in 1922.

The interest in Freud led to the first Institute for Sexual Science. It was founded in Berlin by Magnus Hirschfeld two decades before Kinsey and three decades before Masters and Johnson. The institute published books and magazines to enlighten the general public. It also initiated the *Aufklärungsfilm*, (an educational film) which presented the naked truth about sex—clad in fiction.

Technology and culture, once thought to make up what was called "civilization," have become things apart. A civilization may be able to leave its debris on the moon, but that does not necessarily make it "civilized," in the old, Jeffersonian sense of the word. In this respect, too, Berlin in the twenties also seemed different.

We don't know whether the great theologian of the time Adolf von Harnack ever sipped coffee and slurped soft-boiled eggs at the Romanische Café. But, back in 1911, Harnack, who was also director of the Prussian State Library, founded the Kaiser-Wilhelm-Gesellschaft, a scientific research institute in wealthy, verdant Dahlem, a suburb of Berlin. The proliferating academic and industry-sponsored research institutes had, of necessity, become very specialized and were thus in danger of leading to dead ends. What is more, the time and budgets of scientists were, also of necessity, largely devoted to education and administration. Too little was left for research, pure research, and interdisciplinary contact, exchange, and inspiration. Significantly, it was a theologian who founded the Kaiser-Wilhelm-Gesellschaft, which kept its name through the Weimar Republic but is now known as the Max Planck Institute for the Advancement of Science. Its idea was to provide an opportunity for outstanding scientists to follow their own ideas and to create a center for pure research rather than for a specific scientific purpose. It was—and is—in fact, a place for search, rather than research. Among the institute's luminaries at various times in the twenties were Albert Einstein, Lise Meitner, Fritz Huber, Walter Nernst, and Max Planck. They were part of the intellectual life of Berlin and, although they did not know it, began to change the world even more profoundly than the two world wars through which they lived.

The headquarters of the German book publishing industry was Leipzig. But the avant-garde, as in other fields, centered on Berlin, where Samuel Fischer had founded his remarkable publishing house in 1886 whose authors titillated the well-read German middle class with the new literature of a new era. Fischer introduced Thomas and Heinrich Mann, Stefan Zweig, Gerhart Hauptmann, Knut Hamsun, Sigrid Undset, and other major authors. Other, smaller publishers, who represented the younger generation, were Erich Reiss, who published Klabund (the pseudonym of Alfred

Albert Einstein was one of the luminaries at Berlin's Kaiser-Wilhelm-Gesellschaft who changed the world even more profoundly than two world wars. [*Landesbildstelle, West Berlin*]

Franz Werfel. [*Staatsbibliothek, West Berlin*]

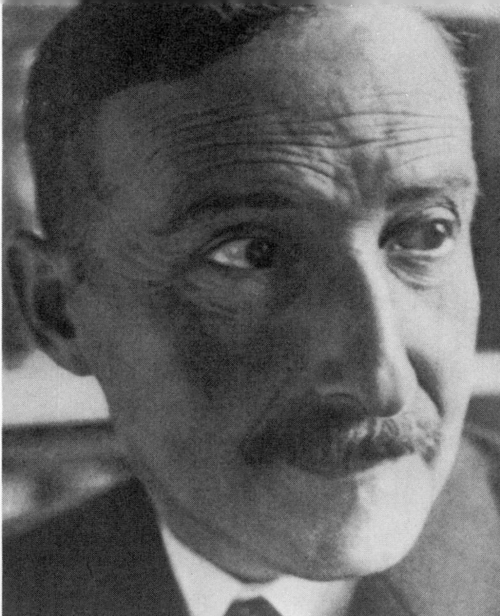

Stefan Zweig. [*Staatsbibliothek, West Berlin*]

Erich Maria Remarque. [*Staatsbibliothek, West Berlin*]

Erich Kästner. [*Landesbildstelle, West Berlin*]

Carl Zuckmayer. [*Staatsbibliothek, West Berlin*]

Stefan George. [*Private Collection, Gilman*]

DER STURM

MONATSSCHRIFT / HERAUSGEBER: HERWARTH WALDEN

DREIZEHNTER JAHRGANG / DRITTES HEFT

Die Weltbühne

Der Schaubühne XXVIII. Jahr

Wochenschrift für Politik · Kunst · Wirtschaft

Begründet von Siegfried Jacobsohn

Unter Mitarbeit von Kurt Tucholsky

geleitet von Carl v. Ossietzky

Inhalt:

Hellmut v. Gerlach . . . Papens Sündenregister
Johannes Bückler . . . Wahl-Interviews
S. Grumbach . . . Frankreich sieht nach Deutschland . . .
Hanns-Erich Kaminski . . . Lehrmeister Reaktion
K. L. Gerstorff . . . Die Zahlen vom 31. Juli
Gerhart Pohl . . . Der große Brockhaus als Literaturbetrachter
Peter Panter . . . Schnipsel
Alice Ekert-Rotholz . . . Der Mann, der verzeiht
Werner Hegemann . . . Weltretter oder -verderber Henry Ford
Wochenschau des Rückschritts / Wochenschau des Fortschritts
Bemerkungen — Antworten

Erscheint jeden Dienstag

XXVIII. Jahrgang 9. August 1932 Versandort Potsdam

Verlag der Wel

Charlottenburg-

Direktion r. hausmann
Steglitz zimmermann
strasse 34

DER dada

50 Pfg.

dadadegie

hausmann · baader

3/ 3333/3333

5,0

Ach

3,14159

Jahr 1 des Weltfriedens. Avis dada

Hirsch Kupfer schwächer. Wird Deutschland verhungern? Dann muß es unterzeichnen. Fesche junge Dame, zweiundvierziger Figur für Hermann Loeb. Wenn Deutschland nicht unterzeichnet, so wird es wahrscheinlich unterzeichnen. Am Markt der Einheitswerte überwiegen die Kursrückgänge. Wenn aber Deutschland unterzeichnet, so ist es wahrscheinlich, daß es unterzeichnet um nicht zu unterzeichnen. Amorsäle. Achtuhrabendblattmitbrausendeshimmels. Von Viktorhahn. Loyd George meint, daß es möglich wäre, daß Clémenceau der Ansicht ist, daß Wilson glaubt, Deutschland müsse unterzeichnen, weil es nicht unterzeichnen nicht wird können. Infolgedessen erklärt der club dada sich für die absolute Preßfreiheit, da die Presse das Kulturinstrument ist, ohne das man nie erfahren würde, daß Deutschland endgültig nicht unterzeichnet, blos um zu unterzeichnen. (Club dada. Abt. für Preßfreiheit, soweit die guten Sitten es erlauben.)

Die neue Zeit beginnt mit dem Todesjahr des Oberdada

Ad 1

Mitwirkende: Baader, Hausmann, Huelsenbeck, Tristan Tzara.

[*Landesbildstelle and Akademie der Künste, West Berlin*]

Henschke), and Herwarth Walden, whose Sturm Publishing House first introduced Marc Chagall in one of its inexpensive art books.

The most outstanding and most controversial book to come out of Berlin in those days was, without doubt, Erich Maria Remarque's *Im Westen Nichts Neues* (*All Quiet on the Western Front*). It was published in 1929 by Ullstein.

Remarque was a sports writer for one of the Ullstein papers when he wrote the novel, which, cutting through all the patriotic cant, said that war is hell. Those who had been there in 1914–18 gave a sigh of relief. Those who had stayed home or at rear command posts thought it sacrilege, if not treason. Remarque became famous overnight.

Most of the popular magazines were also published by Ullstein, a huge, Hearstlike enterprise. *Der Querschnitt* (*Cross-section*) had been founded by Alfred Flechtheim, the famous art dealer, and brought culture to the multitudes. *Die Koralle* (*Coral*) was a popular science magazine. *Das Blatt der Hausfrau* (*Housewife's Journal*) offered helpful hints to homemakers. *Die Dame* (*The Lady*) dealt with fashion in a fashionable way. *Uhu* (*Owl*) was a satirical magazine that also included some notable literary writing.

But of far greater historic significance were a number of struggling, independent journals. The most important of them were *Der Sturm* (*The Storm*), the magazine of the Sturm Publishing House and a catalyst of modern art, and Siegfried Jacobsohn's *Die Weltbühne* (*The World Stage*).

Die Weltbühne began publication before World War I under the title *Die Schaubühne* (*The Theater*) as a journal of dramatic criticism. During the war it became ever more political and in 1918 Jacobsohn changed the name. It became the most influential journal of opinion in Germany. Its essays tried to avoid intellectual snobbery. Left-wing without being Marxist, *Die Weltbühne* tried to inform rather than incite and to guide liberal readers gently toward pacifism and socialist reform.

In 1926, after Jacobsohn's death at forty-five, Kurt Tucholsky, the satirist, assumed the editorship, which he handed to Carl von Ossietzky a year later. Ossietzky, a pacifist, was one of the most brilliant journalists of his time. His independence and forthrightness, not surprisingly, aroused the hatred of the extreme right and the Reichswehr generals.

In 1931 he was convicted for betraying military secrets in a 1929 article about the German air force, written by Walter Kreiser, an aircraft engineer. The article contained nothing that had not previously appeared in trade publications. It criticized fiscal waste by the military. Both editor and author were sentenced. Ossietzky told his readers:

It is certainly not necessary to defend Kreiser and myself to the readers of the Weltbühne, *but we have been slandered before a public which does not know us and which bases its opinions on allegations in the nationalistic press and we were unable to defend ourselves. Behind locked doors, we were judged to have given military secrets to foreign powers. The* Frankfurter Zeitung *wrote that the damage to our reputation is even worse than prison . . .*

Joachim Ringelnatz, whose real name was Hans Bötticher, was a humorous poet, cabaret comedian, and painter who liked to perform in a sailor's suit. [*Staatsbibliothek, West Berlin*]

Brecht contemplating the bust of Brecht. [*Brecht Archiv, East Berlin*]

We stand at a fateful turning point. In the foreseeable future open fascism can come to power. It is unimportant whether this is achieved through "legal" means or through those stemming from the hangman's fantasy of a Hessian judge. The most probable is a combination of the two: a government which closes both eyes, while the streets are given over to the hooligans and murder commandoes of the Stormtroopers to quash all opposition under the common label of "communist." There is still the possibility for the union of all antifascist forces. Still! Republicans, Socialists, Communists, in the large party organizations or alone—you will not for long enjoy the chance to make your decisions in freedom and not at the point of bayonets! The time of individual action is passed. The civil war among the socialists has suddenly become questionable even to its most enthusiastic supporters. In these momentous times, the trial of the Weltbühne *is but a small incident . . .*[3]

But it was significant. Shortly after he was released from serving his term, Ossietzky's prediction came true. Fascism had come to power. The Nazis arrested him again and tortured him in a concentration camp. In 1936 he was awarded, in absentia, the Nobel Peace Prize for 1935. But he was a broken man. He spent the remaining two years of his life in a hospital.

Carl von Ossietzky, one of Germany's most brilliant journalists and winner of the 1935 Nobel Peace Prize, in a Nazi concentration camp. He had predicted the winning combination: a government that closed both eyes and streets given over to Stormtroopers. [*Staatsbibliothek, West Berlin*]

6

NEWSPAPERS AND RADIO

Much Heat and Little Light

Even under the Kaiser, Berlin's newspapers had been dominated by three names, Leopold Ullstein, August Scherl, and Rudolf Mosse. Ullstein, who published the *Berliner Illustrirte*, the world's first picture magazine, the tabloid *Tempo*, and the oldest and most prestigious of the Berlin newspapers, the *Vossische Zeitung* (often called "Auntie Voss"), had followed strongly monarchist lines. Scherl created the first "American-style" newspaper in Germany, the *Lokalanzeiger*; it merged popular journalism and the serial novel, which did for newspapers what soap opera does for television. The House of Mosse began as an advertising agency and entered the newspaper business with the *Berliner Tageblatt*, which reflected moderate middle-class views.

These newspaper empires survived the fall of the Kaiser's empire in 1918, and none of these papers changed its name, though most changed their political character.

The number of newspapers increased as the influence of the metropolitan press (or the myth thereof) decreased. Two more names became prominent in the news business: Alfred Hugenberg and Willi Münzenberg.

Hugenberg represented a consortium of conservative Ruhr industrialists which, in 1916, had bought the Scherl papers. Hugenberg also owned the Berlin news agency Telegraphen Union and the largest German film studio, Universum Film A.G., or UFA.

Vossische Zeitung
Berlin
B.Z. am Mittag
Der Reise-Rekord des englischen Thronfolgers
In 9½ Tagen mit Bahn und Schiff von Ostafrika nach London
Von heute ab: Internationale Automobil- und Motorrad-Ausstellung in Berlin
Die größte Auto-Schau
Tempo
Präsident Hoovers erste Rede: „Rüstet endlich ab!"
Explosion in Sofia: 28 Tote
Dienstag beginnt der Minderheiten-Streit
Berliner Morgenpost
Macht Platz für Stresemann!
Berliner Montagspost
Mit ausführlichen Sportberichten
Begeisterter Flieger-Empfang in New York.
Köhl kündigt einen neuen Ozean-Flug an
Die Wahl-Entscheidung in Frankreich.
Die Grüne Post
Sonntagszeitung für Stadt und Land

Alfred Hugenberg in 1931. The leader of the German Nationalist party, Hugenberg owned a number of newspapers, a news agency, and UFA, the largest German film studio. Left: Hugenberg (facing camera) with leaders of the Stahlhelm, a paramilitary organization. Right: With Oberhofprediger (Chief Court Preacher) D. Doehring. Opposite: A selection of popular German magazines. [*Landesarchiv and Landesbildstelle, West Berlin*]

He was a politician, the leader of the German National People's party, whose views dominated his publications and films. He made clear where he stood, which was more or less in Hitler's corner, though on a less crudely made soap box. In 1931 Hugenberg wrote:

During the election of 1930 I said: "Make the right wing strong!" Thousands of people understood this as a demand that they vote for the Nazis, because "they are today's right wing." A short word about this: Today, we, the German Nationalists, are still the right wing. No one exceeds us in the spirit of national reawakening. The struggle against Marxism and its supporters was led by my party of vision. Our basic economic and other programs are open for anyone to see. We need a national lifting of spirit and determination in Germany. But we also need sobriety and clarity in this time of confusion, hesitation, and extreme danger. Whoever wants to lead us, must make us strong. When I say, therefore, make the right wing strong, I mean make the German Nationalist party strong.[1]

Willi Münzenberg stood at the other extreme. He was a Communist Reichstag deputy and the ruler of the Communist press. Unlike Hugenberg, he managed to make his doctrine lively reading. The foremost of his publications was the *Arbeiter Illustrierte Zeitung*, or AIZ (*Workers' Illustrated*

20. Mai 1928
Nummer 21
37. Jahrgang
Berliner
Preis des Heftes
20 Pfennig
Illustrirte Zeitung
Verlag Ullstein Berlin SW 68

PREIS: M 1,50
DER QUERSCHNITT
BEGRÜNDET VON ALFRED FLECHTHEIM
HERAUSGEBER: H. V. WEDDERKOP
IM PROPYLAEN-VERLAG / BERLIN

Ullsteins
Blatt der Hausfrau
Großer Gratis-Bügelbogen für Buntstickerei
Ahoi!
Aus dem Inhalt:
Segen des Elternhauses / Die Wohnung ist keine Palette / Budapest, die Stadt am Strom / Takt in der Musik und im Leben / Dichterinnen der Gegenwart / Die Landpomeranze / Pflanzen im Zimmer

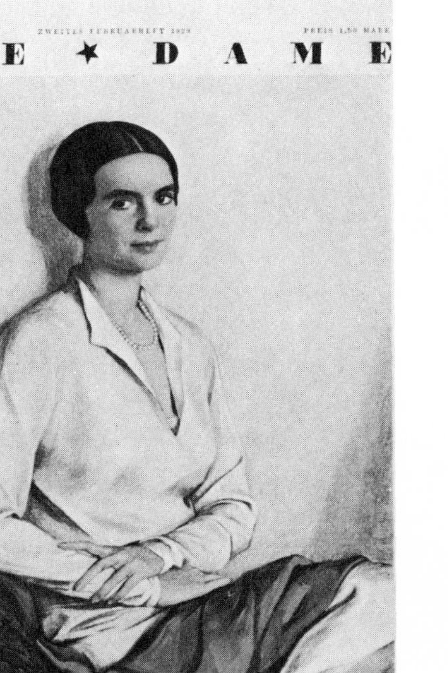
DIE ★ DAME

1 MARK
UHU

HEFT 6 / 4. JAHRGANG
BERLIN ENDE SEPTEMBER 1928
1 MARK
DIE KORALLE
Monatshefte für alle Freünde von Natür und Technik
Das Schiff ganz ohne Eisen

Newspaper), which used photojournalism to hawk the party line. As Münzenberg put it:

The AIZ is basically different from all other modern illustrated newspapers. It is completely oriented to the lives and struggles of the worker and the working class. It publishes pictures of factories, strikes, unemployment, demonstrations, rallies, and starvation.[2]

The Communist press was not the only one to mix fact and opinion into a kind of poisonous amphetamine for the mass of the German readers. Almost the entire German press became politically as confused as it was polarized. "What, when, where, and how" became matters of the editor's *Weltanschauung*.

It was hard for a reader to tell, from reading his newspaper, just what had happened on June 24, 1922, the day Walther Rathenau was murdered.

Rathenau was the son of the founder of the Allgemeine Elektrizitäts Gesellschaft, or AEG, Germany's largest electric company, which held Edison's German patent rights. Walther Rathenau was an inventor, philosopher, economist, political scientist, and, in 1922, Germany's Foreign Minister. He was conservative and exceedingly learned and cultured. But he was also a Jew, a fact which the right-wing conservatives would not forgive him. He favored Germany's reconciliation with the Allies, which the right found perhaps even more unforgivable.

The Freikorps and other fanatical nationalist groups, such as the Organization Consul, had already assassinated Karl Liebknecht and Rosa Luxemburg, former Finance Minister Matthias Erzberger, and several others. They had attacked Philipp Scheidemann with acid, though he escaped unhurt. Now they marched through the streets of Berlin and sang:

Shoot down the goddam Jewish sow,
Murder Walther Rathenau!

Rathenau knew his life was in danger. Everyone knew it. It was known as far away as New York. When Alfred Kerr, the theater critic, returned from a trip to the United States and met Rathenau, a neighbor in suburban Grunewald, he urged him to seek protection. Rathenau smiled, said it was all a matter of fate, and that he had just sent his three bodyguards away.

In the morning of that June day, riding in an open car from his home to the Foreign Ministry on the Wilhelmstrasse, Rathenau

Walther Rathenau was one of the most brilliant and erudite men of the Weimar Republic. He was a businessman, philosopher, inventor, and political scientist. As Foreign Minister in 1922, he negotiated the Treaty of Rapallo with the Soviet Union. The treaty established friendly diplomatic and trade relations between the two countries and did much to make the Western allies reconsider their harsh treatment of Germany. Rathenau was assassinated by German rightists on June 24, 1922. [*Landesbildstelle, West Berlin*]

Preis 2 Mark

Völkischer Beobachter

Kampfblatt der national-sozialistischen Bewegung Großdeutschlands

Leiter: Dietrich Eckart

Ausgabe 51 — München (Mittwoch), den 28. Juni 1922 — 36. Jahrgang

Der Tod des Walter Rathenau

Schutz der Republik

The *Völkischer Beobachter* was subtitled "Battle Organ of the National Socialist Movement of Greater Germany." It was published in Munich every Wednesday and Saturday, but sold—partly by Stormtroopers—all over Germany. [*Collection of the Institut für Zeitungsforschung, Darmstadt*]

was murdered by three former members of the Imperial Armed Forces.

Here is how, on their front page "news" columns, four different newspapers, the Nazi *Völkischer Beobachter* (*National Observer*), the Communist *Die Rote Fahne* (*The Red Flag*), the liberal non-partisan *Vossische Zeitung*, and the middle-of-the-road non-partisan *Berliner Tageblatt*, wrote about this same event:

VÖLKISCHER BEOBACHTER

Munich (*Wednesday*), *June 28, 1922*

The early death of Walther Rathenau understandably has caused great excitement in all levels of the population. After the event, we would not seem to have any further reason to concern ourselves with Rathenau's personality. But we must again turn to this subject because his death could be used as a new means of deceiving the working class.

The well-organized "Liar Press" has succeeded in presenting this man as the great friend of the working class and as a leader born to direct our fate. The goals, however, for which he strove, which he concocted and preached in his vanity and later out of his sense of total power, were never mentioned by our entire internationalist press. And this in spite of the fact that RATHENAU STOOD AT THE HEAD OF THE LARGEST CAPITALISTIC ENTERPRISE IN GERMANY, *the AEG, the stock value of which stood at 1,000 billion, 100 million* [*marks*] *in November of 1921:*

Eighteen years ago Rathenau already announced what was to become public knowledge in 1918: Three hundred men, "each knowing the others," determined the fate of the world and the hour struck for INTERNATIONAL FINANCE *to take the reins of government in place of Emperor and King . . . International high finance, embodied in a dozen Jewish bankers, should reign dictatorially over Europe.*

On the other hand, the capitalist Rathenau welcomed seemingly anticapitalistic Bolshevism and met frequently with its Jewish leaders. He told the Czech engineer Fleichner proudly that Lenin was basing his work on his (*Rathenau's*) *economic plans. He often visited Radek-Sobelsohn* [*Karl Radek, Berlin Marxist leader*] *in the Moabit prison. In 1919 Rathenau wrote: "The communes will replace western parliamentarianism . . ." He explained to a reporter of the Parisian* Liberté *that northern Germany had "fallen totally to Bolshevism" which was being "methodically organized" since "the intellectuals are its most zealous leaders." Rathenau, the richest employer in Germany, ends his pamphlet* Autonomic Economics *with the words: "There can be no peace between employer and employee. When strikes stop, the age of employment stops."*

At Cannes Rathenau stood for an international bankers' government. The name of this same man is written under the Treaty of

Die Rote Fahne was the official newspaper of the German Communist party. It first appeared on November 18, 1918, jointly edited by Karl Liebknecht and Rosa Luxemburg. It was frequently banned by the Weimar authorities. [*Collection of the Institut für Zeitungsforschung, Darmstadt*]

5. Jahrg. / Nr. 290 — Abend-Ausgabe — Sonnabend, den 24. Juni 1922

Die Rote Fahne

Zentralorgan der Kommunistischen Partei Deutschlands (Sektion der Kommunistischen Internationale)

Begründet von Karl Liebknecht und Rosa Luxemburg

Rathenau ermordet!

Heraus zum Aufmarsch gegen die Reaktion!

An den Pranger!

Vor dem Einmarsch der Reaktion in Berlin?

Die systematische Mordhetze.

Die „Campagne" der Unabhängigen.

Auf, in die Versammlungen der KPD.!

Heute 7 Uhr abends: Kliems Festsäle, Hasenheide; Prachtsäle des Ostens, Frankfurter Allee; Moabiter Gesellschaftshaus, Wiclefstraße 31.

Die Ermordung Rathenaus das Signal der Reaktion / Mobilisierung der Arbeiter gegen den Angriff

Rapallo, which binds Germany to the Bolshevik, supposedly anticapitalistic Soviet Union. Here we have the PERSONAL CONNECTION BETWEEN INTERNATIONAL JEWISH HIGH FINANCE AND INTERNATIONAL JEWISH BOLSHEVISM . . .[3]

DIE ROTE FAHNE
Saturday, June 24, 1922

The reactionaries have given the signal. The penultimate deed in the chain of the reactionary acts has been carried out. The general plan which began with Erzberger's murder continued with the attempted assassination of Scheidemann, terminates with [Karl] Helfferich's announcement of the new empire. The reactionary forces are on the march and have announced their arrival with the murder of Rathenau.

The intention of the reactionaries is clear to all workers. Yet they were, until recently, attempting to deny their involvement in the most basic of economic questions, the grain question. It is our opinion that the moment when the bourgeoisie risks making the basic source of nourishment, our daily bread, the object of a struggle between itself and the working class, it cannot remain at a halfway point, but must also mobilize its political arm to underwrite its struggle.

The murder of Rathenau is the signal that these preparations are finished, that the forces collected by the reactionaries are ready . . .

Rathenau's murder radically changes the entire domestic as well as foreign political situation . . . His death is capitalism's announcement that the solution can only be found at the cost of the workers. Rathenau's death puts an end to the illusion shared by a segment of the proletariat and the petit bourgeoisie that the bourgeoisie is ready to assume a minute share of the burden which its war, the war of capital, had placed upon the entire nation.

The workers must understand this fact in all its ramifications. The murder of Erzberger was the initial signal. The workers answered it. But the workers were satisfied with a single show of strength, formulating demands which were supported by no party except the KPD [German Communist party].

Today the workers must answer differently. In opposition to the united front of the bourgeoisie, the worker must create his own unified front. And it must mass its strength where its opponents have massed theirs: outside of the parliamentary system.

The proletarian parties cannot delay. The workers must be mobilized. Demonstrations and proclamations are not sufficient . . . The gauntlet has been cast down to the working population. It will be picked up!

RESIST REACTION!

DISARM THE COUNTERREVOLUTION!

MOBILIZE THE WORKERS!

A UNIFIED FRONT OF ALL THE WORKERS![4]

The *Vossische Zeitung* was founded in the eighteenth century and continued to carry its traditional subtitle "Berlin Gazette Concerned with Political and Learned Matters." Although owned by the conservative Ullstein concern, "Auntie Voss," as Berliners called it, managed to maintain its liberal policy. Its editor was Georg Bernhard. [*Collection of the Institut für Zeitungsforschung, Darmstadt*]

Nr. 296 · B 146 · Abend-Ausgabe · Berlin · Sonnabend, 24. Juni 1922

Vossische Zeitung

1 Mark

Berlinische Zeitung von Staats- und gelehrten Sachen

Schriftleitung: Berlin SW 68, Kochstraße 22-26

Reichsminister Rathenau ermordet.

Organisierte Verschwörung gegen den Staat.

Berlin, 24. Juni. (Amtliche Meldung.) Der Reichsminister des Äußern, Dr. Walter Rathenau, ist heute vormittag einem Meuchelmord zum Opfer gefallen. Das Reichskabinett ist sofort nach Bekanntwerden der ruchlosen Tat zu einer Sitzung im Reichstage zusammengetreten, an der auch der Reichstagspräsident und der preußische Ministerpräsident teilnahmen.

Der Reichskanzler widmete dem ermordeten Ministerkollegen Worte des verehrungsvollsten Dankes für die Aufopferung und die treue Arbeit, die der Tote zunächst als Reichsminister des Wiederaufbaus und dann als Reichsminister des Äußern dem Vaterlande geleistet hat.

Das Kabinett trat sodann in eine Beratung der durch den Mord scharf beleuchteten innerpolitischen Lage ein. Da an dem politischen Charakter der Tat jeder Zweifel ausgeschlossen ist, wird das Kabinett noch heute die schärfsten Maßregeln bestimmen, um die Republik und ihre durch organisierte Verschwörungen bedrohten Einrichtungen zu schützen.

Wer schützt die Republik?

Von Georg Bernhard.

Die Tat und die Verfolgung.

Die Maßnahmen der Regierung.

Die Täter.

Die Trauerfeier.

Der Eindruck auf die Börse.

VOSSISCHE ZEITUNG

Saturday, June 24, 1922

The shots which murdered Walther Rathenau this afternoon in the Grunewald are warning shots. It is a warning which should awaken all the healthy instincts of the German people and unify those who still believe that morals and logic must hold political passion in bounds. Now, finally, the Republic must pull itself together and protect those men who serve it in the rebuilding of Germany. For the Republic itself is in danger.

The German revolution has had a remarkable result: the revolutionaries and their supporters were the only ones who paid for the change in political relationships with their lives. Some were brutally murdered, some hunted down like animals. Only the boundless good nature and the oppressed state of the German people after the collapse could have permitted the situation to be accepted so passively. The men of the old order, who at first believed that they were threatened with the fate of all legitimists in all historical revolutions, brought themselves quickly to safety. They now walk with their heads higher than before. They have lost all their fear. The decent attitude of the revolutionary parties in Germany, who used their authority in the most difficult period of the revolution to safeguard the existence of all levels of society, did not make the slightest impression on these people. On the contrary. They mockingly organized the opposition to the Republic and through this they opposed any reconstruction of national independence. A political banditry has developed in Germany with their passive support and under their influence, a banditry whose terror makes itself ever more felt.

The trial which was held in Offenburg of the accomplices of Erzberger's murder opened the eyes of all those who wanted to see to the connection of this murder to right-wing political circles. It illuminated the crudeness of their murderous intent which in Germany passes as political theory . . . Rathenau himself always felt that his life would end violently. Not a day passed in which he did not receive threatening letters. And if the fanatic makeup of his character did not permit him to accept the offer of police protection which was made repeatedly, it does not mean that he underestimated the threat to his life or of the brutality of his enemies . . .

Today is June 24. For weeks there has been a rumor abroad that "something's going to happen" on June 24. On John the Baptist's Day it was assumed that there would be demonstrations against the Republic. Demonstrations of the worse sort. Now we know what was planned. We don't know whether the shots fired at Rathenau were signal shots to introduce a further "festival program" . . .[5]

The *Berliner Tageblatt*, published by Mosse, was perhaps the most democratic and most independent newspaper in Berlin. It was widely read abroad, where it created a favorable impression of the German Republic. The editorials by *Tageblatt* editor Theodor Wolff often had greater influence outside Germany than at home. [*Collection of the Institut für Zeitungsforschung, Darmstadt*]

Abend-Ausgabe

Berliner Tageblatt

Nr. 294

und Handels-Zeitung

Walther Rathenau ermordet.

Berlin, 24. Juni.

Nach einer amtlichen Mitteilung wurde heute vormittag Minister Rathenau, kurz nachdem er seine Villa im Grunewald verlassen hatte, um sich in das Auswärtige Amt zu begeben, erschossen und war sofort tot. Der Täter fuhr im Auto nebenher und sauste nach vollbrachter Tat weiter.

Die Einzelheiten der Mordtat.

Der Handgranatenanschlag.

Das Attentat von langer Hand vorbereitet.

Walther Rathenau.

BERLINER TAGEBLATT UND HANDELS-ZEITUNG

Saturday, June 24, 1922

We are obligated to use the moment in which we must report the news of the murder of Walther Rathenau to express our emotion and horror. We are moved by the fact that this man, brilliantly gifted, so far above the ordinary, so full of warmth for his nation, should be, like so many before him, murdered by a lackey of a conspiracy lurking in the shadows. Our horror is rooted in the unspeakable conditions in which we live and under which we must be governed. It is, at this moment, impossible to describe the personality of Rathenau in all its intellectual importance and it is also unnecessary, for his personality stands clearly before the eyes of all right-thinking Germans and the entire civilized world. Only those who out of their nationalist fanaticism and hate so madly cursed, attacked, and finally murdered him, or ordered him to be slain, have falsified his desires and distorted his opinions. We do not want to beatify him, we do not want to shroud our own point of view with incense, as it has been masked by the poisonous gas of German Nationalist demagogues, but we must state that this damnable bullet laid low that one man who enjoyed, throughout the entire educated and moral world, an extraordinary authority. This has shown the nations of the world Germany's horrid moral confusion.

We do not wish to accuse entire groups of the actions of individuals, but the guilt is so clear here, the answerability so evident, that it is impossible not to accuse and to gloss over the presence of the truth . . . It must be recognized that the day before yesterday, when Rathenau made his sharply patriotic speech against the rape of the Saarland, some of the Nationalist Berlin papers, such as the Tägliche Rundschau, *publicly admitted that the foreign minister could not have spoken more nationalistically. But others, like the* Deutsche Tageszeitung, *mocked even this speech and are still of the opinion, contrary to fact, that Rathenau bowed before France . . . There are even so-called moral conservatives who support this, who drag this filth along on the coattails of their party and are unwilling to separate themselves from this rabble because it is too valuable to them . . .*

When, eight days ago, some of the Socialist newspapers assured us that the 28th of July would be a new St. Bartholomew's massacre, it was dismissed as an illusion. Today we had a foretaste of such a massacre. And if the government pulls itself together and assumes control, then the entire right wing will cry out against this attack on the freedom of the press and organization. Thus the attacks continue with horrible success.[6]

If Berlin's newspapers were rooted in the traditions of the eighteenth century, radio emerged as a twentieth-century means of communication.

In contrast to the unabashed bias of most Berlin newspapers, the ubiquitous radio, which was publicly owned, did not attempt to exert political influence. It offered a happy blend of entertainment, education, and culture. [*Rundfunkmuseum, West Berlin*]

Hans Bredow, "the father of the German radio," wrote in 1927:

The fact that I was able to hold a public demonstration of wireless radio on November 16, 1919, indicates that the idea of a publicly operated radio was developed quite early in Germany. This public demonstration, sponsored by the Post Office, was held before a large number of representatives of the government and the press in Berlin's Urania lecture hall. A tube transmitter, built by the telegraph office, transmitted voice and music, which was broadcast to the audience by loudspeaker. On this occasion I stated for the first time the incredible future potential of the radio. This potential has meantime been realized.[7]

As in all Europe, radio was publicly owned, but the government exercised little, if any, political influence. The loudspeakers offered a medley of news, popular and serious music, and earnest educational programs. The schedule for Friday, September 11, 1925, for instance, included homemaking tips on storing eggs, a lecture on gardening as a means to uplift the young, a lecture on ancient Indian religions, and a live Mozart concert.

Albert Einstein opened the seventh German radio exhibition in August 1930. He said:

When you listen to radio, consider how mankind came to possess this wonderful tool. Think of [Hans] Oersted, who first used the magnetic field generated by electricity. Think of [Johann] Reis, who first used this effect to create sound, of [Alexander] Bell, who, through his use of sensitive contacts in his microphone, first transferred sound waves into variable electric current. Then think of [James Clerk] Maxwell, who mathematically proved the existence of electric waves, of [Heinrich] Hertz, who first created them and then proved their existence with the help of the wireless. Think especially about [Robert von] Lieben, who created in the cathode tube an incomparable generator of electric waves. Think gratefully about that army of nameless technicians who simplified the instrument, allowing it to be mass produced so everyone could own a set. We ought not use the wonders of science and technology without giving a thought to all these people and without understanding the wonder any better than a cow understands the botany of the plants it contentedly consumes. Remember that it was the technicians who made true democracy possible. They have not only simplified daily work, they are also disseminating true thought and art, . . . to the public at large. Radio, furthermore, has a unique capacity for reconciling the family of nations. Until now nations got to know one another only through the distorting mirror of the daily press. Radio acquaints them in the most immediate form and from their most attractive side.[8]

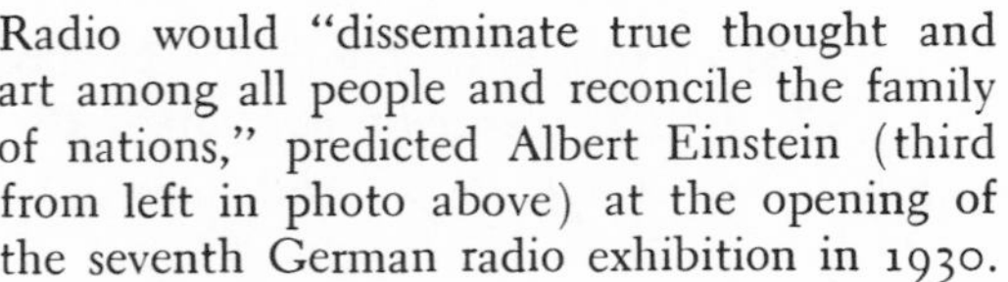

Radio would "disseminate true thought and art among all people and reconcile the family of nations," predicted Albert Einstein (third from left in photo above) at the opening of the seventh German radio exhibition in 1930.

The photos at right show the use of radio as a teaching aid, in a beauty salon, and a means of easing the work of an organ-grinder. [*West-deutscher Rundfunk and Rundfunkmuseum, West Berlin*]

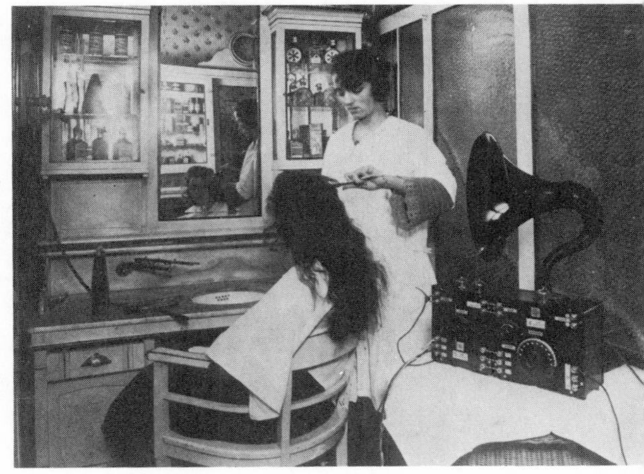

Denes von Mihaly, a Hungarian scientist, came to Berlin late in the twenties to help German broadcasters develop television. He is shown with one of his early TV receivers. A more confidence-inspiring set of the twenties is shown at right. [*Rundfunkmuseum, West Berlin*]

By 1930 just about everyone was within earshot of a radio. Two years earlier, at Berlin's fifth radio exhibition, there was, however, something to see. On display were the first experiments by the American scientist V. K. Zworykin, who pioneered the transmission of pictures.

Denes von Mihaly, the Hungarian scientist, had come to Berlin, under the auspices of the official radio broadcasters, to work on television. He used the "Nipkow wheel," which had been patented back in 1884 by the Berlin engineer Paul Nipkow and which was able to reproduce a flickering picture on the first primitive screen. Similar experiments were made in London by the Scotsman John Logie Baird. But the German Post Office, under Hans Bredow, made the most rapid advances. The Post Office launched its first television broadcast at the end of 1929. The first television personalities were two young Berlin women announcers. But you still had to go to a special television studio, much like a film theater, to see them. By 1930 the Germans were beginning to give thought to color television. Television was one of the sensations of the 1936 Olympics in Berlin.

By that time Hitler had thrown Bredow's associates into concentration camps. Bredow sent him a telegram demanding the same treatment and was hauled before a court. The publishing industry, the newspapers, radio, and budding television were *gleichgeschaltet*—switched to Goebbel's wave length.

7: ART

Manifestoes at the Crossroad

George Grosz, "The Pillars of Society," 1926.
[*Nationalgalerie, West Berlin*]

Before World War I Berlin lacked all the prerequisites of an artistic center.

The Prussian kings despised cultural refinement. The Hohenzollern mind was culturally as barren as the Brandenburg heather. The Muses, like musketeers, were pressed into service only to establish martial glory.

Even after Berlin became the capital of the German Reich in 1871, the Emperor belligerently upheld his dynasty's traditional animosity toward all but military art. In 1908 Kaiser Wilhelm II fired the head of Berlin's National Gallery, the brilliant Dr. Hugo von Tschudi, for favoring modern trends. His Imperial Majesty also refused the gentle, sensitive Käthe Kollwitz the gold medal his Academy of Arts had awarded her for probing the human shadows of his empire.

The repression spawned protest. And the protest, first against the hypocritical sham of imperial mediocrity and then against the sentimental romanticism of the original protesters sparked an astounding, if chaotic, artistic vitality in Berlin.

By 1929 one journalist, Paul Westheim, observed:

Berlin is a city for artists, for the young, for the creative. Not for idyllic artists, who wish to sit on the bank of a pond, dreaming; but for those to whom a melody can come from the struggles of life . . . Berlin has taken a massive step toward becoming a center, if not the *center of artistic force in Germany.*[1]

Westheim was right. In Rome art is eternal. In Paris you would think it was. In Berlin—Berlin was suddenly at the crossing of new roads.

The first influx came from the North, from Norway, back in 1892, with an exhibition of Edvard Munch's haunting and gloomy paintings of almost frantic anguish. Munch's prophecy proved so disturbing that the organizers of the exhibition themselves closed it within days. The scandal established Munch's international fame and prompted Berlin's foremost artist of the time, Max Liebermann, to desert the Imperial Academy and lead the first "Berlin Secession."

Liebermann, a wealthy, witty, and worldly Jew—a cousin of Walther Rathenau's—painted the essence of landscapes, lyric scenes, and portraits by means of fluid color and shimmering air. He was, under the influence mainly of Manet and Monet, the first and foremost German Impressionist. He also introduced turn-of-the-century Germany to the new experiments west of the Rhine, a contribution perhaps even greater than his own cool and pleasant work. With the support of some adventurous art dealers, notably Paul Cassirer, his Secession displayed Van Gogh's new work from Holland, as well as the Impressionists, Postimpressionists, Fauvists, and Cubists from France in the German capital. The seed instantly sprang to life. German art, charged with emotional expression of social concern, joined the great currents of European painting.

From the South, from Italy, the Futurists came to Berlin. They were confused prophets of the technological age, who in their paintings, sculptures, and graphic visions of new skyscraper cities, attempted to capture motorized movement and idolized speed. "Universal dynamism must be rendered as dynamic sensation," said the *Technical*

Max Liebermann, the dean of Berlin's artists, in his studio in 1932. [*Landesbildstelle, West Berlin*]

Manifesto of Futurist Painting, written in 1910.

That same year, from the East, from Russia, came Wassily Kandinsky. When, as a young man, Kandinsky learned that the structure of the atom had been discovered in 1911 by E. Rutherford and others, he wrote: "The discovery hit me with frightful force, as though the end of the world had come. All things became transparent, without strength or certainty." Art historian Werner Haftmann tells us that from this point on, art began to become abstract, replacing old concepts of matter with new concepts of energy, space, and time and the outer view with the inner vision.

A decade later, after the German and Russian revolutions, came the Russian Suprematists and Constructivists, notably El Lissitzky and Kasimir Malevich. Taking the Italian Futurists one step further, as it were, the Russians employed technology—the logus, or knowledge of making things technical—to create new artistic perceptions.

Germany's foremost Constructivist was the Hungarian-born Laszlo Moholy-Nagy, who began his career as an artist in Berlin. Moholy became a leading force at the Bauhaus, the school of design founded by Walter Gropius in Weimar in 1919. The Bauhaus was as much influenced by Russian Constructivism as it was by the Dutch *de Stijl,* the geometric style perfected by Piet Mondrian. Moholy used the Russian-

From the North, in 1892, came the haunting influence of the Norwegian painter Edvard Munch. The closing of his exhibition led to the first "Berlin Secession" from the Imperial Academy of Arts. This woodcut, dated 1905, is entitled "Primitive Man." [*Nationalgalerie, West Berlin*]

From the West, introduced largely by Liebermann, came the influence of Van Gogh and the French Impressionists, Postimpressionists, Fauvists, and Cubists. Van Gogh's "The Olive Orchard" (above) was exhibited in Cologne in 1912. [*National Gallery of Art, Washington, D.C., Chester Dale Collection*]

Dutch blend not only to innovate methods of teaching art, but also to create functional forms of industrial design.

The young prewar avant-garde soon went further than Liebermann's Impressionist Secession. A second Berlin Secession occurred in 1910, advancing not evolution but revolution. The second revolt included groups of artists who called themselves "Die Brücke" (The Bridge), "Der Blaue Reiter" (The Blue Rider), "Die Neue Kunst" (The New Art), "Aktion," and "Revolution." The names of Erich Heckel, Karl Schmidt-Rottluff, Otto Müller, Wassily Kandinsky, Franz Marc, August Macke, Paul Klee, Oskar Kokoschka, Alexei von Jawlensky, Emil Nolde, Ernst Ludwig Kirchner, Lyonel Feininger, Max Beckmann, and Ernst Barlach became known. Not all of them lived in Berlin, but they all exhibited there. Their art got its national and, eventually, international boost mainly from one man—Herwarth Walden.

This poet and playwright had founded the magazine *Der Sturm* in 1910 and became the chief propagandist of Germany's avant-garde. He was often sketched, painted, and sculpted by his artist friends. The portraits show him a pale, owlish-looking man, gazing nervously at a new world of turmoil, his thick spectacles tucked under a huge, bulging forehead. In 1913, the year of New York's famous Armory Show, which introduced modern art to America, Walden summed up the artistic upheaval in the first German Autumn Salon. The exhibition was held in three back rooms in the Potsdamer Strasse which served as Walden's studio, editorial office, and gallery. It included 360 works of German innovators, as well as paintings by Marc Chagall, Robert Delaunay, Constantin Brancusi, Alexander Archipenko, Piet Mondrian, Max Ernst, and Hans Arp.

Thanks to Max Liebermann and Herwarth Walden, the new forces had thus been gathered in Berlin well before the revolution. Once the Kaiser had fled, they were eager to take over, with art as a weapon against social injustice, bourgeois values, and military arrogance, to achieve a new *Gesamtkultur*, a new totality of culture and "unity of art and life," to realize a utopian blend of socialism, religion, and idealism.

A by-product of this surging was a militant vegetarianism and a preoccupation with mystic, pseudo-Oriental cults, notably a weird sect called "Mazdaznan." It was a strange gastro-religious cult that can be traced back to one Mr. Hanish, a Californian of German extraction, who called himself H'a Nish, or something like that, claimed to be a Persian prince, and preached what he called the gospel of Mazdak, he of whom Zarathustra spake. "One gets frightfully spiritual on crackers and apple butter," recalled Moholy-Nagy some years after those cold, hungry winters. Oskar Ko-

From the South came the Italian Futurists, with their infatuation with motorized motion and technology. "Let's kill the moonlight!" they cried. This 1913 painting by Umberto Boccioni, one of the first painters to join the Berlin group, is entitled "Muscular Dynamism." [*The Museum of Modern Art, New York*]

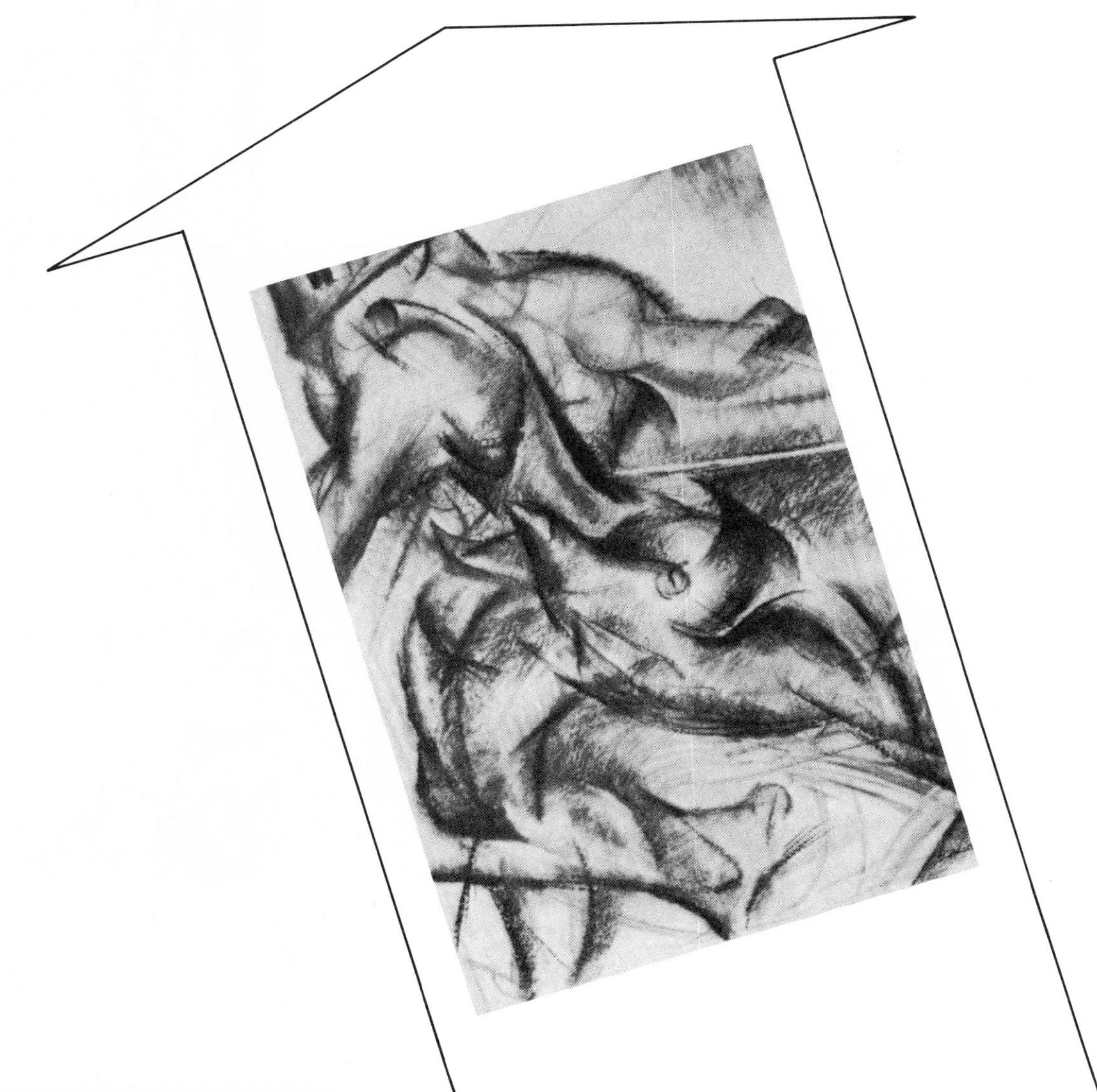

From the East, in 1910, came Wassily Kandinsky, whose work was shown at Herwarth Walden's *Der Sturm* gallery. After a brief return to his native Russia he first joined the "Blaue Reiter" (Blue Rider) group in Munich and later the Bauhaus in Weimar and Dessau. Kandinsky was the first artist to become entirely abstract, depicting his inner vision rather than an outer view. "Homform," shown at right, was painted in 1924 at the Bauhaus. [*Nationalgalerie, West Berlin*]

koschka plotted the new world with his friends in a place called Café Grössenwahn (Megalomania Café).

The strongest force in the upheaval was Expressionism. The term is vague. It connotes an equally vague, always emotional, and often mystic response to the ultramechanized, dehumanized age that Europe was entering at the time. In 1919 *Der Sturm* printed Johannes Molzahn's "Manifesto of Extreme Expressionism." Written in Expressionist style, it said in part:

The work—to which we—as painters—sculptors and poets—are bound—is the powerful energy of experience—it is cosmic will —eternal fire—a living arrow—aimed at you —glowing in your blood—so that it runs livelier and faster—glows better in eternity.

Sun and moon are our images—which we reach out to you—star-covered banner of eternity—blossoming towards you—between beginning and end—thrown between pit and peak—we have no tradition—no pos-

sessions—which are worth claiming. We bear great promise.[2]

One notable dissenter of Expressionism's promise was Otto Dix, whose meticulous work edged on Surrealism without ever abandoning the hyperrealism of the late nineteenth-century naturalists. Dix wrote in 1927:

One slogan has moved the last generation of artists: create new forms of expression. I doubt whether this is really possible. If one only stopped to gaze at the works of the old masters or if one deepened oneself in the study of their creations, I would be proved correct.

In any case, the newness in art lies, for me, in the expansion of the subject matter, in an increase in the modes of expression which are already locked in the heart of the old masters. For me the object remains primary and the form is created only through the object. Therefore it has always been a matter of major importance to me that I come as close as possible to that which I am observing. For more important than the "how" is the "what." Only from the "what" can the "how" emerge.[3]

Deliberately confusing "how" and "what" and paving the way for non-representational art in the process were the Dadaists. Theirs was a form of artistic anarchy that sprang up simultaneously in Zurich (where the Romanian poet Tristan Tzara is said to have given the movement its name), New York (where Marcel Duchamp touted Dadaist celebration of the absurd by exhibiting objects such as urinals), and Paris (where Tzara had organized provocative Dada happenings).

Dadaism blossomed in Berlin's climate of despairing protest. The Berlin "club dada," which held its first exhibition in 1918, included George Grosz and Richard Hülsenbeck. A later show, in 1920, was closed by the police amid considerable violence. Dada's German leader was Kurt Schwitters, who presented his manifesto in play form:

What a fantastic psychological effect is achieved by the wailing of a ship's siren! If one recreated the initial equality of the materials, if one weighed factor against factor and melted them into a new, inseparable work of art . . .

The Public: Ho! ho! perform!—artist, create! don't talk (a bespectacled voice:) right! give us an example!

Schwitters: Ok (calls:) Lights! (stage and audience are darkened)

The Public: (a falsetto:) Lights out! knife out! get him (laughter:) Ha! ha! (a bespectacled voice:) silence! (on the stage a gigantic advertisement appears:)

THE MOST MODERN MEN'S HATS
MADE FROM WOMEN'S HATS

The Public: (an instinctive, naive pleasure at the bright colors of the sign) Ah!—Ah! (laughter, giggling) hi! hi! hi!—what—what is that?! (an upper class voice:) The verb isn't even complete. (an excited voice:) Not even the orthography is correct. (a lady's voice:) Can they really make modern men's hats out of women's hats? (another lady's voice:) Where is this shop? (an excited voice:) Idiocy! pure idiocy! (a falsetto:) Anna Blume! (the bespectacled voice:) Quiet, ladies and gentlemen! Can't

Another strong Russian influence on Berlin's avant-garde, and particularly on the Bauhaus, was that of the Constructivists. One of their leaders was El Lissitzky, who visited and exhibited in Berlin, and whose 1923 sketch for electromechanical puppets (above) illustrates the Constructivist approach. [*Kupferstichkabinett, West Berlin*]

Berlin's foremost Constructivist was the Hungarian-born Laszlo Moholy-Nagy. He became a teacher at the Bauhaus where he applied Constructivism to develop entirely new methods of teaching art and, with astounding versatility, applied himself to typography, film making, and industrial design, as well as painting. Shown above is his "Composition ZUIII," designed in 1924. [*Nationalgalerie, West Berlin*]

you tell that it is a metaphor! New forms are made from old—or? Mr. Schwitters! Mr. Schwitters! Dammit, put on the lights. I can't see anything! Where are you?—(the sign vanishes) Light! (generally:) Light! (stage and audience are illuminated) (the bespectacled voice:) Finally!—well, Mr. Schwitters, explain to us (quickly) no, don't tell us again that art can't be explained—just tell us—what was that?[4]

The attempt to make art an instrument of the revolution began with the Novembergruppe (November Group), founded in 1918 at the instigation of the painter Max Pechstein. Joined by a veritable Who's Who of Berlin's intellectuals, including painters (Feininger, Nolde, Otto Müller), sculptors (Georg Kolbe, Gerhard Marcks), architects (Walter Gropius, Erich Mendelsohn), art historians (Paul Zucker, Wilhelm Valentiner), art dealers (Alfred Flechtheim), composers (Kurt Weill, Paul Hindemith), poets and playwrights (Bert Brecht), industrial designers, and other art professionals —more than a hundred people in all—the Novembergruppe and its Arbeitsrat für die Kunst (Workers' Council for Art) became a focal point of the capital's cultural life. Being German, it also issued *weltanschauliche* manifestoes by the dozen.

The Novembergruppe's first call said:

The future of art and the seriousness of this hour forces us revolutionaries of the spirit (Expressionists, Cubists, Futurists)

Herwarth Walden. Below: In a 1915 sculpture by William Wauer. [*Nationalgalerie, West Berlin*] Right: In a 1926 sketch by Emil Orlik. Walden was the most energetic catalyst and propagandist of modern art in Germany. A poet and playwright, he ran a periodical, a publishing house, and an art gallery, all called "*Der Sturm*." [*Nationalgalerie and Archiv für Kunst und Geschichte, West Berlin*]

toward unity and close co-operation . . The planning and realization of a far-reaching program, to be carried out with the co-operation of trustworthy people in the various art centers, should bring us the closest mingling of art and the people.[5]

Another manifesto, addressed to "all artists," said:

We painters and poets are bound to the poor in a sacred solidarity. Have not many among us learned to know misery and the shame of hunger? . . . Will not the bourgeoisie soon again seize the reins of power through putsches, corruption, and unscrupulous vote manipulation? Will not this Germany of the conquering middle class once again make shameless use of the worker's strength and humble the poor even further? Will it not wish to triumph in spiritual things even more arrogantly and impudently than it had done in Imperial Germany . . . ?[6]

The Novembergruppe held lectures, showed films, and organized a series of exhibitions at the Lehrter Bahnhof, one of Berlin's railroad stations. The exhibits displayed exciting avant-garde art which was directed at the proletarian masses, who scornfully rejected it. The educated middle class of Berlin, which the Novembergruppe scornfully rejected, embraced the group's avant-garde art with delight. In fact, middle-class Berlin accepted modern art earlier and more ardently than anyone else.

As a movement to achieve "a new unity of art and life," however, the Novembergruppe failed. What happened, as Sibyl Moholy-Nagy, the art historian and widow of the artist, observed, was a strange reversal of effects: "For the first time the artist was deprived not of his social acceptance but of his isolation."

Artists withdrew. Despite their slogans, their lack of preparation and organization and the confused social and political situation soon alienated them from the Weimar Republic. They ridiculed it.

Paul Klee, "Moon Play," 1923. [*Nationalgalerie, West Berlin*]

Max Beckmann, "Women's Bath," 1919. [*Nationalgalerie, West Berlin*]

Otto Müller, "Seated Couple," c. 1920. [*Serge Sabarsky Gallery, New York*]

Three outstanding German artists of the period were inseparably involved in the ugliness of life in the big ugly city of Berlin. They were Heinrich Zille, Käthe Kollwitz, and George Grosz.

Zille was to Berlin what Daumier had been to Paris: the chronicler of the urban proletariat, the observer of grim humor and strange beauty in the city's deprivation and decay. Few other artists have succeeded as well in presenting the human side of city life. Zille was the master of Berlin's dank tenement courtyards. "This is my milieu," he kept saying.

He was immensely popular in Berlin. Proudly, he would tell the story of an art student who asked some children to model for him but then complained that they were dirty. "For Zille they can't be dirty enough," the mother replied.

In his autobiography Zille recalled:

In 1872 I began to learn lithography. In the same building was a famous old ballroom, The Orpheum, which had a canteen where we could get beer by helping out, washing the floors or mirrors. In the mornings drunken men and women still lay in

Lyonel Feininger, "Eichelborn," 1920. [*Nationalgalerie, West Berlin*]

Ernst Ludwig Kirchner, "Brandenburg Gate," 1929. [*Nationalgalerie, West Berlin*]

the corners and loges. These were the lucky ones of the Empire, who were reaping the benefits of the victorious war of 1870–1871. I once arrived when a waiter had laid a fat, drunken whore over a chair and was playing solitaire on her naked rump . . .

Only after a long while did people learn to see, judge, and understand me. In the east and north of Berlin they understood me immediately when my work appeared in Simplicissimus *and* Jugend, *which were the first periodicals to print my drawing. I have not worked in the graphics industry since 1907 and have been able to devote my time to that which is closest to me.*

My first apartment was in a cellar in Berlin-East; now I live in Berlin-West, five stories up—evidently I've come up in life. Some of my etchings are in the National Print Collection and a series of drawings and sketches are in the National Gallery. Now, in 1924, I have become a member of the Academy. In this regard, I can quote what the right-wing newspaper Fridericus *wrote: "The Berlin portrayer of toilets and pregnancy, Heinrich Zille, has become a member of the Academy of Arts and has been approved by the minister. —Cover your face, O Muse!"*[7]

The autobiography was written for customary submission to the president of the Academy of Arts. The president at the time was Max Liebermann, who complained about Zille's minuscule handwriting. "You only asked me to write it," said Zille. "You didn't say anyone would want to read it."

If Zille approached modern man's misery with compassionate humor, Käthe Kollwitz made her compassion heroic. She depicts cosmic tragedy. A glimpse at her diaries reveals not so much her view of art as her own being:

April 1921

. . . It was shortly before I became ill. I saw a nanny in the Tiergarten with two children. The older boy, about two and a half years old, was the most sensitive child I have ever seen. As the girl said: He's like a little bird. Therefore she didn't like him. But the boy was sweet. In his tiny face and slim body every experience he had was mirrored. Fear, shyness, joy, hope, and ecstasy, then fear again, etc. Like a butterfly whose wings are constantly fluttering. Moving,

Otto Dix, whose meticulous, almost surrealist representational style is illustrated by this self-portrait (1920), dissented from Expressionism. He preferred to follow the old masters, he said. [*Staatsbibliothek, West Berlin*]

needing help, desiring love, more helpless than I have ever seen a child.[8]

George Grosz, the most sophisticated and versatile of the trio (aside from his brush with Dadaism, he did work which echoed Picasso, Delaunay, and Chagall), took to savage satire to express his disgust with poverty, prostitution, patrioteering, and profiteers. Much of his work is macabre, showing a preoccupation with sordid sex, drug addiction, vice, and violence. He liked to shock the German burgher out of his complacent *Gemütlichkeit.* Charged with the crime of public blasphemy, Grosz answered his judge in 1928:

I have certain obligations as an artist. I belong to the entire German people and I, therefore, feel myself to have a certain mission. I have been placed on this earth as a cat-o'-nine-tails, if but an artistic and therefore reasonably harmless one. . . . I create from my own time, from my own personality, from my own sense of the artistic. . . .

I stand behind my work, I am responsible, and, as an artist, I am in the minority. You have the majority and power on your

Ernst Barlach, though often counted among the German Expressionists, was also a "loner," who, as Max Liebermann put it, "worked from reality, not from the intellect." A mystic, Barlach was not only a sculptor, but also a playwright. The wooden sculpture shown at right is entitled "Reading Monks" and was made in 1932. [*Nationalgalerie, West Berlin*]

The most popular artist in Berlin was Heinrich Zille, the chronicler of the city's ordinary people, whose everyday life he depicted with compassionate humor. He spoke to the heart, the heart of Berlin, this "street urchin of art," as he has been called. To most people who knew Berlin before the Nazis, "Daddy Zille's" sketches are an inseparable part of the memory. [*Kupferstichkabinett, West Berlin*]

Käthe Kollwitz, shown at right in a self-portrait (1921), looked at Berlin's poor in a different way. She transformed her suffering sensitivity into a proletarian heroicism. Kollwitz's art tells us about the craving for love in a world of cruel turmoil. [*Staatsbibliothek, West Berlin*]

"Shut up and keep serving," wrote George Grosz under this sketch of Christ in a gas mask and wearing army boots. The drawing was used as the backdrop for the Piscator production of Brecht's *The Good Soldier Schweik*, a play based on Hasek's novel, and it led to Grosz's indictment for blasphemy. The Weimar Republic found Grosz guilty and fined him 2,000 marks in lieu of two months in prison. [*Kupferstichkabinett, West Berlin*]

side . . . If the times are uneasy, if the foundation of society is under attack, then the artist cannot merely stand aside, especially not the talented artist with his finer sense of history. Therefore he becomes, whether he wants to or not, political.[9]

George Grosz and German modernism lost their political battle. Hitler declared the new art "degenerate" and burned much of it. He announced his "uncompromising cleansing of these last elements of social decay," stating:

Cubism, Dadaism, Futurism, Impressionism, etc., have nothing to do with the German race. For all of these concepts are neither old or new, they are the artificial mumblings of people who have been denied the God-given attributes of the true artist and have instead a gift for deception . . . And this is basic: art which cannot depend on the healthy, instinctive support of popular feeling and relies on a small, interested clique cannot be tolerated. It attempts to confuse the healthy, instinctive feelings of the people instead of joyfully supporting them.[10]

Shortly after Hitler took over in 1933, Max Liebermann looked out of his studio window one afternoon. He saw a parade of Stormtroopers joyfully expressing their healthy, instinctive feelings with their *Horst Wessel Song*. Turning to his guest, Liebermann observed: "Pity one can't eat as much as one wants to puke."

8
THEATER

Poesy, Stairs, and Morality Suspended

In the mid-1920s Berlin had thirty-two legitimate theaters. It had Max Reinhardt, Leopold Jessner, and Erwin Piscator—stage directors with a zest for experiment, who considered the theater not mere entertainment, not even just art, but an essential force in human life. In their time, perhaps in this century, Berlin's theater was unrivaled anywhere in the world.

Reinhardt set the stage. He began as an actor in his native Vienna and was as adept at the business of filling theaters as he was at involving his audience in the play. In imperial Berlin, he had founded the cabaret Schall und Rauch and directed the Deutsches Theater and the smaller Kammerspiele.

In 1919, firmly established and inspired by the revolution's promise of a popular culture, Reinhardt opened his enormous Grosses Schauspielhaus, "the theater of the five thousand." The following year he launched the Salzburg Festival. Every summer to this day, his *Everyman* is faithfully produced there as he conceived it, with all of the town's church bells chiming the grand finale.

Reinhardt was the innovator of a poetic realism on the stage. He was the master of gigantic productions and a genius of the mob scene. His philosophy went beyond making the theater a place of creative amusement:

The theater today is struggling for its existence. Not merely because of economic troubles; they are general. It is suffering, rather, from anemia. Neither literary nutriments, on which it was exclusively fed for too long, nor a purely theatrical diet can aid it . . .

Salvation can come only from the actor, for it is he and he alone who owns the

Max Reinhardt. [*Akademie der Künste, West Berlin*]
Leopold Jessner. [*Private collection, Gilman*]
The silhouette of Erwin Piscator projected on a Constructivist stage set. [*Akademie der Künste, West Berlin*]

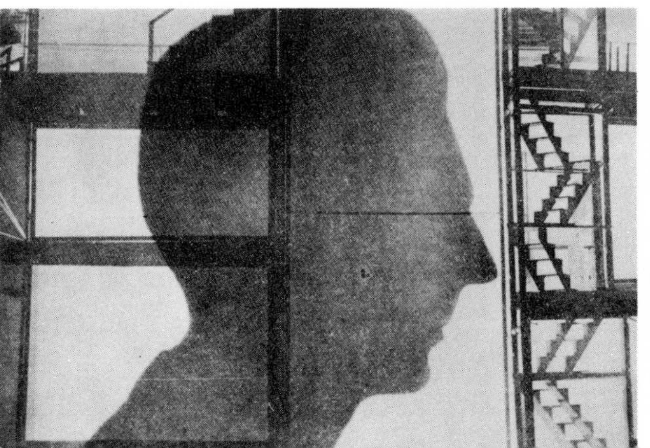

Eingang
zum
Trianon-Theater

Bert Brecht's Berlin had about three dozen theaters, if you count some of the basements where performances were given. The three most popular boulevard theaters were (opposite, top row, left to right) the Renaissance, the Trianon, and the Admirals-Palast where musical comedy reigned. Opposite, middle row, left to right: The Theater des Westens was the home of operetta. At the Thalia German classical drama held sway. At the Deutsches Theater Max Reinhardt rose from actor to director to owner. Opposite, bottom row, left to right: Erwin Piscator turned the Theater am Nollendorfplatz into the home of political theater. Brecht's *Threepenny Opera* was first performed at the Theater am Schiffbauerdamm. The Volksbühne offered popular entertainment. On this page: The Berliner and *Schiller* theaters and the *Kammerspiele* (or Little Theater) of the *Deutsches Theater*. [*Willy Springer,* Das Gesicht des Deutschen Theaters; *Landesarchiv, and Landesbildstelle, West Berlin*]

theater. All great dramatists were born actors, whether or not they ever stepped behind the footlights. . . .

The art of the actor [not only his manifestation of emotion] frees man of life's conventional stage. For the art of the actor is to expose life, not to suppress it. In our age we can fly and communicate across the ocean. But the path to ourselves and to our neighbors remains infinite. An actor walks this path. With the light of the poet, he explores the unchartered abyss of the human soul, of his own soul, he mysteriously transforms himself, his hands, eyes, and mouth full of miracles, and then reappears . . .

The actor is at once artist and work of art; he is the man at the border between reality and fantasy . . .

Abandoned by its good spirits, the theater can sink to the level of the prostitute. But passion for theater, for acting, is one of the basic urges of man. It is this urge which will always lead actors and audiences to the theater, which is man's most noble and satisfying edification. Whether he knows it or not, everyone has the urge to transform himself. We all carry in us the potential for all passions, for all fates, for all forms of inner life. "Nothing human is foreign to us." If it were not so, we could not understand other men, neither in life nor art . . .[1]

Reinhardt's Grosses Schauspielhaus had first been a market hall and was then converted into a circus arena, Zirkus Schumann. Reinhardt had it elaborately rebuilt into a huge legitimate theater. His architect was Hans Poelzig, the young leader of a visionary, architectural Expressionism.

Poelzig turned the arena into a stalactite cave, a fantastic *tour de force,* which was to realize Reinhardt's dream of bridging the gap between actor and audience and making the spectator part of the action. The spectator, if critic Franz Ferdinand Baum-

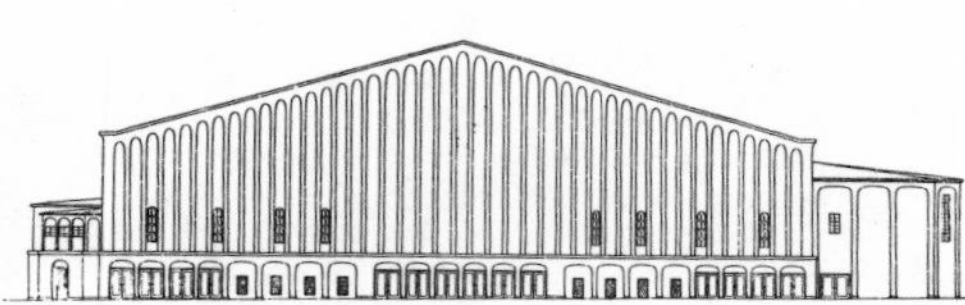

garten's opinion is any indication, remained skeptical. Baumgarten wrote in 1919:

The auditorium seems small, because one can only see the center section under the dome. The rest of the hall slumbers behind supports and columns . . . This ugly room makes people ugly. The one positive feature is the dome, its form pretty but its function and acoustics impossible. The dome of the Pantheon rests, Brunelleschi's dome soars, St. Peter's dome hovers. This dome hangs. It never rests. The hanging "icicles," intended to carry the sound into the audience, should relieve the heaviness, but they don't. The dome seems to be falling on our heads . . .

The value of a theater is determined by the view of the stage. Here the view is painfully ugly . . . Poelzig is an end, not a beginning. His building wobbles in all its joints. It has a touch of the Asiatic and the American, like all the buildings housing the

---

Some called Hans Poelzig's Grosses Schauspielhaus a "*coup de théâtre.*" The building had been a market hall and later a circus arena, which made it eminently suitable as a home for Reinhardt's theatrical empire. What amazed Berliners about it was not only Poelzig's spectacular, exotic fantasy, but also the speed with which it was realized. The stalactite-dripping dome was designed in July 1919 and despite some strikes and other disruptions was finished four months later. [*Akademie der Künste, West Berlin*] *amusements of this metropolis. I feel something quite frightening about it. It is a spiritual Luna Park in the shadow of the* danse macabre.[2]

Bad architecture or not, the opening performance—Aeschylus' *Oresteia*—was a critical success. Fritz Engels, the drama critic of the *Berliner Tageblatt,* wrote in November 1919: "For the first time we were shown the entire trilogy. What was distant beauty eight years ago has become a real experience. A war between the hemispheres is over, Europe has fought with Asia over a whore, a warrior returns home."

To the avant-garde of the twenties, however, Max Reinhardt represented the Establishment. Brilliant as they were, Reinhardt's productions (and he directed more than fifty in Berlin) were outdated, if not degenerate, in the eyes of the young. The first successful challenge to Reinhardt's preeminence came from Leopold Jessner. In December 1919, less than a month after the opening of Poelzig's "cave," Jessner staged his production of Schiller's *Wilhelm Tell,* starring Albert Bassermann, at the Staatliches Schauspielhaus. In the past, *Tell* had been played as a soapy melodrama, a kind of Robin Hood in the Swiss Alps. Jessner stripped the pathos from the production and presented it on a bare stage dominated by the now-famous "Jessner stairs."

Felix Ziege, a contemporary critic, wrote:

The world before the war was illusory . . . We saw appearances, externals. Effects were explained irrationally. Romantic idolatry of the machine dominated all thought. Romantic illusion even dominated where realism should have reigned—in politics.

The war disillusioned the world. Necessity became dominant. "Imagination" was not important; what was vital was to "conceptualize."

Before the war a social-humanistic ethos was dominant, what rules now is social-revolutionary politics. In place of illusion, we now have the idea—not only in life, also on the stage.

Correction: Also in life. Above all on the stage.

Thanks to Leopold Jessner.

Leopold Jessner's productions of Wilhelm Tell *and* Richard III *demonstrated the beginning of the predominance of the idea.*

The Tell *set: a single mountain wall. Generating the idea of the Alps. Not illusion, as we had been accustomed to.*

The desire for the idea is proclaimed with reckless energy: through the stairs. Stairs, not steps. The word is important. It determines the concept.

Leopold Jessner defined the difference between stairs and steps more successfully in his production of [Hauptmann's] Die Weber *than in words. Thirty stairs lead from the factory to the dwellings. On these stairs Dreissiger pleads for the weavers. The stairs divide the upper world from the lower. They divide.*

*Steps connect. Always. Stairs—*may *connect. But more often they divide. They express the difference between above and below. Stairs are not a substitute for the use of illusion through decoration. Stairs are the replacement of vision by concept.*[3]

Siegfried Jacobsohn wrote in his review of *Wilhelm Tell* that "Jessner achieves a persuasive effect. A mighty, thrusting green flight of stairs fills the stage from right to left, top to bottom. On both sides shorter, lower stairs lead to vertically placed bridges, over which one comes to Tell's or Stauffacher's house. No limits are set on fantasy."

It was the set, then—or, rather, the ab-

A bare stage, dominated by the famous "Jessner stairs"—"the replacement of vision by concept." This one was designed for Shakespeare's *Richard III.* [*Akademie der Künste, West Berlin*]

sence or at least abstraction of it—which heralded this approach to the theater. Jessner's stairs freed the Berlin theater—and with it, the Western theater—of representational scenery and the staging it demands. Like painting, theater had moved from the Impressionism and later the Expressionism of Reinhardt into the realm of abstract art.

Erwin Piscator, perhaps the most daring of Berlin's three great directors, was influenced by yet another of the new approaches to art: Constructivism.

Theater, what with the startling experiments of Vsevolod Meyerhold (nerve-wracking, anti-aesthetic combinations of Greek drama, circus acrobatics, and shock therapy) and Alexander Tairov (*Romeo and Juliet* played on a kind of scaffolding as "a symphony of bold and passionate, mighty and consuming, cruel and splendid erotic power"), had been an essential facet of the Constructivist movement in Moscow. Piscator sublimated, as it were, Russia's drastic new techniques to make them somewhat less shocking and more comprehensible. He introduced the multimedia approach, using lectures, electrical sound effects, dramatic lighting, movies, and myriad mechanical devices on Constructivist sets. Every play he produced was turned into a social and political message, an appeal to the intellect rather than the emotion. Along with Bert Brecht, he would make theater a weapon of revolution.

Piscator began his experiments at the Volksbühne, which produced good plays at low prices. But it was not until he moved to the Theater am Nollendorfplatz in 1927 that he perfected his "political theater." Two years later he wrote:

The Volksbühne was first to produce a one-hundred-per-cent chemically pure human being on the stage, raising the "thing itself" to the center of the drama and the theater. The thesis "art for the people" was changed, passing through the phase "the greatness of the masses" to its direct opposite: "the supremacy of art." It was a long road, winding through the state of bourgeois individualism with its vast private woes. What irony that the dramatic thesis of the Volksbühne led to a dead end, permitting no escape into the world.

Bourgeois individualism was finally buried by the war . . . As Remarque observed: "The generation of 1914 died in the war, even if it escaped its grenades." Those who returned no longer had any relationship to the greatness of man, which had served as the symbol of the eternity of divine order in the parlors of prewar society . . . For us, the individual on the stage serves a social function. Not his relationship to God but his relationship to society stands center stage. Where he appears, he represents his class.[4]

Piscator literally dramatized this theory in 1928 in his production of the play *The Good Soldier Schweik,* Brecht and others' adaptation of a novel by Jaroslav Hašek, as well as in a number of plays and revues on current political topics, such as rearmament and abortion. But he was a superb director as well as theorist and propagandist. Critic Max Lenz described a Piscator rehearsal:

The scenery on stage can only be sensed. The extras are rehearsing a war song . . .

Suddenly everything stops. Piscator and the stars appear. One is reminded . . . of the parade ground . . . Only here it happens with comradery . . .

The director's desk stands in one of the first rows of the orchestra. Piscator places

The Piscator Theater, as seen by cartoonist Karl Arnold. Piscator is the man on the wagon, which is as mechanized as his productions. [*Akademie der Künste, West Berlin*]

The Berlin theater attracted the best talent from all German-speaking countries. Among them were, top row, left to right: Fritz Kortner, Peter Lorre, Oskar Homolka; bottom left: Max Pallenberg; and bottom right: Hans Albers. [*Landesbildstelle, West Berlin*]

Heinrich George. [*Akademie der Künste, West Berlin*]

his briefcase on it, takes out a manuscript, the ever-ready pencil, other things. The stage director, the scenic designer, the set painter, and others approach him and present their needs . . .

Suddenly: "Attention!" Silence on the stage. "Are you ready?" He is casual with some, more formal with others—but despite his pleasantness, despite all the comradery, one has the feeling that the director is in charge.

He has the scene played through. The actors, scripts in hand or on tables, act as they want, asking each other's advice, giving each other inspiration. Piscator tosses a word in here or there, but generally lets them work as they see fit. But they all work under his direction and accept his idea of how the scene should go. Each one is independent and yet each is influenced by his personality. One has the feeling that the actors speak what Piscator is thinking.

[*But he*] *does not demand blind acceptance of what he says.* [*Heinrich*] *George, for example, . . . gives him many suggestions, often suggests things to his colleagues, and directs the extras. One might think George were in charge, which doesn't irritate Piscator. . . .*

Only if there is disorder, or if someone doesn't understand, or if the extras are too loud, will his voice cut shrilly, his excitement turn to anger . . . Once again one is reminded of the parade ground.[5]

Heinrich George was one of the three most notable actors of the Berlin theater in the 1920s. The other two were Albert Bassermann and Elisabeth Bergner. These stars were supported by a remarkable ensemble. Berlin attracted the country's best talent—talent which, in all the ups and downs of theatrical experimentation, gave Berlin's theater a rare standard of quality. The same actors would play under different directors. You could see the best of them not only under Reinhardt, Jessner, and Piscator, but also in one of the five theaters directed by Heinz Saltenburg, or in one of the three theaters directed by Victor Barnowsky, or in the three others directed by Arthur Hellmer. They might also play at one of Martin Zickel's many United Theaters, or at Theodor Tagger's Renaissance Theater, or at a host of others. Tagger "discovered" one of the most original playwrights of the time. He was billed as "Ferdinand Bruckner," which turned out to be a pseudonym for—Theodor Tagger.

Here is what one critic wrote about Heinrich George's performance in Ehm Welk's *Gewitter über Gottland* (*Thunderstorm over Gottland*):

. . . This "knight" [*the character Klaus Stoertebekker*] *shines with anger . . . He pounds the table with a fist of blood and iron . . . Then some runt attacks him. He lifts his paw—bash!—and his opponent lies on the side of the road. All one movement. But what a movement! It was perfect, it was accurate, just the way the medieval warriors must have fought.*

At the same time, Klaus Stoertebekker possesses a comic affability. He helps to his feet the one he has just beaten. Up you go! You didn't hurt yourself, did you? He pounds him on the shoulder, pacifies him, speaks a few helpful words to him. As if Klaus, the giant, wanted to apologize for the blow. No, no, it wasn't so bad. There

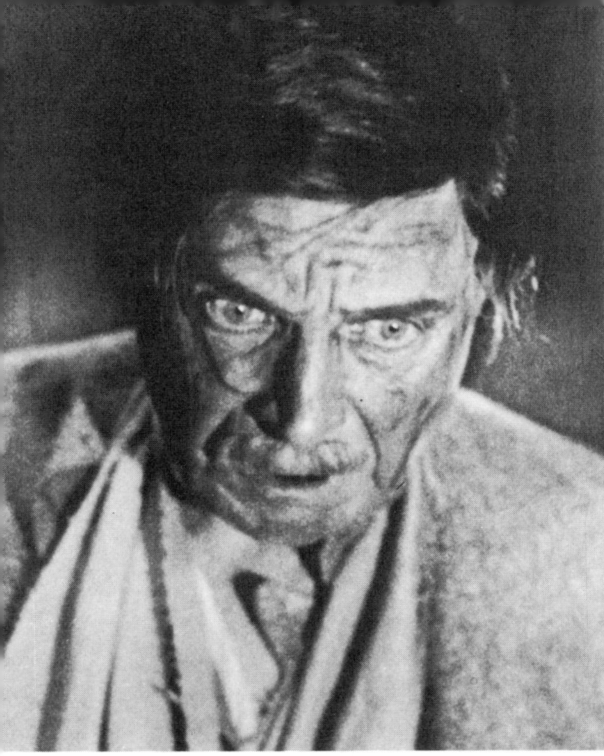

Albert Bassermann. [*Landesbildstelle, West Berlin*]

are worse blows in me! The words swing in a melody, the roaring heartiness is unforgettable.[6]

Another critic wrote about Albert Bassermann playing the title role of Schiller's *Wallenstein:*

Beaming, hurrying, bursting with energy, Bassermann descends . . . from the steps of the observation point in the background: "Let it be, Seri. Come down." Everything moves as if generated by a great force, as if created in an assured mood. His steps reach out into space, his gaze pierces forward, his speech is quick: "Now we must act, with dispatch!" This is the central line, receiving all the power of his intonation. A brilliant man, in the height of his power. The height has been built up for the coming downfall.

During the ensuing discussion with Terzky and Illo, this powerful force falters. One sees how he draws back from the plot of these two, resolved in his decision. And then comes the monologue, which Bassermann in no way "declaims." He plays it stormily instead, setting it completely into the dramatic flow of the action . . . He pauses before he begins: "Thus was I the traitor." And now defends himself with the intensity of a lawyer pleading to demolish his own accusations: "Only an act of violence can tear me loose."[7]

But Elisabeth Bergner surpassed them all. She was at once the Eleanora Duse and Sarah Bernhardt of her time, except that, as you sat in her spell, she was neither. She was whoever she played that night. When she played George Bernard Shaw's *Saint Joan,* a critic wrote:

I don't know whether the wise old man ever really visualized the Maid of Orleans who was canonized a second time by his play. But she certainly wasn't a tiny thing like our Elisabeth. To turn the Maid into intelligence incarnate, the intelligence must be coupled with imagination, a sense of humor must be superimposed over a slightly irritating superiority. I believe that among all the Saint Joans in London, New York, Paris, or elsewhere, our tiny Joan is the most creative. Cognoscenti support this view. No actress other than Elisabeth Bergner is so rooted in the childlikeness and innocence, in the obstinacy that springs from delicate impertinence. Our Joan is a child-woman, almost arrogant in her impatience with man's indolence and stupidity. Her intelligence is that of a monarch who learned to rule as she herded sheep. How delightful is her naïve slyness when, at the opening of the play, she demands a horse, a horse to serve her kingdom. How innocent, trusting, and sisterly is her lack of due respect for the Dauphin. Bergner, above all, has intelligence, has certainty, has purity of form; but if she only had those, she would still not be the best Saint Joan by far.

One believes her, her voices, her calling out. She presents an elfin little creature who surely hears what no other mortal has heard, who has come, suddenly, from her sheep pastures and from another world. She makes one believe, not with the glib, strong-lunged ecstasy of today, but with her silence, her depth, her baptism in the nameless sources of life.[8]

There were also a few new playwrights. One of them caused a scandal. He was Arthur Schnitzler, who, at the *fin de siècle* in Vienna, was Sigmund Freud's literary

Elisabeth Bergner. Above: In the title role of George Bernard Shaw's *Saint Joan*. Right: As Juliet in Max Reinhardt's production of *Romeo and Juliet*. "She makes one believe, not with the glib, strong-lunged ecstasy of today but with her silence, her depth, her baptism in the nameless sources of life." [*Staats- und Universitäts-Bibliothek, Hamburg, and Max Reinhardt Archive, Binghamton, New York*]

Doppelgänger and had privately printed *Reigen* (*La Ronde*) in 1900. The play had its first authorized production on December 20, 1920, not in Vienna but at Berlin's Kleines Schauspielhaus. The codirectors, Gertrud Eysold and Maximilian Sladek, along with the entire cast, were promptly hauled to court for "immoral behavior in public." Supporting the charges were the usual guardians of public morality—the League Against Alcoholism, the League Against Public Immorality, the League for Culture and Morals. Defending the play were just about all of Berlin's intellectuals.

The trial went, as most of these morality trials go.

Defense Attorney Heine: Did you actually speak to any young people who claim that the play gave them license to "have sex when they feel like it"?

Witness: Sort of.

Heine: Did anyone actually say that?

Witness: Yes. Especially about the bed scenes . . .

Heine: Never mind. My question was, did you actually speak to anyone who said that?

Witness: Yes . . . I no longer know the name. I spoke to a young girl . . . seventeen years old.

Heine: And what did she say?

Witness: Approximately?

Heine: All right, tell us what she said approximately.

Witness: That the play presented a new view of life which had little resemblance to what had been preached to youth before. That she saw a completely new view of the holiness of matrimony and of what was and was not permissible.

Heine: Did she also say that anyone should be allowed to do what was done in the play?

Witness: I don't believe she said that.[9]

The critic of the *Berliner Börsen-Courier,* the city's equivalent of the *Wall Street Journal,* testified that prewar French comedies and postwar operettas he had seen were far more explicit about moral matters than *Reigen.* Why, at the Deutsches Theater, you could actually see Shakespeare's Romeo and Juliet in bed together.

The play had already closed before the trial ended, so the guilty verdict was moot. But after a subsequent reversal by a higher court, Berlin's stage was set for a great deal more frank probing of sexual morality.

Other new playwrights who filled the gaps between Shakespeare and Shaw were Carl Zuckmayer, Frank Wedekind, and Georg Kaiser. But the shining light was Bertolt Brecht.

After that first, bitter taste of the city in 1920, Brecht moved permanently to Berlin in September 1924 to work as a script reader at Reinhardt's Deutsches Theater. He came not without laurels. His *Trommeln in der Nacht* (*Drums in the Night*) had been performed in Munich and earned him the coveted Kleist Prize. A month after his arrival in Berlin, his *Lebens Eduards des Zweiten von England* (*Life of Edward II of England*), also first produced in Munich, opened at the Staatstheater. That same month, October 1924, his *Im Dickicht der Städte* (*In the Thickets of the City*) was produced by Erich Engel with sets by his Augsburg classmate Caspar Neher.

The *Berliner Börsen-Courier* critic wrote:

After this litmus test, the name Bert Brecht will be remembered for reasons other than its attractive alliteration. Spheres of light and confusion revolve about this young man: his emotions are rooted in primordial sounds: his hands uncover fragments of life. They can balance humanness with humanity and conquer human frailty in the earthly spirit. He has a wild, prize-worthy, young talent, as long as one does not demand that a twenty-year-old begin at his peak.[10]

For Brecht, these plays were the beginning of a new theater:

Today's stage is completely makeshift. To view it as having to do with the intellect, with art, is a misapprehension. Theater deals with a vaguely comprehended public . . . The despairing hope of the theater is to keep a hold on its public by constantly capitulating to its taste . . . But unless the public is seen in terms of the class struggle,

The most famous German legs of the twenties (and in subsequent decades) were first seen on stage in a show called *Broadway.* They belonged to the last girl at the left, Marlene Dietrich. [*Landesbildstelle, West Berlin*]

it must be rejected as the source of a new style.[11]

Brecht's success in Berlin was, indeed, based on his view of the audience as representatives of a class. After *Baal* (a parody of Expressionist excesses) and *Mann ist Mann* (*Man Is Man*), he moved straight to his great and eventually international triumph.

Die Dreigroschenoper (*The Threepenny Opera*), with a book by Bertolt Brecht after John Gay's *Beggar's Opera* of 1728 and music by Kurt Weill, opened under the direction of Erich Engels at the Theater am Schiffbauerdamm on August 31, 1928. It was an instant hit with the public.

Herbert Ihering, Brecht's critical mentor, called it "the breakthrough, not of a worldly or a society-oriented theater . . . not because beggars and criminals appear in a drama that is not a mystery story, not because a threatening underworld disregards all social relationships, but because morality is neither attacked nor negated, but simply suspended . . . Here is a world where the line between tragedy and humor has vanished."

Others were disgusted. The *Kreuz-Zeitung* wrote that *The Threepenny Opera* "can be most easily summed up as literary necrophilia, of which the most notable factor was the worthlessness of its subject matter. What simple-mindedness—naïveté is too weak a word—for [the manager of the theater] to believe that he can fill his house with emptiness!"

The most outstanding critic, the dean of Berlin's theater world, was Alfred Kerr, who wrote for the *Berliner Tageblatt*. His review was devastating, but even worse was his charge that Brecht had plagiarized some of the songs from K. L. Ammer's translation of François Villon's poetry. Brecht admitted this some months later in an article in the *Berliner Börsen-Courier*. "I am quite sloppy when it comes to matters of intellectual ownership," he wrote.

Kerr reviewed not only the premiere, but also what he called "the dernière," *The Threepenny Opera*'s last performance. He deplored the fact that, "the joyful Zuckmayer aside," few modern German plays were performed on Berlin's stage, *The Threepenny Opera*, being, after all, basically an English play. He noted with some glee that it was succeeded on Schiffbauerdamm by *Charlie's Aunt*. "We have," wrote Kerr, "after the Russians, the most experimental theater in the world. But these efforts produce directors, not playwrights."

What does The Beggar's Opera *have to do with our time? Good lord! Does the threatening march of the beggars' battalion or a little pseudo-Communism make it relevant? Pah! Without the magnificently simple music of Weill it is nothing. Rubbish. Junk. The thirteenth in the baker's dozen.*[12]

But *The Threepenny Opera* had a long run. The public liked it. And if it was "a delight, rather than a platform," as Kerr complained, that may have been the secret of its success. Perhaps the public had grown tired of political productions.

Brecht kept writing political plays. His *Happy End* was a failure. His *Rise and Fall of the City of Mahagonny* yielded some wonderful tunes by Kurt Weill, but had none of the impact, let alone success, of *The Threepenny Opera*. A radio production of *Saint Joan of the Stockyards* aroused interest only because Carola Neher, the inimitable *Threepenny* star, played the title role. Brecht, influenced by such friends as Karl Korsch and Walter Benjamin, delved deeper and deeper into Marxist philosophy. But he was never a Communist:

As I read Das Kapital *by Karl Marx, I understood my dreams. You can see that I want a wider public for this book. I did not suddenly discover that I had written a whole collection of Marxist dramas without knowing it, but Marx was the only audience I had come across for the dramas. A man of his interests would have been interested in such plays. Not because they are brilliant, but because he was . . .*[13]

Brecht left Berlin on February 28, 1933, the day after the burning of the Reichstag —a historic event which no theater could have arrested.

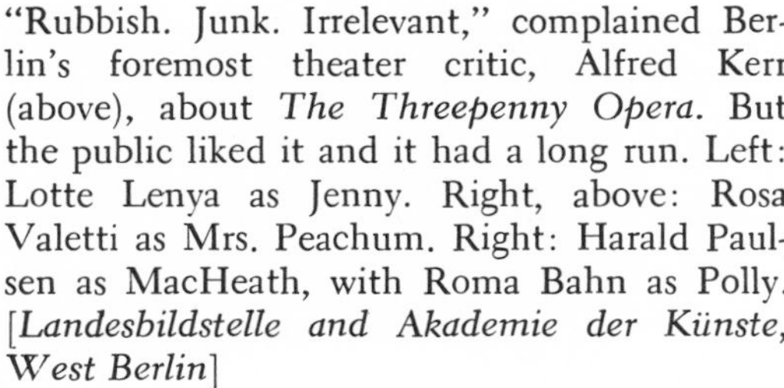

"Rubbish. Junk. Irrelevant," complained Berlin's foremost theater critic, Alfred Kerr (above), about *The Threepenny Opera*. But the public liked it and it had a long run. Left: Lotte Lenya as Jenny. Right, above: Rosa Valetti as Mrs. Peachum. Right: Harald Paulsen as MacHeath, with Roma Bahn as Polly. [*Landesbildstelle and Akademie der Künste, West Berlin*]

This scene sketch for the first production of Brecht's *The Threepenny Opera* is by Caspar Neher, who was the stage and costume designer for most Berlin productions of Brecht's plays. [*Max Reinhardt Archive, Binghamton, New York*]

9

FILM: *Magic, Mountains, and Mirrors*

Max Skladanowsky, who, with his brother Emil, invented the first movie projector in 1895, here proudly exhibits his gadget. [*Staatsbibliothek, West Berlin*]

The Lumière brothers were first to patent a satisfactory movie projector. They opened their public cinematograph show on December 28, 1895, in the basement of the Café de Paris in Paris. But Berlin had beaten them to it.

Two months earlier, Berliners had seen the world's first public screening of a film. The projector had been invented by Max and Emil Skladanowsky and the film was made by Oskar Messter, who was to become the world's first professional film producer. It was a comic pantomime—what else?—and it was presented as the not-so-grand finale of a variety show at the Wintergarten, Berlin's music hall, on November 1, 1895. The audience was not impressed.

No wonder:

The room is darkened. Suddenly floats on the Ganges, palms, the temple of the Brahmins appear.
A silent family drama rages
with bon vivants, a masquerade—
a gun is pulled. Jealousy inflamed.

A scene from one of Skladanowsky's early films, entitled *Die Jungfrau von Orleans* (*The Maid of Orleans*). [*The Museum of Modern Art, Film Stills Archive, New York*]

Lilian Harvey flaps butterfly wings to help her audience escape grim reality in UFA's *Die keusche Susanne* (*Chaste Susan*) (1926). Though an English actress, Harvey was one of Germany's most popular movie stars in the twenties. [*Staatsbibliothek, West Berlin*]

Mr. Piefke duels headlessly
and they show us, step by step,
mountaineers climbing the steep, demanding paths.
The paths lead down through forests,
they twist and climb the threatening
cliff. The view into the depths is enlivened by
cows and potatoes.
And into the darkened room—into my very eyes—
flutters that, that . . . oh, dreadful!
One after the other!
Then the arc lamp hissingly announces the end, lights!
And we push ourselves out into the open . . .
horny and yawning.[1]

Yet it did not take long before people became addicted to the new art form. Movies provided an escape during World War I. Berlin became Germany's Hollywood. The first film studio was built in the Tempelhof district, where the Skladanowsky brothers lived. The Kaiser's crafty First Quartermaster General, General Erich Ludendorff, recognized the motion picture as a potential instrument of war propaganda. He established the Photograph and Film Office in the German War Ministry and subsidized the young film industry.

After the revolution, the military remembered. There was a scandal, early in the Weimar Republic, when it became known that the Phoebus Film Company had received millions from a secret War Ministry slush fund to make patriotic films which treated militarism as a paradise lost thanks to the Treaty of Versailles. The War Minister had to resign, and the administrator of the fund, a Commander Lohmann, died shortly after the story broke, probably by suicide.

The generals might have saved their money. Alfred Hugenberg, the political agent of the armament manufacturers and a Junker, had bought the Universum Film A.G. (UFA), the largest German film company. It soon inundated Germany's movie palaces (many of them UFA-owned) with well-produced patriotic kitsch that made Germans cry—and cry out for a *Führer*.

Hugenberg's propaganda from the right was counterbalanced somewhat by high-quality emotional appeal from the left. The Soviets showed a number of their films in Berlin, not with tedious subtitles, but dubbed with German dialogue. Sergei Eisenstein's *Battleship Potemkin*, shown in 1926, was particularly well received—so well, in fact, that the authorities banned this Bolshevik epic for a while. "The German repercussions made us realize the progress we had made in the art of the film," said the Russian People's Education Commissar A. V. Lunacharski later. In March 1933, shortly after he came to power, even Hitler found it necessary to praise *Battleship Potemkin*. He tried to assure German film makers that he would not compromise their art.

Their art was also an industry. German film production became second only to that of the United States. In 1927, protected by a quota that allowed only one foreign film to be imported for every German one, Germany produced 241 feature films, compared to 743 American movies. The French made 74 and the British, 44. Of all the films made in the twenties, German ones were among the most memorable and influential.

But most filmgoing was a mere pastime, though an immensely popular one. In 1920 there were twenty seats for every thousand Berliners. At the end of the decade this figure had increased to thirty seats per thousand.

Here is how one Berliner remembered the early movies:

Standing in an endless line of ticket addicts, I can only shrug my shoulders. Finally after a quarter of an hour I get to the ticket box.

Two in the loges—nine marks eighty.

For that much I could have attended Parsifal!

Black space receives us. The flashlight of the ticket taker glows like a will-o'-the-wisp before our noses.

A program—forty pfennig.

For forty pfennig I could buy a paperback of Götz von Berlichingen—*and Mark Twain's essays.*

"Look, the feature has begun—" We sat down. Mitzi pulls out her handkerchief.

"Knöppchen isn't in a hurry"—a subtitle flashes on the screen.

"This isn't the main feature—it's only the comedy," I remarked with acumen. "You're here only as a viewer—not as a critic," Mitzi whispered.

Right. Not one more word.

Knöppchen's antics loose waves of laughter.

Intermission. Candied nuts! Mumbling. Someone sprays pine scent. Yech!

Darkness . . .

"The Stepmother Visits Her Daughter at the Boarding School."

Yesterday the "boarding school" was a bordello, the day before yesterday, a gambling den, and the day before that, the embassy in Malaleppe.

The old servant comes in.

From Klösschen naturally. Forty-five marks a day and overtime.*

In the meantime, the girls have crawled into a car. It begins to move—there's no one behind the steering wheel.

Screams—horror—breathless excitement—then the crash. Dummies fly in all directions, the model car burns to a crisp—

* *Temporary help, somewhat like the American "Kelly Girls."*

Henny Porten, who made her first appearance in 1907, in Oskar Messter's earliest films, became one of Germany's earliest movie stars. She and her steed look longingly from a picture postcard towards the never-never land of *kitsch*. [*Private collection, Gilman*]

Wege zur Kraft und Schönheit (*Roads to Strength and Beauty*) was the title of this 1925 "sex education" film. There were many others, all of which escaped the censor because their producers disguised prurient intent under noble protestations. But there were also as many hard-core porno films in the Berlin of the twenties as you could find half a century later on New York's Forty-second Street. [*Private collection, Offermanns*]

Madame du Barry (1919), with Pola Negri, was Ernst Lubitsch's first great feature film, inaugurating a spate of romantic historical films with spectacular displays of costumes and sets. Lubitsch, born in 1892 in Berlin, was one of Max Reinhardt's actors. The famous "Lubitsch touch" eventually attracted some of the best artists to German cinema. [*Private collection, Offermanns*]

But now you must really pay attention!

Second act: In the palace of a "rich" millionaire.

Aha, it's the Walser Room at Friedmann and Weber—they haven't spared themselves any costs. It runs 1,200 marks a day, without extras.

Guests have been invited to the millionaire's. They stream in from all sides. If one could only see an unfamiliar face. No such luck. A few young people want to go off on a lark. They want to drive to Longfellow in Yellowstone Park. A swarm of tuxedos (forty marks and overtime) run down the stairs and pile into the car.

The chauffeur doesn't budge. They haven't rehearsed this shot. At the price of rubber today, I don't think he's going to move. Normally he drives five people, and there must be at least eight—he's simply not driving.

Where's the director? He doesn't appear but from off camera an invisible hand offers the chauffeur an extra fifty marks. Then he suddenly nods in acquiescence, puts the car into gear, and drives off.

The romantic vistas of Yellowstone Park appear . . . One glance is sufficient to recognize the limestone hills around Rüdersdorf. Ah, there is the turn to the lake and there—right, that's where May filmed Mistress of the World, *that's the place where the flight to Egypt was shot . . .*

I leap up. I can't stand another second. It's dreadful but we can't seem to get rid of it. I can't stand to see another film![2]

If these films, nevertheless, pandered to Mitzi's emotions, others simply pandered. They were as pornographic as anything that occupied the attention of the United States Supreme Court in 1973. The Reichstag felt compelled to take action. In a debate in February 1920, the Minister of the Interior, having viewed pornographic films in the company of a parliamentary committee, observed:

To be honest, it was dreadful to see what an extensive collection of filth it was. The thought that this repulsive stuff could be shown to children makes me blush. One cannot find worse poison for the soul . . . The worst films were not even screened. The police were ashamed to show them in the presence of women. Only the male members of the committee could be exposed to such a performance. What a morass of immorality the players must wallow in to let themselves be used for such a performance! And in what murky depths must those exist who photograph such scenes and act as directors.

Reporting this speech, *Vorwärts*, the Social-Democratic party organ, commented:

Who are the connoisseurs who consume

Expressionism dominated the best of the early German movies, as it did all German art of the period. One of the earliest films in that genre was also, perhaps, the most notable: *Das Kabinett des Dr. Caligari* (*The Cabinet of Dr. Caligari*), 1919. "The phenomena of the screen are the phenomena of the soul," said Carl Hauptmann, the novelist. *Caligari* showed the extent to which the German soul seemed beset with fatalism, which was transformed into violent art—at times, an art of hallucination rather than mere fantasy. *Caligari*, directed by Robert Wiene, featured Lil Dagover, Conrad Veidt, and Werner Krauss and became better known abroad than in Germany, where it was at first turned down by a distributor and rarely shown afterward. [*Private collection, Offermanns*]

Mädchen in Uniform (*Girls in Uniform*) was made in 1931, just before cinema became a means of Nazi propaganda. The film tells the story of a girls' school in Potsdam, where the iron discipline leads to a suicide attempt by a young student after she naïvely confesses to being in love with one of her teachers. Produced by Carl Froehlich for an independent company, it was directed by Leontine Sagan, a stage director. [*The Museum of Modern Art, Film Stills Archive, New York*]

Der alte Fritz (*Old Fritz*), as Frederick the Great of Prussia was known with misdirected fondness, was a favorite subject of Alfred Hugenberg's patriotic films. Shown here in *Das Flötenkonzert von Sanssouci* (*The Flute Concert of Sans Souci*), 1930, he is portrayed by Otto Gebühr under the direction of Gustav Ucicky. Nostalgia for the martial virtues of the Hohenzollerns made German movie audiences cry—and cry out for a *Führer*. [*Private collection, Offermanns*]

The Gloria Palast near Berlin's Zoo was one of the city's proliferating movie palaces, most of which were owned by UFA and as lush as any in America. [*Landesbildstelle, West Berlin*]

---

these tasty treats for dessert? Not inhabitants of Berlin North and East. These were, and are, the habitués of Berlin West gambling halls and clubs. There the police can find such things. There they seize films straight out of the projector to the general dismay of the audience.

The Interior Minister replied:

As if the inhabitants of Berlin North and East would not view these films with the same enjoyment if they had the opportunity! Is the moral makeup of a society determined by income? Does proletarian morality stand at a higher level than the bourgeois? Only circumstances are different, people are the same.[3]

After the censorship law was passed in

Der Kongress Tanzt (*Congress Dances*), 1931, with Lilian Harvey, Willy Fritsch, and Conrad Veidt, was one of the first—and most successful—operatic musicals. Inspired by René Clair's work in *Sous les toits de Paris, Kongress* combined song, humor, and romance in the setting of the Congress of Vienna which, in 1814–15, founded the Holy Alliance between Prussia, Russia, and Austria after the exile of Napoleon to Elba. [*The Museum of Modern Art, Film Stills Archive, New York*]

Luis Trenker in *Die Weisse Hölle von Pitz Palu* (*The White Hell of Pitz Palu*), 1929, enchanted the masses of movie fans by leading them up the "narrow track of the elite" to conquer mountains. [*The Museum of Modern Art, Film Stills Archive, New York*]

1920, underground films flourished in Berlin, often competing with girlie shows in the same clubs. Nor did the 1920 Reich Film Act hint at anything more censorious than the protection of children. It specifically stipulated that no film could be banned because of its politics. But even benign censorship can become a cancer. As the antidemocratic forces grew in Germany's body politic, artistic merit was increasingly confused with political merit—as the right wing saw it.

The art in films, like the art in the modern galleries and architectural offices, was chiefly Expressionist. In films, it was a matter of psychological simplifications and symbolism, distraught "souls" caught in the web of "fate." Even the review by Rudolf Kurtz of *The Cabinet of Dr. Caligari* (directed by Robert Wiene from a script by Hans Janowitz and Carl Mayer and released in 1919), is Expressionist:

There is a primordial energy with which all factors interact, a freshness, an atmosphere of risk, of excitement, surprise. The creative process is a delirium, a hallucination, stemming from a much wilder time: darkened streets, the shouted commands of republican troops, from somewhere the harsh screeching of street-corner rhetoricians —a city clothed in the deepest darkness, occupied by radical revolutionaries, with the rattle of machine guns, chains, rooftop snipers, and hand grenades . . .

A delicate girl vanishes, stolen by the dark phantom, dragged over the sharp, high walls, past steep, pointed roofs. Murder shines from the feverish, wide eyes. Murder looses its dark purple cloak over the roofs of the little city . . .

And then a cry, a scream: Murder! Murder! And the murderer is there, is seized: the dark phantom from Dr. Caligari's cabinet . . . Where is Caligari?

A great stone building! There is Caligari! Like lightning, banners stream across the sky: Caligari! Caligari! Frenzied is the carrousel of the city, frenzied the murder and the blood, raging circles of mankind in high hats and fluttering capes—a dark, black point—Caligari—it is he—surrounded by men, trusted by men.[4]

In addition to Expressionism, German film makers contributed another genre to their art: the mountain films, the drama of nature and the courage of man. Their originator was Arnold Fanck, a geologist turned mountain climber. There were many such films—among them *Ski Wunder* (*The Wonder of Skis*) (1920), *Der Kampf um den Berg* (*Struggle with the Mountain*) (1921), *Der Heilige Berg* (*The Holy Mountain*) (1926), and *Die Weisse Hölle von Pitz Palu* (*The White Hell of Pitz Palu*) (1929)—but only two stars: Luis Trenker and Leni Riefenstahl, who was to become the foremost film maker of the Third Reich.

Co-starring with Trenker in *Pitz Palu*, and in most other German mountain pictures, was Leni Riefenstahl, who later became Hitler's favorite film maker. She gained world acclaim for her documentary on the 1936 Berlin Olympics. [*The Museum of Modern Art, Film Stills Archive, New York*]

The myth of the mountains became part of the German nationalist credo. Trenker and Riefenstahl personified this myth much as Jeanette MacDonald and Nelson Eddy, a decade later, were to personify the American myth of eternal springtime. Both myths were antidotes to the corruption of civilization. There was as much comfort in the heroic ideal for the Germans, as there was in the idyllic ideal for Americans. Said Luis Trenker:

Mountain climbing demands unparalleled performances . . . It is not the broad path of the masses but the narrow track of those who have selectively and systematically strengthened their talents, of those who know the technical aspects of climbing, of those who have grown to conquer the mountain.[5]

The greatest film, perhaps, of Berlin's great decade was *Der blaue Engel* (*The Blue Angel*). It was released in 1930 and made Marlene Dietrich famous around the world. Ironically, this satire of prewar German society, produced by UFA, was quite contrary to Hugenberg's political tendencies. Professor Rath (played by Emil Jannings), who is seduced by the cabaret singer Lola-Lola, was not unlike Hugenberg. But *The Blue Angel*, based on a novel by Heinrich Mann and directed by Josef von Sternberg, was more than a portrayal of the decline and fall of a petty tyrant. It spoke to the heart of the Berlin experience during the twenties. The humorist and poet Munkepunke (a pseudonym for Alfred Richard Meyer) wrote at the time:

I couldn't fall asleep for a long time after the premiere. I struggled to repress in my dreams those dim days before my comprehensives. It had been my senior teacher, now transformed into Professor Rath, who began his sentences with "Well then . . .", who peered over his glasses, who moved from desk to desk in the classroom only to turn suddenly on one of the slightly worn soles of his high-laced boots: "Well then . . ." Many years later I heard a rumor that that man, whom we often mocked but to whom our sympathy really belonged, had committed suicide "for unknown reasons." Committed suicide—perhaps he finally had enough of student mockery.

It was a tradition to go to the Blutige Knochen (Bloody Bones) . . . That old, smoke-filled vaudeville palace probably doesn't even exist any more. It was in the Kamengiesser Strasse, which everyone who went to Pastor Brake at the Brother's Church or to the old Petritor to get a schnapps had to pass. It may well have been only a guilt-ridden, old legend that our "Professor Rath" searched for his senior class at the Blutige Knochen.

We had our own Blue Angel . . . Our Lola-Lola was called Hedy—her calling card identified her as "The Lady Barber." Her hit in 1899 was not "Falling in Love Again"

Der blaue Engel (*The Blue Angel*), 1930, told the tragic story of an elderly professor who is seduced by a cabaret singer. One of the most frequently revived German films of the period, it still moves many into "Falling in Love Again" with Marlene Dietrich. [*Staatsbibliothek, West Berlin*]

If Dietrich's Lola-Lola continues to seduce, Emil Jannings still shows himself to be one of the greatest actors in cinema history. Under the direction of Josef von Sternberg, Jannings' Professor Rath gave this sound film its haunting poignancy. Words, music, song, and natural sound are almost incidental to the psychological drama expressed in Jannings' face and gestures. [*Private collection, Offermanns; Private collection, Gilman*]

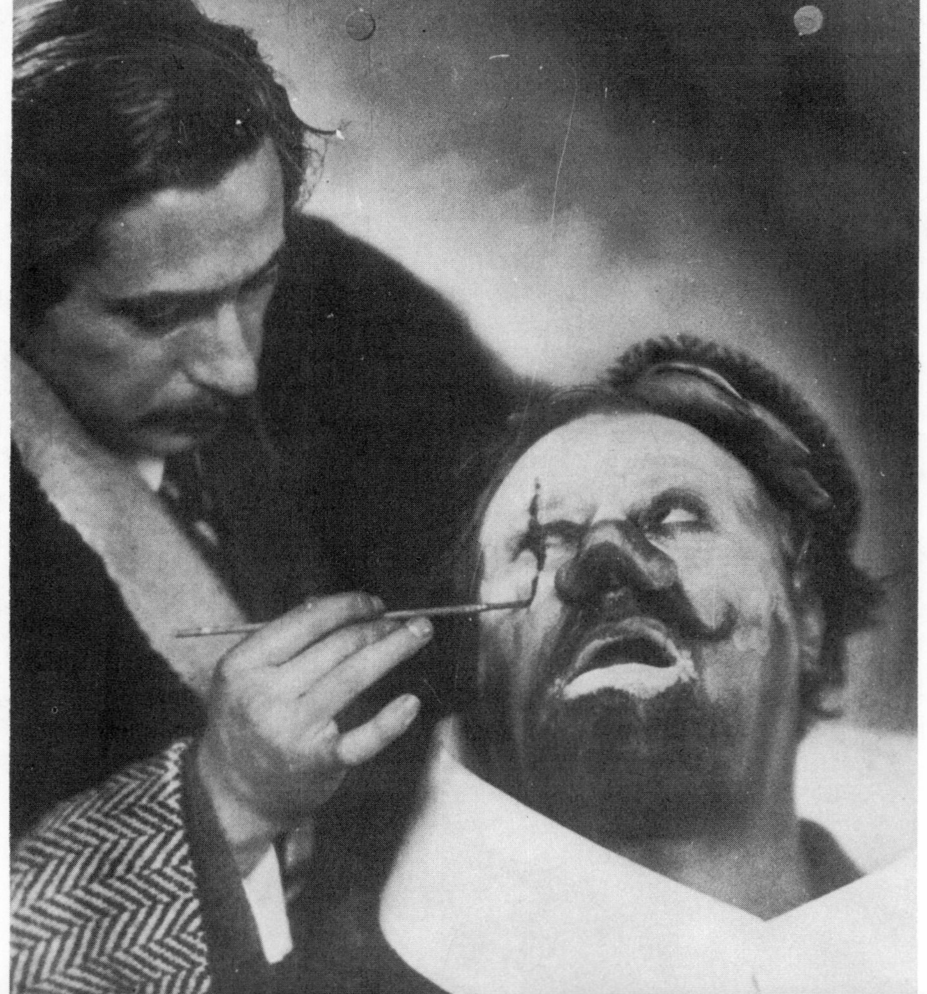

Lola-Lola, [*Private collection, Offermanns*]

("*Ich bin von Kopf zu Fuss auf Liebe eingestellt*") *but rather:*

When the wind doesn't blow,
And the mill doesn't go,
My miller turns me
In the straw, in the straw.

And we believed in her nightly transformation into the most elegant of miller's wives. This gold-bespangled soubrette, who allowed us, when we had the means, to buy her a beer, this temptress was our local Lola-Lola. Above us always hung the Damocles sword—that our Rath would show up any instant and that our diplomas would vanish . . .

And suddenly Professor Rath did appear. We seniors dived under the table while the Professor's glance followed us over his glasses, not sparing a glance for the professionally tempting charms of Hedy-Lola.

And whose collar did he grab under the table? —Mine![6]

There were many other good films, besides all the lavishly produced comedies about Monte Carlo, the dancing Congress of Vienna, and miscellaneous heartless vamps. Producers, directors, and stars won the hearts of millions of fans and some of them won contracts in Hollywood. One film that stood out for the stark beauty of its emotional power was *Mädchen in Uniform* (*Girls in Uniform*), released in 1932. Directed by Leontine Sagan and starring Dorothea Wieck, it exposed the cruelty of insensitive, authoritarian discipline in a girls' boarding school. The film was a humanitarian triumph, as well as a box-office hit.

The film version of Brecht's *Threepenny Opera* was also a considerable success—but not in the mind of its playwright. Marlene Dietrich, American Ambassador Frederic Sackett, and other notables attended the premiere at the Atrium. Bert Brecht stayed away. Angered that fundamental parts of his message had been disregarded or eliminated, he sued the producers.

Brecht expressed his views in an interview printed soon after the premiere:

In reworking existing stage plays for the talking film, more changes are necessary than just technical alterations. In many cases, changes are needed in the poetic substance of the work.

The rights the author has in the theater must be extended to film. This is not yet legally clear, but the trial covering The Threepenny Opera *will create a precedent.*

I kept trying to see what was going on in the studio. Not even once did they let me see the final script. From a third party I learned that the script had two additional authors. They barred me from the studio. Since no one consulted me about the style of The Threepenny Opera, *the public will find something totally different than it expected.*[7]

Some six months after the premiere of the film, which took place on February 19, 1931, Brecht started to make his own film: *Kuhle Wampe, or Who Owns the World?* Directed by Slatan Dudow, written by Brecht and Ernst Ottwalt, with music by Hanns Eisler, *Kuhle Wampe* was the first German Marxist film for the masses. The Berlin censor first demanded that certain scenes (including a nude bathing scene) be cut, and then banned the film in toto as "potentially dangerous." This was 1932. The misery of unemployment was rapidly increasing, and, just as they did during World War I, Berliners sought escape in their proliferating movie houses. A year later there was no escape from Goebbels' propaganda.

Brecht took his *Kuhle Wampe* abroad, changed its title to *Whither Germany?* and showed it as a document of the struggle of the German intelligentsia against Fascism.

Before that, however, Berlin had made

a contribution to cinema technology. While the studios at Tempelhof and Neu-Babelsberg were grinding out silent movies, three young Berliners, Vogt, Masolle, and Engl, who had served together in the German Navy during World War I, had gotten together in the sleepy district of Mariendorf and developed sound pictures. There had been other attempts to match sound and image—mostly with the use of the gramophone. But it was the achievement of this trio, who aptly called their process "Tri-Ergon" ("the work of three"), to place the sound track directly on the film. In 1922 they patented the first "talkies." Their first cackling sound flick starred chickens in a barnyard.

Berlin film studios rejected the Tri-Ergon innovation. Talkies? Films, they said, were not supposed to talk. So the trio sold its patent to a Swiss concern which, in turn, sold it to Hollywood, where, in 1928, the world's first all-talking picture, *Sights of New York*, was produced. The Germans showed *Die Nacht gehört uns* (*The Night Is Ours*), with a talking Hans Albers, a year later. By then, movies and Hollywood had become synonymous.

A contemporary montage of stills from the film based on the Brecht-Weill *Threepenny Opera*, made in 1931. Brecht was not as pleased by this film version as was most of its large audience. [*Private collection, Offermanns*]

Scenes from *Kuhle Wampe, or Who Owns the World?* (1932), a film written by Brecht, directed by Slatan Dudow, with music by Hanns Eisler. It was an attempt to present "a Marxist film for the masses." Banned in Germany, it was later shown abroad as *Whither Germany?* [*Private collection, Offermanns*]

Wilhelm Furtwängler, conductor of the Berlin Philharmonic, caricatured by Olaf Gulbransson. [*Archiv für Kunst und Geschichte, West Berlin*]

10

MUSIC AND DANCE: *...And All That Jazz*

Next to New York, Berlin was the most musical city in the world, proclaimed Eugen Szatmari in his guide to Berlin of 1927, which was subtitled *What Baedeker Won't Tell You*. Berlin "has absorbed a good part of the musical life of the old Danube monarchy—using American business methods. German music managers have become as smart as any Americans, paying musical stars enormous sums."

One thing Baedeker didn't tell was that the violinist Fritz Kreisler would get five to eight thousand marks for one concert in Berlin. The singer Richard Tauber or Heinrich Schlusnus would get between two and two and a half thousand, and the pianist Arthur Schnabel about the same. It was a lot of money. Even Szatmari doesn't tell us the salaries paid to Berlin's famous resident musicians, such as Wilhelm Furtwängler, who conducted the Berlin Philharmonic from 1922 to 1934 (when he resigned for a year because Hitler banned Paul Hindemith's music), or Bruno Walter, who conducted Berlin's Municipal Opera from 1925 to 1929. But he does reveal that some of the younger musicians shelled out as much as a thousand marks to give a public concert. It was worth it to them. Once you played one of Berlin's some six hundred annual concerts (and were accepted by the city's many discerning music critics, notably Hans Heinz Stuckenschmidt), you had it made in the provinces, if not in the rest of Europe.

Szatmari also tells us about an unnamed violinist who rose to fame only after a piano manufacturer hired a hall and sent out five thousand free tickets for his first concert. The violinist, in return, promised that he would be forever accompanied on a piano made by his benefactor. The second concert also had a full house—with all tickets bought at the box office.

More important than manufactured fame and genuinely honored stars with astronomical honoraria was that Berlin was instrumental in launching modern music.

Arnold Schönberg, born in Vienna, had lived in Berlin from 1901 to 1903 and then again from 1911 to 1918. In 1925 he returned to teach at the Prussian Academy of Fine Arts.

Paul Hindemith was born in Hanau, Germany, and came to Berlin in 1927 to teach at the Academy of Music.

The two were officially sponsored by the Prussian Ministry of Culture, thanks mainly to Leo Kestenberg, the daring bureaucrat in charge of music. Kestenberg also appointed the Austrian Franz Schreker, the most widely performed modern composer of the twenties, to direct the Academy.

The Academy had been founded in the previous century of Brahm's friend Joseph Joachim, the Hungarian violinist. Between 1919, when it first presented Hans Pfitzner's opera *Palestrina*, until 1930, when it presented Darius Milhaud's *Christophe Colomb*, the Berlin Academy was a sounding board for the most interesting avant-garde—and some of the best—music of the early twentieth century.

Arnold Schönberg, one of the leading composers of the twentieth century, returned to Berlin in 1925 to teach at the Prussian Academy of Fine Arts. [*Staatsbibliothek, West Berlin*]

The music was, of course, also controversial. When Schönberg's 1912 song cycle *Pierrot Lunaire* was presented in the Academy's auditorium on January 5, 1924, there was a riot no less ferocious than the bedlam at the Paris premiere in 1913 of Igor Stravinsky's *Le Sacre du Printemps*. Some hotheads rose to condemn the "Jewish Bolshevism" of Schönberg's "cacophonic garbage" and went on with tirades against the Weimar Republic, modern art, Schönberg, Jews, and music in general.

But they could not silence the new voices. Almost two years later Berlin was the scene of another landmark event in musical history: the premiere of Alban Berg's *Wozzeck*, directed by Erich Kleiber. Berg was a pupil and close friend of Schönberg, somewhat tempering the master's atonality and, later, Schönberg's twelve-tone technique with his own, more pleasingly Viennese lyricism and drama. *Wozzeck*, an opera based on Georg Büchner's fragmentary play of jealousy and murder, was Berg's masterpiece. It had been considered unperformable, but Kleiber dared. Berg was in Berlin to watch the rehearsals. He wrote his wife:

December 4–5, 1925: Again optimistic about Wozzeck. *A fantastic accordion player, an American, a virtuoso. So the great danger is eliminated. Rehearsal with the doctor. Very good. A bel canto voice, just what I wanted. Everything singable . . .*

December 5–6, 1925: . . . The way the Wozzeck *rehearsals are going, you haven't missed much. On the contrary, the fact that you are being spared much of the irritation and upset makes our separation easier to take. Otherwise, I am very, very alone in this sea of people . . . I am up sixteen to eighteen hours without a break . . . How all of this—orchestra and stage—will be ready in eight days is beyond me, and I am comforted only by the conviction that Kleiber will not let anything unfinished out of his hands. He knows the success of the premiere depends on him . . .*[1]

Paul Hindemith, who also stood in the avant-garde of modern music, came in 1927 and taught at the Berlin Academy of Music. [*Staatsbibliothek, West Berlin*]

The protests during *Wozzeck*'s public

Left to right: Wilhelm Furtwängler, conductor of the Berlin Philharmonic; Otto Klemperer, conductor of the Berlin State Opera; Erich Kleiber, conductor; Arthur Schnabel, pianist and professor at the Academy of Music; Kurt Weill, composer. Below: Bruno Walter, director of the City Opera from 1925 to 1929, returning from one of his frequent trips to New York. [*Landesbildstelle and Archiv für Kunst und Geschichte, West Berlin*]

dress rehearsal were Schönberg's *Pierrot Lunaire* performance in 1924 all over again. The public did not understand the radical use of orchestral forms in opera, the use of atonal scale, the strange *Sprechgesang*, Schönberg's innovation of using voice halfway between song and speech. Nor did it want to.

But the actual premiere of *Wozzeck*, with Leo Schützendorf in the title role and Sigrid Johanson as Marie, came off without a hitch. Georg Büchner, the German poet and revolutionary agitator, who died in 1837 at the age of twenty-four and who is best known for his powerful drama *Danton's Death*, would have been amazed to see his last, unfinished work set to music. As an avant-gardist he would probably have approved, although not everyone did.

The Social-Democratic *Vorwärts* wrote:

A historic event. An audience, not partial to moderns, accepted this most problematical work of new music without great resistance. A number of supposedly unproduceable scenes were produced . . . The impossible occurred. The hard logic of this drama was ennobled, humanized, psychologized through the spirit of music . . . Physical actions torture the senses with horror and murderous certainty, but the composer raises the brutality of a single fate to the spirituality of an unreal, dreamlike, unworldly experience . . .[2]

The critic of the conservative *Kreuz-Zeitung* wrote:

. . . Alban Berg, who has been known up to now as a composer of chamber music,

Alban Berg's *Wozzeck,* long considered unperformable, was first performed at Berlin's State Opera in 1925, conducted by Erich Kleiber. Above, left: The composer and conductor are shown, front row center and right, with some members of the cast. Above: A scene from *Wozzeck,* which is based on a fragmentary play by Georg Büchner. Left: Kleiber (center), meeting the Vienna Philharmonic on the orchestra's arrival in Berlin. [*Private collection, Offermanns; Landesbildstelle and Akademie der Künste, West Berlin*]

has revealed himself [in this opera] as a progressive in the "moderate" sense of Schönberg. *The subject gave him a field in which his intellectual and antiemotional fantasy could blossom . . . The drama remains a proletarian play with a specific moral: not the murderer but the society in which he lives is guilty . . .*

. . . [Berg's] Tonmalerei *seldom supports the singers with singable melody. But since the color and expression often achieve the effect, the ear accepts the multitude of noises, hoping it will discover a melody. But the final act more than makes up for this. Here the composer explores new paths, becomes less harsh in his harmony—indeed, every once in a while he is "simply old-fashioned pretty" and the listener can relax. Applause, sparse up to this point, increased. In all, the music is not refreshing but exhausting and exciting, not at all ethereal.*[3]

The *Berliner Tageblatt* wrote:

Where anarchism will eventually lead the nations may be a political question to be answered in the future. Where it is leading art is a question that must be answered today. Young talents have exhausted themselves and left us a field full of ruins which will be barren for years. Every limitation has been destroyed . . . In literature and art the crisis seems to have passed. The artist's self-awareness is slowly reawakening. But music, as ever, limps behind and is still trapped in dim confusion . . .

All those today who purposely create the ugly (dissonant, impoverished, overdone, distorted) are damned to vacuity. It is no accident that their music is boring . . .

Is the State Opera House the right place for such experiments? Last evening's response says nothing about the future of this opera. There were applause and foot stamping and curtain calls. There was even a special ovation for Kleiber. But there was no dissenting view. The audience consisted of invited guests and friends who had rushed here from Vienna. Only later performances will show . . . whether this is a work of permanent value.[4]

The critic of the Catholic *Germania* wrote:

. . . Pretense! Ingenious pretense, sensational pretense, but, in any case, pretense! And this is what "German" composers, controlled by unseen strings, call art. The time is approaching to rebel against giving this inspired methodological nonsense a respectable backdrop . . . It is a witch's brew of broken orchestral sounds, twisted throats, animalistic screeching, shouting, rattling, contradicting every concept of music . . . Open the doors and windows! Fresh air! Respectable music, which pays back ticket buyers with joy and pleasure—and not at inflated prices![5]

There was no lack of "respectable music," and not at inflated prices either. High society could hear it gratis with its caviar and champagne. Concerts at home were the rage of those who happened to be both cultured and wealthy. It was considered a mark of great distinction to have celebrated musicians perform at one's house. A number of bankers and corporation executives held regular musicales in their spacious Dahlem villas, with artists like Richard Strauss or Arthur Schnabel as guests. Music filled the refined home of the publisher S. Fischer. The most important musical salons, however, were those of Marie von Bülow and Louise Wolff.

Frau von Bülow was the widow of Hans von Bülow, a composer, conductor, and the first husband of Cosima Wagner. She would charge her guests one mark or a mark fifty and give the money to needy musicians. The world's most prominent artists would perform in her house on Uhlandstrasse to help the cause. Frau Louise Wolff, on the other hand, was an impresario and a musical kingmaker. Her salon was often a steppingstone to world fame. It was also a meeting ground not only for the artists themselves but also for people of the press, the government offices, and the academies who could help advance them.

But the greatest influence on the music of Berlin, on the very sound of Europe, came from across the ocean.

"Duke" Ellington hit Berlin in the summer of 1925 with his all-black revue *Chocolate Kiddies*.

Jazz had been known for some time along the Spree. The night clubs were full of saxophones. Paul Whiteman's name was a household word. But a full-length jazz show? That was new. That was different. That was *knorke*, as the Berliners said in their inimitable dialect, which can't be translated even into German. "Nifty," perhaps.

Ellington had a lot of young Berlin composers running for score paper, and it was not long before one of them, Ernst Krenek, came up with a jazz "opera" of his own. It was called *Jonny Spielt Auf* (*Johnny Strikes Up*), and what he struck up was world unity: jazz conquers all. Krenek also wrote the libretto. The opera was first performed under Georg Sebastian at the Berlin City Opera on November 21, 1927. It concluded with a bang-up finale:

The curtain parted slowly. The audience saw a railroad station with the train about to leave. Girl waits for Boy. The conductor shouts: "All aboard!" Boy makes it, but rather than jump on the train, boy jumps on the big station clock, riding down with its hand and playing a violin.

Chorus: The hour of the past has struck, the future is approaching. Don't miss your connection. We are off to the unknown land of the free.

(The clock is lowered to the floor of the stage, turns into a globe, starts to glow, and then to rotate, while Johnny stands on the North Pole, fiddling away. Everyone dances around him.)

Chorus: The journey has begun. Johnny is calling the tune. A new world is dancing across the seas to take over old Europe . . .

Curtain.[6]

Kurt Weill was the most talented of those who called the new tune. In the fall of 1928 he presented two one-act operas, based on texts by Georg Kaiser, in the City Opera—as well as his *Threepenny Opera* performed in the Theater am Schiffbauerdamm. Jazz opera was established. Duke Ellington proved to have had as much influence on the new music as Schönberg.

Spreading the new sounds across the city and across the Western world was the phonograph. Everybody had one. Mamma would play the big hand-crank-and-horn one for her guests in the parlor. Lovers would take portables along picnicking in the woods or canoeing on Müggelsee.

At the Bauhaus, Moholy-Nagy, suggested —prophetically, if you consider electronic music—that musicians be done away with and music be created directly on the gramophone disk:

1. *Through the creation of a means of notation—an alphabet for the grooves of the record—a general instrument would be created, making all existing instruments superfluous.*

2. *Such a graphic series of symbols would make a new graphic-mechanical scale, which, in turn, would make new mechanical harmony possible. Through this, one could examine the various individual graphic signs and place them into a system. Here one can mention a possibility which is still utopian today: the conversion of graphic presentations into music based on specific equivalences.*

3. *The composer could create his compositions directly for reproduction and would therefore not be dependent on the ability of the interpreter. The latter has, until now, managed to smuggle his own emotions into the written composition. The new possibilities of the gramophone would place contemporary music education on a healthier basis. In place of the performer, who has nothing to do with the creation of music either actively or passively, people would be educated to become real musicians, that is, composers or listeners.*

4. *The introduction of this system of musical creation would also introduce considerable simplification: independence from large orchestras; expanded encouragement of creative originality through the simplest possible means.*[7]

As music changed, so did dance.

Isadora Duncan had moved dance from the traditional rigidity of ballet to a free interpretation of Greek classical art. From there, mostly in Germany, under the influence of the occult "spiritual science" of

Rudolf Steiner's "anthroposophy," it moved into the realm of religious Expressionism. This movement had its center at the Dalcroze School at Hellerau, near Dresden, which called its dance form "eurythmics."

The most renowned, most creative alumna of this school was Mary Wigman, a student and assistant of the innovative Swiss dancer Rudolf von Laban. She was the leading pioneer of modern dance.

In contrast to Isadora Duncan, who often interpreted familiar music, Mary Wigman experimented with dances in silence or accompanied only by flute or percussion instruments. She wanted, she said, to rid dance of the "dictatorship of music," and, much like the German Expressionist painters, she was given to stark and mythical moods. Her dances had titles like "Death Call" and "Dance for the Earth." She once expressed her philosophy as follows:

Dance is the language of the living, moving body.
Dance expresses invisible movement by means of visible movement.
Dance is an avowal of human existence.
Dance is the unity of force, time, and space, bound and unbound by inborn rhythm.
Dance is mankind, it exists for man, and turns to man.
Dancing can be done by anyone who has the desire and love.
Dancing as an art form can be created and produced only by the anointed dancer.
Living movement is rooted in all.
From this natural fact, dance receives its force in the creation of communal feeling.
The obligation of all creative dancers is to recognize this power and to make it work for the future.[8]

Mary Wigman had her school in Dresden. But she frequently performed in Berlin, where modern dance schools proliferated. Hundreds of Berlin girls, disdaining ballet, took to the new art form, which soon produced a galaxy of star performers. Not all of them were female. One of the brightest of the stars was Harald Kreutzberg, the Nijinsky of modern dance.

Much of all this, to be sure, was highbrow. But there was reason to raise one's brow about popular music as well, and not only because the operetta and night club songs were often risqué. Just as often, they had a surprising artistic quality.

The hits on Radio Berlin, on gramophone records, and in sheet music—the blues, the Charleston, Black Bottom, the "Yes, We Have No Bananas," along with flat-chested

Mary Wigman moved dance into the realm of religious Expressionism. Dance, she said, "expresses inner, invisible movement by means of visible movement." At left Miss Wigman is shown in "Balkan Dance." [*Staatsbibliothek, West Berlin*]

Jonny Spielt Auf (*Johnny Strikes Up*), composed by Ernst Krenek, was Germany's first jazz opera, written under the influence of Duke Ellington's visit to Berlin. The theme of the opera is that jazz conquers all and thus brings about world unity. [*Private collection, Offermanns*]

flappers—came from where Duke Ellington had come from. In fact, the only American madness of the twenties that Berlin did not share was Prohibition.

And yet Berlin added its own unique flavor to the American style: a somewhat bitter, satiric note. The tune of the 1920 hit, "Wandering St. Peter," for instance, might have been written on Broadway. But on Kurfürstendamm, the lyrics went like this:

Everywhere there's a lack of coal,
Even Heaven is upset.
St. Pete can light just one little star,
Even up there, that's all you get.
The starlight turns off at nine p.m.
And all little angels, big or small,
Have to be in bed by then.
Only wandering old St. Peter
Turns in kind of late,
For he often sneaks out of heaven's gate
With a date.

Nineteen-twenty was also the year of Dada, so "Beda," whose real name was Fritz Lohner and who was one of the most gifted song writers of the twenties, came up with this Dadaist number:

Gallipoli, Molly Dolly,
the whole Manoli Bridge.
Hairpins, ham and eggs,
Brush stroke, paint smear, great!
Vaporetto, Cavaletto,
Tintoretto kitsch.
A green point.
Forstad jaunt.
Painted scream:
Spinach and eggs.
Creosote, a bit of Iodine,
Oh Dawn. Idiot!

During the inflation, Berlin sang "Broke, broke, the whole world is broke!" and "How about selling Granny's house to buy booze?" And if Americans had their "Yes, We Have No Bananas," Hermann Frey gave Berliners his 1928 hit: "My Parrot Won't Eat No Hard Boiled Eggs."

The French, of course, invented the "chanson" (a cabaret, rather than dance-hall, song), which is a ballad of sorts, a ballad of the moods and sentimental joys and frustrations of modern life. Berlin's chansons were rarely sentimental. They had a frantic air about them. Berlin also had Friedrich Holländer, the composer, and Marlene Dietrich, the singer— if that's the word for the way Dietrich breathes chansons.

Holländer had written "Falling in Love Again" in 1930 for Marlene Dietrich to sing in *The Blue Angel.* But the team's most popular chanson was "Johnny." Miss Dietrich says it was the first she ever recorded, and she always sings it in German, asserting that it just can't be translated. She is probably right, but there is a try:

Johnny, I like your birthday best,
Then I will be your guest
All the long night.
Johnny, it's you who in my dreams I see.

Paul Lincke's *Frau Luna,* first produced in 1899, was one of the ever-popular operettas that kept Berliners humming schmaltzy tunes. Berlin absorbed much of the musical life of the old Danube monarchy. [*Archiv für Kunst und Geschichte, West Berlin*]

Why don't you drop in on me
Some afternoon for tea?
Oh-oh, Johnny! I like your birthday best
When in your arms I rest
All the long night.
Johnny, I cannot help but say
You should have a birthday every day.

Four decades later Dietrich returned to sing some of the songs of her youth for the Berliners. She held them in her memory, word for word and note for note, she said. The wildest applause came when she sang:

Durch Berlin fliesst immer noch die Spree . . .
Wenn die tollsten Dinge in der Welt passiern,
Der Berliner wird nie den Humor verliern.
Er hält stolz die Nase in die Höh'
Denn durch Berlin fliesst immer noch die Spree.

[And through Berlin still flows the Spree . . .
Even though the whole world goes mad,
Berliners keep their humor. Never sad,
Their nose high in the air, they say:
"And through Berlin still flows the river Spree."]

The Spree still does. And through all the madness, Berliners did keep their humor—well, some of them did, some of the time.

Ludwig Mies van der Rohe, charcoal sketch for a glass skyscraper, 1920. [*The Museum of Modern Art, New York*]

11

ARCHITECTURE

"The Crystal Palace of a New Faith"

We reject { *all aesthetic speculation,*
all doctrine,
and all formalism. }

Architecture is the will of an epoch translated into space. Living. Changing. New.

Not yesterday, not tomorrow, only today can be given form. Only such architecture is creative.

To create form from the nature of the function with the means of our time, that is our job.

LUDWIG MIES VAN DER ROHE, 1923

Much of the "new architecture"—the "modern" architecture around us today—was born in Berlin at the time Mies made this pronouncement.

It was a creative architecture, although the epoch and the nature of the function were confused.

The challenge was enomous:

The first city plan for Berlin had been drawn up in 1853—by the Chief of Police and his Royal Privy Councilors.

The plan had been ordered by the King of Prussia, Friedrich Wilhelm IV, and was prompted by the increasing influx of people into the city, which remained impoverished as the result of the Napoleonic Wars and Prussia's vast military expenditures. The King wanted and needed more people to man new industries and furnish soldiers, but he wanted to spend as little as possible for streets and parks to accommodate them.

The Chief of Police seemed the logical person to draw up building ordinances, for he was in charge of drawing up safety and fire regulations.

What the Chief of Police came up with was a layout of narrow streets with tightly packed, seven-story tenements with as many as five successive inner courts to provide a minimum of light and air. These courts were just large enough to turn a fire hose around in. Half of the windows opened on these small, dark "light-shafts." The apartment houses were about 60 feet wide and 150 feet deep and housed anywhere from 1.5 to 3 persons per room—a total of as many as 650 people per building.

In 1861, the year of Berlin's first official census, it was discovered that one tenth of the total population of 521,933 lived in basements. Only half of the rooms could be heated. Almost a third of all Berliners lived in one-room apartments which were occupied by an average of 4.3 persons.

But the plan was orderly and Prussian and many other German cities dutifully copied it.

It was not until 1874 that housing reformers, notably the German Association of Architects and Engineers, demanded street widening and new avenues to accommodate increasing traffic. The officials, including Prince Otto von Bismarck, the first Chancellor of the German Empire, also noted an increase in tenant revolts and health and sanitation problems. The Police Chief's building ordinance had to be improved.

After victory in the war against France in 1871, Berlin, furthermore, became the prosperous capital of the new Reich, and the Kaiser built ostentatious imperial avenues and vast squares, lined with clumsy, monumental buildings.

But housing conditions behind these imperial façades had not noticeably improved when, in 1919, the red flag of revolution was raised on Brandenburg Gate. Nineteen of twenty Berliners still lived in crowded *Mietskasernen* (rental barracks), as the tenementlike apartment houses were called. The twentieth Berliner lived in a single family house in the suburbs.

A decade and countless architectural manifestoes and proclamations later, little had changed. The famous Berlin architects of the time—Peter Behrens, Bruno Taut, Hans Poelzig, Hans Scharoun, Erich Mendelsohn, Walter Gropius, and Mies van der Rohe—were concerned with style and form and the *Weltanschauung* of building. They gave little thought—they were given no opportunity to give thought—to the real world in which cities are built, the world of finance, profit, construction problems, real estate, bureaucrats, tenants, and landlords. All during World War I and the revolution they believed that major social and spiritual change was imminent. Political and artistic revolution was one and the same to them. They looked forward to the political revolution mainly as an opportunity to introduce the new architectural style they craved. The November revolution, however, soon disap-

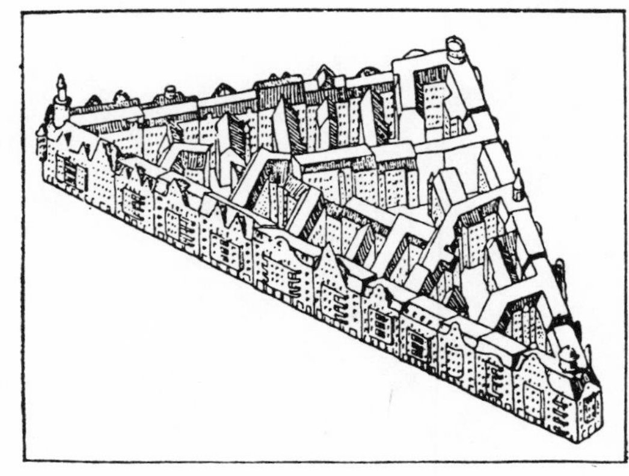

Above: Housing blocks, according to the development plan drawn up by Berlin's Chief of Police in 1897 (an improvement over the original plan of 1853). Right: The inner court of one of the resulting tenements, shown during the rent strike of 1932. Both Communist and Nazi flags are displayed. The inscription on the back wall reads FIRST FOOD, THEN RENT. [*From Werner Hegemann,* Das Steinerne Berlin; *Landesbildstelle, West Berlin*]

pointed them. That wasn't the revolution they envisaged. They were preparing for bigger things. Utopia was a most serious matter, and they worked hard at it. "Social architecture," Gropius recalled, "came later." As Albert Einstein once put it, "perfection of means and confusion of aims seem to be characteristic of our age."

Yet the architectural form and *Weltanschauung* that came out of all this soon spread all over the world as the "International Style." The Berlin architects did, as they set out to do, shape a "totally new, man-made environment."

But Berlin's environment, though lively, remained unchanged and abominable. The results of poor housing, according to Werner Hegemann, were high mortality and low birth rates—almost a zero population growth. An estimated two to three thousand abortions were performed in Germany every day. In the capital, the so-called "housing crimes"—sexual perversion, prostitution, incest, and venereal disease, particularly among children—were steadily increasing. Many Berliners had no homes at all, but rented beds by the hour.

Yet, because of in-migration, the city kept growing. In 1920 a number of surrounding municipalities, long considered part of Greater Berlin, were incorporated into the city, bringing its population to four million inhabitants. By the end of the decade, there were almost a quarter million more.

The new republic responded to Berlin's housing problems with the same sense of helplessness that the United States Federal Government and its Department of Housing and Urban Development display today. In Germany low-cost housing, to be sure, was to be given priority. The slogan was "internal colonization." Government subsidies were to give preference not to more high-rise housing projects, but to small houses and low-rise buildings. In 1919 the Weimar government passed a law to promote large-scale resettlement for no fewer than six million people in rural areas. The German industrial city was considered beyond redemption. What is more, Germany had neither money nor building materials (under the Treaty of Versailles, Germany lost almost three quarters of its iron-ore deposits) to build either in town or country. Architects had nothing to do.

"My life is suspended in thin air like Mohammed's coffin," Gropius wrote to Poelzig at the time. "I have nothing to design to earn myself a penny." Bruno Taut, as historian Wolfgang Pehnt tells it in his book *Expressionist Architecture*, wrote a friend that he was "all alone again, lost in the middle of Berlin, at my drawing board, now become more of a desk."

They all joined the revolutionary Arbeitsrat für die Kunst (Workers' Council for Art) and later the Novembergruppe of which Taut and Gropius were the most prominent leaders.

The Arbeitsrat used its time to dream dreams and the empty drawing boards for drafting manifestoes. It urged co-operation

After Prussia's victory over France in 1871, Berlin became prosperous and the Kaiser adorned the capital of the new Reich with vast squares and clumsy monuments. [*Landesbildstelle, West Berlin*]

With no money for housing, architects dreamed up utopian schemes like Bruno Taut's proposal to rebuild the Swiss Alps. "The realization," Taut noted under the sketch at the right, "is surely terribly difficult, but not impossible. 'How rarely one asks the impossible of man' (Goethe)." [*Photograph courtesy The Museum of Modern Art, New York*]

of artists and craftsmen to create the *Gesamtkunstwerk*, the total work of art. It urged the co-operation of industry to marry art and technology.

In a memorandum to the Arbeitsrat, Gropius said:

The most important goal of the Arbeitsrat program is the union of all the arts under the wings of a great architecture. Art will no longer serve the pleasure of the few, but the happiness and life of the masses.

Architecture is of concern to all the people. Interest in architecture has almost completely disappeared in our time. Only a very few recognize that the buildings of a period are the cultural form of its intellectual content. This recognition must be aroused by every means . . .[1]

At one time the Arbeitsrat also demanded vacant sites and the support of the government to experiment with a new *Volkshaus*, a people's house, something akin to Hitler's later Volkswagen. The demand was not met and the architects went on dreaming their Expressionist dreams.

No one used the time or the drawing boards to design that *Volkshaus*.

Taut, who had made a name for himself with his glass pavilion at the 1914 Cologne Exhibition and who later designed International Style housing projects, encouraged the romantic notion of abandoning cities and drew up a scheme for an "Alpine" architecture. His pamphlet, published in 1919, showed how the very peaks of the Swiss Alps might be turned into architecture, for just whom and why he did not say. Taut proposed:

Pillars and arches of emerald-green glass above the snow-capped summit of a high mountain tower above the sea of clouds. The architecture of Framework of Space open to the Universe. Architecture and the House are not inseparable ideas . . .

Walls of colored glass in rigid frames are set up on slopes. The beams of light bring out many changing effects, both for those who walk in the valleys and between the valleys—and for those who see them from the air. The aerial view will bring great changes to Architecture—and to Architects.[2]

There were other such schemes, an architecture of escape from reality and mediocrity. The architects all got high on it—and most later denied the hallucinatory trip. Gropius would get angry three decades later at Harvard when critics recalled that he, and his Bauhaus, too, had been largely inspired by these flights into Expressionist fancy.

Sigfried Giedion, the Swiss architecture historian, who, with his famous book *Space, Time and Architecture*, gave us the gospel according to Gropius, declared that "men who were later to do grimly serious work in housing developments abandoned themselves to a romantic mysticism, dreamed of fairy castles to stand on the peak of Mount Rosa. Others built concrete towers as flaccid as jellyfish . . .

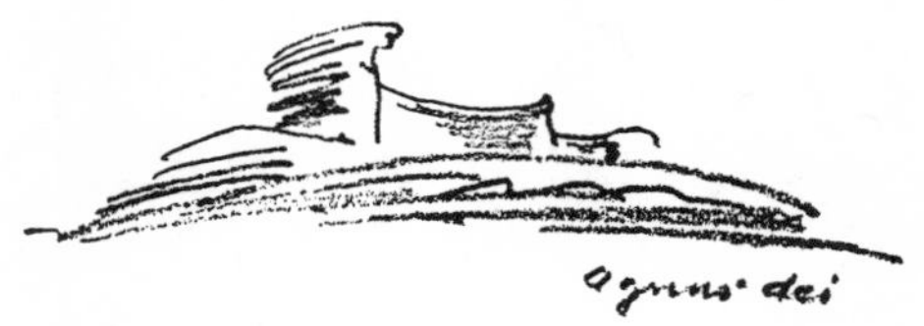

"Expressionism could have no influence on architecture . . ."

Not so. No one, to be sure, polished the rocky Alps to make them an inspired habitat. But Erich Mendelsohn's "flaccid" Einstein Tower at Potsdam and Poelzig's Grosses Schauspielhaus did get built. The Einstein Tower, commissioned by the physicist, served as an astrophysical laboratory with small, medieval study rooms. It had a profound influence on what was to come.

What is more, the ecstatic faith that art and architecture would redeem us all, that it would bring about a total man-made environment, which in turn would generate a new culture and new religious spirit, was, and largely still is, the credo of modern architects.

In the spring of 1919, all these messianic intentions found a focal point. Gropius was given the opportunity to realize his ambition to effect "the union of all the arts under the wings of a great architecture." He was summoned to Weimar and asked by the new provisional Socialist government of Saxe-Weimar-Eisenach to head both the Arts and Crafts School and the Weimar Academy of Fine Arts across the street. He decided to combine them under the name "Das Staatliche Bauhaus Weimar."

The Bauhaus set out to join art with industrial production and search for new forms in architecture and industrial design. It concerned itself with "everything from the coffee cup to city planning," as Mies van der Rohe, the last Bauhaus director, was to put it later.

The first Bauhaus proclamation reflected, often in the same words, what had been said, planned, and plotted at the Arbeitsrat:

The ultimate aim of all visual arts is the complete building! To embellish buildings was once the noblest function of the fine arts; the arts were the indispensable components of great architecture. Today the arts exist in isolation, from which they can be rescued only through the conscious, co-operative effort of all craftsmen. Architects, painters, and sculptors must recognize anew and learn to grasp the composite character of a building both as an entity and in its

Below: One of the few Expressionist designs actually built was Erich Mendelsohn's Einstein Tower in Potsdam, an astrophysical laboratory. Left: Mendelsohn became famous for his visionary sketches, most of which he drew in the trenches during World War I. [*The Museum of Modern Art, New York*]

Mendelsohn with Frank Lloyd Wright, whom he visited in 1924 at Taliesin, in Spring Green, Wisconsin. Wright's work inspired German architects long before it was recognized in the United States. [*Photograph courtesy The Museum of Modern Art, New York*]

separate parts. Only then will their work be imbued with the architectonic spirit which it has lost as "salon art . . ."

Architects, sculptors, painters, we all must return to the crafts! For art is not a "profession." There is no essential difference between the artist and the craftsman. The artist is an exalted craftsman. In rare moments of inspiration, transcending the consciousness of his will, the grace of heaven may cause his work to blossom into art. But proficiency in a craft is essential to every artist. Therein lies the prime source of creative imagination. Let us then create a new guild of craftsmen without the class distinctions that raise an arrogant barrier between craftsmen and artists! Together let us desire, conceive, and create the new structure of the future, which will embrace architecture and sculpture and painting in one unity and which will one day rise toward heaven from the hands of a million workers like the crystal symbol of a new faith.[3]

The Bauhaus managed to collect some of the most remarkable artistic talent of its time. In architecture and furniture design, there were Marcel Breuer and Mies van der Rohe. Painting was taught by Lyonel Feininger, Paul Klee, Wassily Kandinsky, and Josef Albers. Photography, typography, and industrial art were taught by Laszlo Moholy-Nagy. Herbert Bayer taught graphics. Anni Albers taught weaving. And there were many other important artists, less well known in the United States, such as the painter and stage designer Oskar Schlemmer and the sculptor Gerhard Marcks.

If the initial style in Berlin and at the Bauhaus was clearly Expressionism, the basic philosophy of that "crystal palace," of that *Gesamtkunstwerk*, came from the Deutsche Werkbund, an association of craftsmen, architects, and industrialists, its architecture was inspired by an eccentric German poet, Paul Scheerbart.

The Werkbund had its origins in the nineteenth-century English arts and crafts movement of William Morris and John Ruskin. Morris revived craftsmanship with all its medieval connotations in romantic protest against industrial production. The Werkbund, however, felt that craftsmen should not oppose the machine but make it the servant of the artist.

The Werkbund, an association of artists, designers, and industrialists, had been launched by Hermann Muthesius, a commercial attaché in the German Embassy in London from 1896 to 1903. Impressed by British predominance in world trade, he felt German products needed better design to compete, but he also thought there was need for a "spiritualization of German production." Art was to have a social purpose. The Werkbund was much concerned with introducing better design into everyday life, in everything from that coffee cup to city planning. Both industry and artists responded. The Werkbund became an important movement in Germany, particularly before World War I.

Opposite page: Walter Gropius in 1923. Gropius founded the Bauhaus, the famous school of design at Weimar in 1919. Above and right: He designed the school's new building when it moved to Dessau in 1926. [*Photographs courtesy The Museum of Modern Art, New York*]

The Bauhaus, as Gropius saw it, was at once less and more ambitious. In July 1919 Gropius told Bauhaus students:

Before the war we put the cart before the horse and sought to carry art to the general public backwards, through organization. We designed artistic ashtrays and beer mugs and sought by that means to rise gradually to the level of great architecture. Everything through cool organization. There was a boundless presumption, on which we foundered. Now it will be the other way around . . .

No large intellectual organization, but small, secret, self-contained groups, lodges, workshops, conspiracies, whose mission it is to keep watch over and give artistic form to a secret kernel of faith. Such groups will not come into being until the day when once more there takes shape out of the individual groups a great general spiritual and religious idea which will find its crystalline expression in the total work of art. This communal work of art, this cathedral of the future, will then shine with the fullness of its light into the smallest aspect of everyday life.[4]

Paul Scheerbart, who lived in Berlin, was a wit, a bohemian, an "arbitrary" poet, who, said one critic, strove "to bring to expression a spiritual content derived from a fantasy of soul." Scheerbart's *Glasarchitektur* was published in 1914 by Herwarth Walden's Sturm Publishing House. The first of its numbered paragraphs gives an idea of its prophetic bent:

1. *Environment and its influence on the development of culture:*

We live for the most part in closed rooms. These form the environment from which our culture grows. Our culture is to a certain extent the product of our architecture. If we want culture to rise to a higher level, we are obliged, for better or for worse, to change our architecture. And this only becomes possible if we take away the closed character from the rooms in which we live. We can only do that by introducing glass architecture, which lets in the light of the sun, the moon, and the stars, not merely through a few windows, but through every possible wall, which will be made entirely of glass—of colored glass. The new environment, which we thus create, must bring us a new culture.[5]

Scheerbart goes on predicting many architectural developments which we now take for granted: heated floors, self-opening doors, air-conditioning, and movable glass partitions. He also anticipated the illumination of buildings, or as some architects call it today, "night architecture," and demanded that "towns and other places should always be distinguished by towers.

Every effort must naturally be made to lend enchantment to towers by night. Under the rule of glass architecture therefore, all towers must become towers of light."

In most architectural minds, the marriage of art and technology, *Gesamtkultur*, and the New Architecture were suddenly associated with glass. No one blew Scheerbart's glass horn harder, however, than Mies van der Rohe.

Mies's first and only building in Berlin at the time was his 1926 memorial to Rosa Luxemburg and Karl Liebknecht. It was of brick and was Expressionism pure and simple. But far more important were his experiments in glass architecture, the most decisive of which was his entry in the 1920 competition for a high-rise office building at Berlin's Friedrichstrasse. No building could be more glass. The only opaque things about it were the elevator core and the steel skeleton—the "bones," Mies called them—back inside the uninterrupted glass "skin." All else was transparent. The transparency gave Mies what he was after all his life: "universal space." That space could not only be subdivided and thus used at will, but it also let in, as Scheerbart demanded, "the light of the sun, the moon, and the stars"—the cosmos.

In his Berlin days Mies also experimented with brick and concrete. But for his greatest work of that time, the German pavilion for the International Exhibition in Barcelona in 1929, he returned to glass. The pavilion was a beautifully proportioned and detailed glass box, supported by chromed steel columns and relieved by panels of honey-colored marble. There was nothing in it except a pool, a Georg Kolbe sculpture, and a few of Mie's now-famous steel and leather "Barcelona chairs," designed for the occasion. The exquisite building was Germany's contribution to the exhibition and, it turned out, to world architecture.

The Barcelona pavilion was dismantled

Below: Mies van der Rohe's first building in Berlin was a monument to Karl Liebknecht and Rosa Luxemburg, erected in 1926 and no longer in existence. Right: His foremost preoccupation was with abstract schemes to exploit the potentials of glass which he considered most expressive of the new age. [*Photographs courtesy The Museum of Modern Art, New York*].

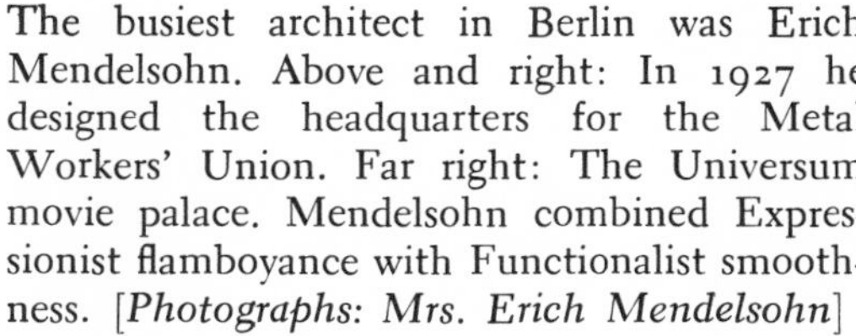

The busiest architect in Berlin was Erich Mendelsohn. Above and right: In 1927 he designed the headquarters for the Metal Workers' Union. Far right: The Universum movie palace. Mendelsohn combined Expressionist flamboyance with Functionalist smoothness. [*Photographs: Mrs. Erich Mendelsohn*]

when the show was over—incredible as that seems—and lost in transit on its way back to Germany. In the 1960s Mies repeated this feat of demonstrating his credo that "less is more" with his glass pavilion for Berlin's Gallery of Twentieth-Century Art.

Berlin's busiest architect in the 1920s was Erich Mendelsohn. In 1919, at the famous art gallery of Paul Cassirer, he had startled people with his architectural visions, prophetic little thumbnail sketches he had drawn in the trenches during World War I. Among them were sketches that look like famous later buildings by other architects such as Dulles International Airport in Virginia, the Air Force Academy Chapel near Denver, and the Watergate Apartments in Washington, D.C. This is not to say that the architects of these buildings copied Mendelsohn's strange forms, though they were, consciously or not, certainly influenced by them. It is to say only that Expressionism is by no means dead and that Erich Mendelsohn, with the prescience of a great artist, anticipated the spirit of our time.

Mendelsohn, at any rate, could not have realized his wartime visions. The necessary technology of tension structures and reinforced concrete had not been developed. What he did build, after the Einstein Tower, was an addition to the newspaper offices of Mosse's *Berliner Tageblatt*, a large department store, the headquarters of the Metal Workers' Union, the Universum movie palace, the Columbus House office building, and an exquisite house for himself. What he accomplished with these buildings, and others throughout Germany, was something no one else accomplished. With his flamboyant, curvaceous forms, rendered in the smooth and severe manner of his "functionalist," glass-obsessed contemporaries, he made the New Architecture genuinely popular. That was probably why he was so busy.

Mendelsohn had set forth his belief:

What today is a problem will one day be a task; what today is the vision and faith of a single individual will one day become a law for all.

Therefore all trends seem necessary to achieving the goal, and hence to solving the problem of a new architecture:

The apostles of glass worlds,

The analysts of spatial elements,

The seekers for new forms of material and construction.[6]

As the German economy improved, others, too, were given the opportunity to build rather than just scheme. Bruno Taut had warned in 1919 that it was not the business of a New Architect to be serious about building. "Down with seriousness!" he proclaimed in his column, entitled *Frühlicht* (*Daybreak*), published in the periodical *Stadtbaukunst alter and neuer Zeit* (*Urban Architecture Old and New*). He wrote:

"Important! Important!" This damned habit of acting important! Tombstone and cemetery façades in front of junk shops and old clothing stores! Smash the shell-limed Doric, Ionic, and Corinthian columns, demolish the pinheads! Down with respectability of sandstone and plate-glass, fragment the rubbish of marble and precious wood, to the garbage heap with all that junk!

Oh, our concepts: space, home, style! Ugh, how these concepts stink! Destroy them, put an end to them! Let nothing remain! Chase away their schools, let the professorial wigs fly, we'll play catch with them.

Marcel Breuer's "House for a Sportsman" (1931), displaying his tubular chairs, was typical of the bare and square interiors that came out of the Bauhaus. The designs found more favor with the editors of fashion magazines than "the masses" for which they had been designed. [*Photograph courtesy The Museum of Modern Art, New York*]

Blast, blast! Let the dusty, matted, gummed-up world of concepts, ideologies, and systems feel our cold north wind! Death to the concept-lice! Death to everything stuffy! Death to everything called title, dignity, authority! Down with everything serious! . . .

In the distance shines our tomorrow. Hurray, three times hurray for our kingdom without force! Hurray for the transparent, the clear! Hurray for purity! Hurray for crystal! Hurray and again hurray for the fluid, the graceful, the angular, the sparkling, the flashing, the light—hurray for everlasting architecture![7]

In 1925 Gropius made his contribution to lasting architecture with his building for the Bauhaus in Dessau, where the school moved from Weimar that same year. The building helped establish the International Style. Two years later Gropius worked with the stage director Erwin Piscator on a new "total theater" in Berlin. It was designed to be adjustable for all kinds of productions, from semicircular Greek theater to arena stage. It was never built, however, but architects everywhere still reach for its plans to do flexible theaters.

In 1929 Groupius was commissioned to design some buildings for Siemenstadt, a housing project for the workers of the Siemens electrical concern in Berlin. The buildings were still essentially apartment houses, although they were also a vast improvement over what Berliners were used to. These ten-story buildings were essentially narrow slabs, placed perpendicularly, rather than horizontally, to the street and spaced widely enough apart to avoid those dark inner courts and to bring light, air, and cross-ventilation into the rooms. They had balconies. And the spaces in between the buildings were sodded and landscaped with trees. Today Siemenstadt looks like most other apartment house projects around the world, but it was a welcome novelty at the time.

Other apartment house blocks at Siemenstadt were designed by Hans Scharoun and showed more flair. Scharoun introduced curves and living rooms extending across the entire width of the building.

Gropius, Mies, Scharoun, and some of the others worked hard on new systems to "industrialize" building, that is, to design components that could be factory-produced and easily assembled and so bring down construction costs. But costs would not come down and few new modern, moderately priced homes and apartments went up. For the average Berliner, the New Architecture was scarcely a success.

The only significant attempt to employ the modern forms in the cause of greater livability for the masses was made not in Berlin but at Weissenhof, a suburb of Stuttgart. That was in 1927, and Mies was the co-ordinating architect for this Werkbund

demonstration. He invited sixteen of Europe's leading architects to show what they could do for the average man with a moderate budget. He made no stipulation except that all buildings—both apartment and single family houses—had to have flat roofs.

Most visitors were more excited by the display of Mart Stam's and Marcel Breuer's tubular steel furniture than they were about the architecture. The exhibition failed in its attempt to launch prefabricated building. If it introduced a new life style, its advent was imperceptible, except perhaps in the architectural fashion magazines. But Mies was right when he said three years later:

The new era is a fact. It exists entirely independently of whether we say "yes" or "no" to it. But it is neither better nor worse than any other era. It is a pure datum and in itself neutral as to value. Therefore I shall not spend any time trying to elucidate the new era, to demonstrate its links and lay bare its supporting structure.

Let us also not overestimate the question of mechanization, standardization and modular units.

By 1929 the New Architecture was at last given the opportunity to get down to housing for the average man. Gropius designed this project for Siemenstadt, a housing development in Berlin, that heralded similar projects all over the world. [*Akademie der Künste, West Berlin; photos: Arthur Köster*]

And let us accept the changed economic and social conditions as fact.

All these things go their destined way, blind to values.

The decisive thing is which of these given facts we choose to emphasize. This is where spiritual problems begin.

What matters is not "what" but only "how."

That we produce goods and by what means we manufacture them means nothing, spiritually speaking.

Whether we build high or low, with steel and glass, tells us nothing about the value of the building.

Whether in town planning we aim at centralization or decentralization is a practical question, not one of value.

But the question of value is decisive.

We have to establish new values, to demonstrate ultimate aims, in order to acquire criteria.

For the meaning and right of every age, including our own, consists solely in providing the spirit with the necessary prerequisites for its existence.[8]

Another three years later, the Nazis, to overcome the new architecture's "Bolshevist depravity," put pitched roofs on the Weissenhof houses. And Albert Speer began work on his drawings to rebuild Berlin in the megalomanic image of his Führer.

Ten years later the British and American air forces took care of the *Mietskasernen.*

12

SPORTS: *Mens Politica in Corpore Sano, and Horses, too*

One of the things Napoleon set in motion were young German muscles. Sports came in as training for national liberation from the French.

The French Emperor defeated the Prussian army at Jena and on October 27, 1806, occupied Berlin. The city became a hotbed of patriotic resistance and the catalyst not just of Prussian but also of Pan-German nationalism.

In 1807–8 Johann Gottlieb Fichte, soon to be the first rector of the Berlin University, delivered his *Reden an die deutsche Nation.* These "Addresses to the German Nation" seeded the idea in the minds of his compatriots that the countless, scattered, demoralized and intrigue-ridden German kingdoms, dukedoms, and principalities might find moral, economic, and political strength in nationhood.

And in 1811 out on the old Hasenheide, a large park, now Tempelhof airport, Friedrich Ludwig Jahn, a high school teacher, commanded growing crowds of young Berliners to jump, hop, bend, twist, and run. They called him "*Turnvater* Jahn," the "Father of Calisthenics." He founded the first Turnverein, or gymnastics club, and introduced physical education into the German school system.

In part, Jahn's sweaty muscle-flexing was a response to the industrial city. It was a matter of survival to get the new class of workers out of their crowded tenements and hot factories into contact with nature, including the nature of their own bodies.

In part, Jahn's movement had undisguised political and military aims. The French occupiers restricted military training in Prussia, so another kind of exercise was needed to harden the body and spirit of German youth in the struggle for liberation. Jahn was an ardent German patriot, a nationalist. He was one of those who burned "reactionary" books in a roaring bonfire at the Pan-German Wartburg Festival in 1817, which clamored as much for a narrow-minded Teutonic nationalism as it did for democratic freedom.

Doing push-ups, hiking in the woods to the strains of rediscovered folk songs, basking in the nude, and even kicking soccer balls, was, even a century later in Germany, rarely entirely divorced from a political romanticism. It was all an expression of the social animal, the *zoon politicon.* Sport was political training.

This was as true for the left as for the right. In his book *Arbeitersport* (*Workers' Sport*), Fritz Wildung asserted in 1929:

The progress of history indicates that in every class-oriented society sport served a political function. And the development of that epoch which spawned the modern working class and which continues to nurture it speaks eloquently in support of the division of sport into "ours and theirs," into workers' sports and bourgeois sports. The specific social position of the proletariat de-

Sports club Teutonia jogging through the Brandenburg Gate in 1925. [*Archiv für Kunst und Geschichte, West Berlin*] *mands a different attitude towards sports than that of the ruling class . . . to be neutral would be swimming without getting wet . . .*

When the working class becomes active in sports . . . [sport] becomes the means for the social struggle . . . turning people from lonely, persecuted, tortured, and destroyed beings back to their rightful human dignity.[1]

Games, physical recreation, and gymnastics for just about everyone were a well-organized part of Berlin's life. In 1920 Dr. Carl Diem, the chief organizer of organized sports, who was later in charge of the 1936 Berlin Olympics, had founded a College for Gymnastics in Berlin. It was the clearing house for the city's school game and gymnastics competitions, including the famous Berlin–Potsdam track race. Diem made athletics loom as large as arithmetic in the curriculum.

Ironically, playgrounds, sports fields, and open space were scandalously scarce in Berlin—constant victims of land speculation and developers' greed. For all their professed concern for *mens sana in corpore sano*, the city fathers were deplorably mindless about the physical needs of the citizenry.

In the mid-twenties, for instance, Berlin lost its largest open space, used by no less than fifty-seven soccer clubs. It had been the former parade ground at Tempelhof, and the military finally relinquished it. The city turned the larger part into a public-housing development for 60,000 people—without a single playground. The leftover became an airport.

A famous cartoon by Heinrich Zille was not far-fetched. It showed a little girl in the courtyard of a Berlin tenement, yelling upstairs to her mother: "Mommy, throw down the flower pot; Daddy wants to sit in the garden!"

Better-paid workers found little gardens in their *Schrebergärten* outside the city. Named after a Dr. Schreber and first initiated in 1864, these were tiny allotments in endless rows. There was usually only room for a tool shed, a picnic table, and a few cabbages. For all the political rabble-rousing about "blood and soil," this offered the only fresh oxygen to enrich German blood and the only tillable soil German workers ever saw.

The young fled the city on weekends and holidays with the Wandervögel (Ramblers). This youth movement swept practically all young Germans out into the countryside, where they trudged from youth hostel to youth hostel, camped in the woods, and dreamed up one *Weltanschauung* or another around their campfires.

But there was a more adventurous, increasingly popular way to take care of the body—taking off clothes. Nudism in Germany was and is called "*Freikörperkultur*" (FKK), which means "free body culture." While nudism as a health movement had

its roots in the late nineteenth century, it was in Berlin during the 1920s that the idea caught on.

A gymnastics teacher in a city school in a workers' district, Adolf Koch, gave FKK its big boost with the observation that his students' ragged clothing hid poor posture and lack of personal hygiene. He conducted gymnastics classes in the nude, asserting that he could thereby educate the youngsters to the natural grace of their bodies and give them an incentive to keep clean. It seemed to work and Koch soon had three hundred students in his class. He was also soon arrested and charged with corruption of minors. One of his defense witnesses was Dr. Magnus Hirschfeld, the founder and director of the Berlin Institute for Sexual Science. Hirschfeld testified:

The exercises were an indication of Mr. Koch's high ethical sense, which was shared by the participants. The prejudices against nudity, which are basically post-factum prejudices, immediately vanished in the naturalness, freedom, and earnestness which prevailed in the gymnastics class. One had the feeling that the nude body represented a natural creation in its higher, purer form. (A nude is not undressed, rather he is not dressed.) Absolute nudity is a necessity, because otherwise the observation of movement (especially with the covering of the pelvis) would be impossible and the gymnastic exercises would become superficial and valueless.[2]

The newspapers had a field day and the debate soon reached the Berlin City Council:

Mr. Kunze (German National Party): Now we come to the central point of this issue, and, my dear Dr. Weyl—don't take offense. (City Council member Dr. Weyl: "I could never be offended by you!") If we look at the cause of this movement, we see the puppetmaster lurking in the background. (Shouted interruption: "The Jews!") I'm

Far left: Tossing medicine balls was one of the sports in Berlin's city-wide annual school contest which brought a thousand finalists out to the stadium. Below left: A walking race in 1927 was won by less than a stretch. Below: In the All-Berlin Relay of 1927 the runner passes the baton to a swimmer, who must swim a hundred meters down the Landwehrkanal, then relatively unpolluted. [*Archiv für Kunst und Geschichte, West Berlin*]

Nudism in Germany, called *Freikörperkultur* (free body culture) drew adherents both from among workers and middle-class intellectuals. Right and below: Some members of the Wandervögel youth movement also romped in the nude. But as in other countries, nudism was mostly a family sport. [*Licht-Land and Staatsbibliothek, West Berlin*]

sorry that no one has had the nerve to say it— Yes, it is not a German spirit which envelops our German people. The puppet-masters are always the Jews. Ladies and gentlemen, I can conclude that all of these signs of decay are nothing more than the result of the Jewish infection of our people. It is the product of a pigsty, a Jewish pigsty.[3]

Forced to resign from the public school system, Koch founded a private gymnastics school in Berlin. It drew its students from both workers and middle-class intellectuals. In one of his books, Koch tells of a convert to his cause, a young American engineer named Billy. After a bit of nude proselytizing in the course of a railroad coach encounter, Billy was invited to a skinny-dipping session at Koch's school:

On the way to the pool [*Billy*] *became increasingly silent. I asked him whether he was sorry that he had so quickly agreed to come and he answered: "I'm afraid . . ."*

In 1925 the Brandenburg Gate was the starting point for two walking trips around the world. Far left: Two men and a woman set out on their hike. They figured it would take them four and a half years. Left: The men here went by automobile, which was considered no less daring in 1925. [*Archiv für Kunst und Geschichte, West Berlin*]

Since I did not answer and we were soon to arrive at the pool, he had to overcome his anxiety and replied: "That was just a joke—about being afraid."

I was accustomed to the scene in the pool. Billy looked about: "Impossible, impossible," was all that he could say when he entered. Then he grasped me by the shoulders and looked into my eyes: "How I envy you," he said, "this beautiful hall and nude, too." Soon we were swimming happily and the only thing that Billy could say was "Impossible, impossible."

. . . After gymnastics he shook my hand. "Well," he said, "you Germans are something. You swim together nude, let a nude girl teach you a gymnastics class, invite me —an American, who saw his first nude girl today—and are not at all amazed that in five minutes this American is as used to everything as though he had never known anything else."[4]

Whether or not these earnest calisthenics and nude romps advanced the dignity of the working class, as Wildung had asserted in *Arbeitersport*, the bourgeois class was undaunted in pursuing the pleasures of bourgeois spectator sports.

Berlin had six race tracks; the closest to the city was Grunewald, the most elegant was Hoppegarten, and the most popular was Karlshorst. All of them were replete with beautiful, or at any rate expensively dressed, women, with vestiges of the old aristocracy, monocles and all, with the postwar *nouveaux riches*, and with popular jockeys, who were apt to get more gawks from the crowd than even the beauties, monocles, or Mercedes-Benzes.

To most Berliners, 1919 was the year of bloodshed and turnips. To the horse-racing fans and bookies, it was the year the Hamburg race track was closed for repairs and the German "Derby" was held in Berlin. Let history note that Gibraltar won in an upset, followed by Thor, Eckstein, Rosenritter, Thunichtgut, Tulipan, and Abschluss, in that order.

If you did not believe in horses (or they reminded you too much of those inflation-winter dinners), you could watch race cars go up in flames. Berliners did not have far to go to watch auto races. Even before World War I, a ten-kilometer race track, the Avus (*Automobil-Verkehrs und Übungs-Strasse*, or traffic and training road) had been built smack in the city, running symbolically from the Kaiser's resplendent Heerstrasse to the ritzy suburb of Wannsee. Avus was a forerunner of Hitler's *Autobahnen* and Eisenhower's interstate freeways. The big races were held once a year, and from 1926 on, Avus was the track for the "Grand Prize of Germany," the German Indianapolis-500. The perennial star was Fritz von Opel, son of the car maker. In 1928 he raced the first rocket car on the Avus.

For added chic, you could watch ostrich races. Josephine Baker, the black American dancer, boosted that exotic sport with a publicity picture, although she herself wore more than ostrich feathers.

But if all this was diversion, the Six-Day Bicycle Race was Berlin's passionate craze and crazy passion. It was held in the Sportpalast (Sports Palace), the enormous arena on the Potsdamer Strasse, which had been dedicated in 1910, to the strains of Beethoven's Fifth, conducted by Richard Strauss.

The Six-Day Race meant just that. For six long days and nights, one relay after another, the bicyclists pedaled around and around the wooden track, as the exhaustion of the racers and the frenzy of the crowd accelerated. As one poet put it:

Hard
at the start
Muscles at the ready
Two times a hundred thousand
eyes
peering from the human wall.
Noah's ark filled to bursting!
Firmly
the thighs pressed on the cross bar
Naked and ready
Starting gun, tuxedo clad
spark and shot
Go!
Pedaled,—daled,—daled
Brains on the pedal.
Steel
and tire
hard to the fresh wood of the course
rolling, squealing
where once were forests . . .
Only a breath
tires pumped full!
. . . .
Six
Day
Race
Burning, the brain lies in wait
Six times two hundred thousand eyes
peering from the human wall,
Six times two hundred and thousand
Raging
snorting nostrils
breath-robbing
our breath robbing,
sweat!
Hot and only
on and on
pedaling,—daling,—daling.
Music music
pedaling,—aling to chapel
music music
wheels interlock
overlapping
tires
whistle on the fresh wood
turn somersaults
interlocking
overlapping
wheels wheels
just wheels left
harder
harder
up from the seat
press those thighs
curve into the curve on every curve.
Every hour every turn
brain to brain
racked into the brain.
And the hours are
dissected
into seconds

Berlin had six tracks for horse racing where remnants of the *ancien régime* and the *nouveau riche* joined to crane necks. [*Staatsbibliothek, West Berlin*]

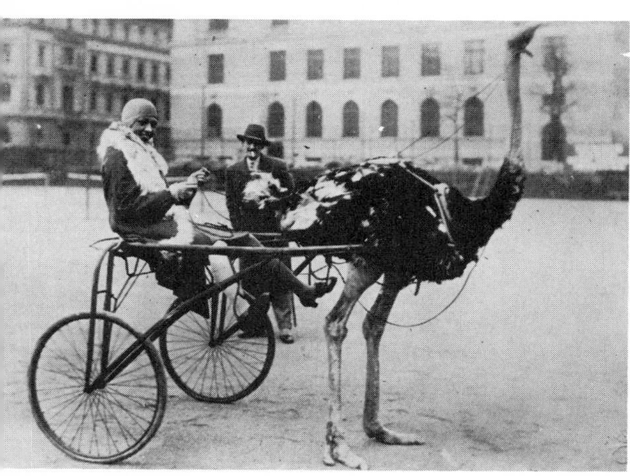

Ostrich racing got a publicity boost from Josephine Baker, the American-born night club star who lived in Paris but was equally popular in Berlin. [*Archiv für Kunst und Geschichte, West Berlin*]

and divide
in rhythm every round.
Hard
at the start
The brain burns
circulation
pause
on
and gone.
Six
day
race![5]

At the end of 1926 the newspaper *Die Literarische Welt* (*Literary World*) held a writing competition to seek out young, new talent. It set up several categories and appointed Bert Brecht as judge of the poetry contest. Some six hundred entries arrived and Willi Haas, the editor, dutifully passed them on to Brecht, who ignored them all. He would have nothing to do with such obsolete bourgeois stuff, he declared. Instead he selected a poem that had not been entered at all but represented, he said, relevant purposes and the best possible work of its author. The author was a young sports fan, Hannes Kuppers, and the poem was a tribute to a bicycle racer:

Hey, Hey! The Iron Man!
About him circles a legend

The hero of the Avus, the automobile race track in the center of Berlin, was Fritz von Opel (at the wheel) who in 1928 reached a speed of 195 kilometers an hour in his rocket car. [*Archiv für Kunst und Geschichte, West Berlin*]

The city's passionate craze was the annual Six-Day Bicycle Race at the Sports Palace. Above: Contestants are ready to go. Right: Two happy winners almost too exhausted to smile. Below, right: A racer grabs a quick bite in the course of the ordeal. [*Archiv für Kunst und Geschichte, West Berlin*]

That his arms and hands and legs
were formed from a smithy's iron
In Sydney on a night bright as day.
Hey, Hey! The Iron Man!
A mainspring of steel in his heart,
free from feeling and human pain,
his brain a bank of switches
controlling the dynamos.
Hey, Hey! The Iron Man!
Thick cables are his nerves
Charged with volts and amperes
For
This artificial man was not
intended to be a Six-Day Racer.
He was to be the new Caesar
which explains his iron strength

Hey, Hey! The Iron Man!
And
If all this is legend,
there is also the truth:
There is a human miracle:
Reggie McNamara
Hey, Hey! The Iron Man![6]

Brecht's favorite sport, however, was not bicycle racing, but boxing. The boxing ring was the central metaphor in his drama *Im Dickicht der Städte*. His collaborator, Emil Burri, and the writer Lion Feuchtwanger introduced Brecht to some of the leading boxers. Burri, a confirmed fan, was an amateur trainer at the Sportpalast and took Brecht to important matches.

Boxing was a new sport in Berlin. Before World War I there had been only a few exhibition matches. Now it was suddenly "in." Boxers, such as Hans Breitenstrater, Curt Prentzel, and Paul Samson-Körner were local heroes. The one who got headlines all over the world was, of course, Max Schmeling. He won the German light-heavyweight title in 1926. Two years later he beat the German heavyweight champion Franz Diener at the Sportpalast. Finally, from 1930 to 1932, he held the world heavyweight championship. It was glamorous to be seen with him and movie stars sparkled around him. He married one of them—Anny Ondra.

Bert Brecht was particularly close to Paul Samson-Körner, whose autobiography he ghosted and with whom he wrote a short story, "The Knock-Out Punch." In it, one of the characters is telling a story:

". . . *Freddy had finished training on the tenth, and on the twelfth at seven o'clock we sat in a bar—Freddy, myself, and his manager, Fat Kampe. You know him, over there, that fellow with the toothpick in his mouth. The fight was supposed to begin in an hour and naturally it was wrong to come here. You can see how smoky and musty this bar is, but Freddy wanted to come and he didn't think much of people who had to shield their lungs from every March breeze. To make a long story short, we sat there in a cloud of smoke which you couldn't have cut with a buzz saw, and Kampe and I ordered glasses of beer. This caused a hell of a situation in the fifteen minutes which remained, but I was the only one to notice. Freddy got it into his head that he wanted a glass of beer too.*

"*He actually called over the waiter. But then Kampe interrupted and said emphatically that it was stupid before the fight. He could just as well eat shoe nails as drink a beer.*

"*Freddy mumbled 'Nonsense,' but sent the waiter away. For Kampe the incident was over but not for Freddy. Kampe again recited everything he knew, positively or negatively, about Freddy's opponent. Freddy read the paper. I had the impression that behind the want ads he became more and more concerned with his beer or, rather, with his desire for beer.*

"*Soon afterward he stood up and moved over to the bar. Kampe didn't notice. He stood there for a while without pushing—once, twice, he allowed others ahead of him. Then he took a few cigarettes, which, with a silly look, he stuck into his vest pocket.*

"*When he returned to the table he looked changed. He played with the cigarettes in his vest pocket and looked sullen. But he sat down and kept quiet behind his* 8-Uhr Abendblatt. *Without paying any attention to Kampe's monologue, I began to curse out the beer. I still remember that I called it a lukewarm, repulsive brew, whose questionable ancestry could be sensed from the taste of the manure pile which pervaded it. Liquid typhus! Freddy smiled.*

"*I think he was about finished with his*

Sonja Henie, the ice-skating champion, was fourteen years old when this picture was taken at Berlin's Sports Palace, where she frequently performed. Born in Norway, she moved to the United States in 1936 and turned professional. [*Archiv für Kunst und Geschichte, West Berlin*]

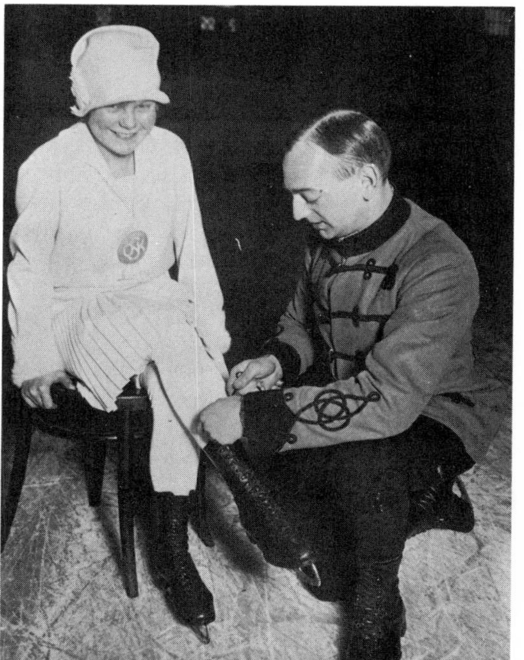

Above: Franz Diener (at left) won the German heavyweight championship from Paul Samson-Körner in 1927. Below: Diener lost the title to Max Schmeling (standing between movie stars Conrad Veidt and Lil Dagover) the following year. Berlin's boxers and film stars liked to be seen together. [*Archiv für Kunst und Geschichte and Landesbildstelle, West Berlin*]

inner struggle. He couldn't stand sitting here without drinking just because he wasn't supposed to weaken himself. He wanted to ingest that lake of typhus, but he didn't have the guts. At the same time, he probably pictured his girl with her engagement face, the walnut bedstead, and the walnut bookcases. He stood up and paid.

"We drove silently in a taxi to the Sportpalast."

At this point, the narrator noticed that his sleeve was resting in a pool of beer and he mopped it off with a handkerchief. We were all fairly sure of the outcome of the bout, but I still asked him: "Well . . . ?"

"He was knocked out in the second round. Did you expect anything else?"

"No, but why do you think he was knocked out?"

"Simple. As we left the bar, I knew that Freddy had lost his confidence."

"OK," I said, "but what should someone in Freddy's situation have done?" The man emptied his glass and said: "A man should always do what he wants to. In my opinion, caution is the mother of the k.o."[7]

Berlin's greatest athletic event took place later, under Nazi auspices. But the Berliners were still good sports. When Jesse Owens, the black American, ran off with four of the 1936 Olympic gold medals, the Berliners cheered and cheered and cheered.

But their Führer refused to shake hands with a black.

13

YOUTH: *The Greening that Turned Brown*

Stenography was surely one of the less exciting courses offered at the Steglitz High School in Berlin. But the teacher of this class, Hermann Hoffmann-Fölkersamb, a young university student from Magdeburg, fascinated his students. He told of his hiking trips through the Harz Mountains, of the joys to be found at the bosom of mother nature, of the true soul of the Fatherland, of the rewards of self-reliance and self-education, and of the uplifting value of truth and youth.

That was in 1890, and like wandering birds, Germany's Wandervögel, in open shirts and knee pants, soon roamed over the countryside, folk-singing, folk-dancing, reciting poetry, searching for what the poet Novalis (Friedrich von Hardenberg) called "the blue flower of romanticism," and seeking, to borrow Charles Reich's phrase, "the greening" of Germany.

Many an idealistic Wandervögel marched into World War I singing folk songs and carrying a volume of Friedrich Hölderlin or Rainer Maria Rilke in his pack. In the battle of Langemarck, in Belgium, it was said, the Imperial High Command needlessly sacrificed a whole battalion of youth-movement volunteers. The legend helped the movement not only to survive war and revolution but also to re-emerge even stronger than before. There was in the post-war period, as much cause as ever for romantic rebellion against parental and educational authoritarianism and what seemed a rotting society.

The lure was adventure and self-assertion, which made the German youth movement different from Lord Baden-Powell's controlled, paramilitary Boy Scouts, a movement that never caught on in Germany.

Friends of Nature, 1916. [*Landesbildstelle, Berlin*]

The youth movement, furthermore, offered all manner of new experiences. One group took up folk dancing with a fanatic enthusiasm reminiscent of some medieval dance hysteria. Led by Friedrich Lamberty, nicknamed "Muck," they would wander from town to town, staying in hostels or barns, performing in the town square, attracting more members, and then moving on.

Der Zupfgeigenhansel (*Guitar Johnny*), the first and most comprehensive of a long series of folk song books, revived and enhanced Germany's musical folk lore, which soon echoed from even the remotest corner of Germany's once quiet forests.

Pure song is a source of strength. Don't sing without a plan; don't sing simply what pops into your head. Be sure of the meaning.

Don't sing without feeling. Don't shout or lapse into sickening sentimentality.

Silence is often better than singing. Don't think you have to sing at any cost, like the fellow who feels obliged to talk "to be sociable" . . .

Sing and play with your whole soul. Music, you should know, is not entertainment, but education.[1]

The campfire was something of a secret ritual:

Marching about an altar,
Swinging our arms together,
Sacrificing together
In the presence of a god,
All of us are one.
When the sacrifice rises in pointed flames
Our blood flows in one stream
We dance joyfully locking arms.
All of us are one.

. . . . .

We reach to the heavens,
Reach to the horizon
With our arms.
We are a cup
From which the gods
Drink.
Amen.[2]

Around that flaming altar in the woods, in village barns, in town squares, and, best of all, in the ruins of medieval castles, these ecstatic young people in their corduroy and cotton uniforms would perform theatrical skits and plays. That, too, was mystical intoxication. As Georg Götsch, one of the early Wandervögel, put it:

Acting for me is a greater joy than watch-

Wandervögel dress c. 1920. [*Staatsbibliothek, Berlin*]

Opposite page, top left: The German youth movement started out with perpetual singing and strumming of guitars. Top right: It dotted the countryside with youth hostels. Bottom row: Wandervögel revived old folk songs as well as the old village customs, such as this wedding under a wreath. [*Archiv für Kunst und Geschichte, Landesbildstelle, and Staatsbibliothek, West Berlin*]

The campfire was something of a secret ritual. [*Archiv für Kunst und Geschichte, West Berlin*]

ing a performance. Crude mechanical truth is rejected, the moment becomes eternal, that which is vital is concentrated into seconds, the happy lie becomes a virtue . . . One can act out the many souls which one harbors within, all the faint memories of ancestral destiny; one can be at once magnificently outside oneself and yet deep inside one's innermost being . . . Oh, what a release, not to be trapped in the identity of one's own ego, to have for once the opportunity to try all the potentials of life, to play many roles, to discover and multiply one's own power. In the theater we have the power of dance and idea, instruction and awareness, the free reign of the spirit—and, related to this, a relationship with the intellect through word and sense, so that young people growing up are given release and restraint at the same time.[3]

The Wandervögel movement was determined to be antipolitical, or at least apolitical. While it was always romantically *völkisch*, that is, ethno-Germanic and thus conservative-nationalist, German youth tried to steer clear of partisan politics. Naturally, this *völkisch*-ness excluded Jews, and some Wandervögel even refused to meet with the Jewish equivalent, the "Blue-White" organization. For the Wandervögel anti-Semitism was not a political matter, but part of their concept of purifying the Teutonic spirit.

Pervading the entire movement was an air of (mostly latent) male homosexuality. Girls were excluded or at least segregated. In the 1930s the Wandervögel gradually disintegrated. Its countless splinter groups, clustered around magnetic local leaders, were loosely organized in the essentially middle-class Deutsche Freischar (German Volunteer Corps).

The youth movement in all its forms shunned alcohol and tobacco and was ignorant of drugs. Nor were its activities entirely confined to outdoor weekend and vacation excursions.

In Berlin and other big cities many of the groups had a *Heim* (home), and some youth organizations had several such "homes" in different neighborhoods. Most were small basement apartments or store fronts, for which the youngsters themselves paid the rent and which they furnished haphazardly, if at all, and decorated with posters, flags, trophies, and mementos of their excursions. Here, the youngsters would play games, sing, rehearse skits, hold poetry readings, get into big discussions, plan and plot the next trip, and in other ways enjoy what they enjoyed most in the woods—an escape from adult authority. It was easy to feel more at home in these "caves," as some called them, than at home.

As Peter Gay observed in his *Weimar Culture,* German youth elevated "adolescence itself into an ideology." But there were too many organized adolescents for the politicians—and for some of their own grown-up leaders—to leave alone in their soggy tent camps and dank city basements.

Hitler addresses a national youth meeting at Potsdam in October 1932, shortly before he seized power [*Landesbildstelle, West Berlin*]

President Paul von Hindenburg inspects a troop of Hitler Youth girls. [*Landesbildstelle, West Berlin*]

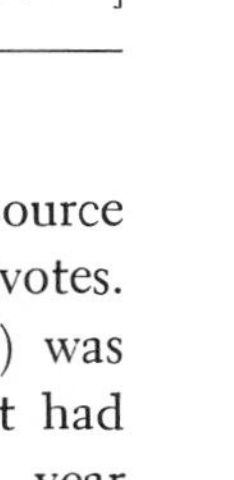

The Socialists were first to tap this resource of confused enthusiasm and potential votes. The Arbeiterjugend (Workers' Youth) was organized as early as 1909. By 1920 it had a hundred thousand members. That year one of its leaders also declared:

The early period [of search for a social program] is past. Romantics may be sorry that vague yearnings have vanished. Young socialists have learned to investigate coldly the process of social change . . . The proletarian youth movement is educational . . . Its goal . . . is the creation of a political human being.[4]

Before long, every political party wanted to create its own young "political human being," to indoctrinate youth not by means of long-winded speeches and tiresome plans of action, but out there around the campfire at the end of exhilarating hikes and exhausting song and dance festivals. The Catholic Center party launched its Windhorstbunde and the nationalists their Bismarckjugend. There were as many youth groups, emblems, and different colored shirts as there were political parties—and the Weimar Republic had plenty of them.

The right wing, on its part, perniciously perverted the naïvely romantic *völkisch* spirit of the Wandervögel. As one observer put it:

. . . a retrogression and simplification has occurred. The earlier breakthrough toward humanism responded to a deep need of

youth. Today there is an overt desire for conflict . . . The undesirable tone and style of the Wilhelmian era made patriotic symbols despicable. The same tone and style now pervade the völkisch *youth movement, which attempts to shape the future through frantic action rather than quiet change.*[5]

The bulk of the youth movement, however, the Freischar, remained rigidly apolitical. Nor did it show much outer change as the years passed. By the end of the twenties, however, the same old *Zupfgeigenhansel* songs seemed sung out, the old Wandervögel corduroy uniforms began to look a little ridiculous, all that *völkisch* lore became a bore. To many youngsters, it all suddenly seemed hopelessly and irrelevantly bourgeois.

Eberhard Köbel, one of the Freischar leaders, took a hiking trip through Lapland, the northernmost part of Scandinavia. The Lapps called their visitor "tusk," which is their word for "German." He kept the name when he returned to Berlin with a knapsack full of new Scandinavian songs (to which he added Cossack and American cowboy tunes), changed those soggy old tents to Laplandish tepees, designed a snappy black flannel blouse for his boys, and, on November 1, 1929, with all these trappings and more, founded his own group. He called it "d.j.1.11" ("d.j." stands for "deutsche Jungenschaft" and "1.11" denotes the fact that the group was founded on the first day of the eleventh month). The lower-case letters and the date were significant. That was the way the Russian Constructivists and the Bauhaus (where everything was written in lower case) would have done it. The designation was symbolic of a new, modern spirit, also reflected in the graphics of "tusk's" magazine, *Das Lagerfeuer* (*The Campfire*) and the balalaikas that were added to the obligatory guitars. It still was most romantic, but the romanticism had a new style and a fresh and exciting international flavor. "Tusk's" *Jungenschaft* caught on.

But so did Hitler's Jugend. The Hitler Youth, founded in 1922, which promptly adopted "tusk's" snappy uniform design for its junior groups, appropriated a good many of his songs, and borrowed the other manifestations of his style. A decade later it had more than a hundred thousand members. It also had an appeal that the apolitical youth movement did not even try to match. Hitler told his young followers in October 1932:

In the past it was possible for German youth to ignore the things that move us today . . . I know there are many among you whose fathers walk the streets looking for work, that many of you do not know what will happen to your families in the weeks and days to come. . . . Our people have been fragmented, corrupted and powerless and, because of this lawlessness [in the streets] lost work and bread . . .

The National Socialist movement wants

"The National Socialist movement wants to educate the German youth to be proud and brave and not to bend when others would lure him into evil deeds . . ." [*Landesbildstelle, West Berlin*]

to educate the German youth to be proud and brave and not to bend when others would lure him into evil deeds . . . We must once again be able to sing proudly about our people in sagas and folk ballads.[6]

"Tusk" thought it wrong that the bulk of the youth movement simply stood aside. On April 20, 1932, Hitler's birthday, he told his growing flock in a letter "to be read at once and then destroyed":

I am going to join the Communist party . . . The misery and difficulties of our homeland are so great that I cannot stand aloof from the political struggle just for my own personal comfort. A lot of people will not understand this. They'll say: "'tusk' has changed." Naturally, I have changed: I have grown . . .

I am becoming a Communist because one cannot let words remain words. Actions must follow . . . The vain, gossipy, smart-alecky youth movement is dreadful . . . Don't fall back into naïveté . . . You have an obligation . . .[7]

A year later, "tusk" was forced to escape to England. Several d.j.1.11. members, not all Communists, carried on for a while. Some took their obligation seriously and were active in the anti-Nazi underground, particularly in the abortive Munich student uprising of 1943.

The "vain, gossipy, smart-alecky youth" changed into brown shirts and became Hitler's.

[*Landesbildstelle, West Berlin*]

[*Staatsbibliothek, West Berlin*]

[*Staatsbilbliothek*, West *Berlin*]

14

COLLAPSE: *No Jobs but a Storm of Heils*

The Weimar Republic did fairly well as long as such able men as President Friedrich Ebert and Foreign Minister Gustav Stresemann were at the helm.

When the currency had been stabilized, the economy improved. Ebert reduced tensions between management and labor. Stresemann reduced the excessive penalties imposed by the Versailles Treaty, made Germany a respected member of the League of Nations, obtained foreign loans, and, jointly with his friend the French statesman Aristide Briand, received the 1926 Nobel Peace Prize for his efforts.

But in Germany the disillusionment, the lack of faith in parliamentary government, and the vilification of moderate leaders continued. Extremists kept fanning the unrest.

"Tusk," the left-wing youth leader, was wrong about one thing: the Germans, including ill-paid and unemployed workers, did not want to be counted among the "proletariat." The rigid Soviet-Communist doctrine seemed alien to them. Hitler was clever with his semantic trick: The "little man" wanted both "nationalism" *and* "socialism," nationalist law and order *and* socialist revolution. He wanted an end to the chaotic party squabbles and he wanted a radical change that would *really* meet the promises of work and bread and a little house with a flock of rosy-cheeked kids romping in the back yard. He never saw the contradiction. After all, *Führer* meant leader, not dictator.

In 1925 Ebert died of a ruptured appendix, having ignored doctors' orders to undergo an operation. In the election for a new President, Field Marshal Paul von Beneckendorff und von Hindenburg, seventy-eight years old, defeated Wilhelm Marx, sixty-two, a leader of the Catholic Center party, with a run-off vote of 14,660,000 to 13,750,000. It was not a clear victory for the near-senile perpetrator of the *Dolchstosslegende*, the myth that Germany lost World War I only because the Jews and Socialists stabbed his glorious army in the back. The third candidate might have saved German democracy by withdrawing from the run-off. He was Ernst Thälmann, the leader of the Communist party, which believed that a Nazi victory would be short-lived and followed by its own. Thälmann received 1,930,000 votes.

Gustav Stresemann, the Foreign Minister, died in office in 1929. He was succeeded by Julius Curtius, who was dismissed the next year by Chancellor Heinrich Brüning, who assumed his job. Brüning was a man whose admirable intentions paved the way to hell and Hitler.

Against this kaleidoscopic background of political faces and fumblings, a fear seized Berlin—the fear of unemployment.

In December 1925, 120,000 Berliners had no jobs. In February 1926, unemployment had risen to 227,500; by April, to 240,000;

Yorck Str

by July, to 277,000; by January, 1927, to 284,000. On March 13, 1927—Black Friday—the German mark began to slip again. Berlin's unemployment problem became a national unemployment problem and catastrophe:

When I walk through the streets
freezing, unemployed,
looking into warm shops,
I ask myself:
"Does that last tooth of yours
have anything to chew?" . . .
Why does the employment office
close at two?
At least it's warm there
while you pass the time.
Between me and the earth
stands my bare toe.
Between my hunger and a steak
only money, that's all . . .[1]

By the end of October 1929, Berlin alone had nearly half a million unemployed and the rate had climbed disastrously in the rest of the country. The New York stock market crashed.

In the darkest days of the Depression, Germany had six million unemployed walking the streets. The Weimar coalition began to lose control of the situation. Berlin again became a city of insurrection, with the police being attacked from the left by Communists and from the right by Nazis.

In one 1929 street battle against the police in the workers' district of Wedding, the Communists threw barricades across the streets and used snipers. A Communist described the scene:

From the darkened entrance of Police Station 95, shining steel helmets appeared. Twenty. Thirty. The young faces were almost covered by the rim of steel . . . For the first time, live grenades hung from their belts . . .

The first five had slung their carbines around their necks. The fifth was Sergeant Schlopsuies. The young policeman's hands shook as he took the tin cap off a grenade. The tiny porcelain ball on a string, by which the grenade is detonated, fell out and dangled between his nervous fingers. He shook so badly he was afraid to touch it. His whole body quaked . . .

Schlopsuies pulled the cord—his helmet hit against someone—he tripped—screamed in fear—the grenade slipped from his fingers—he ran. A few meters behind him, the exploding grenade tore a hole in the sidewalk. Earth and stone splinters covered him . . .

A shadow ran past. Police? Commies? Schlopsuies cried after them, but no one heard. He couldn't get his feet to run— His ears rang with shots and explosions . . .

From the bridge there were two blasts from a police whistle. The company ran back and collected around the corner. The police attack had failed.[2]

It did not look much different from the other side. A Nazi wrote, about a skirmish with the law:

A few days later Cohrs was arrested again, this time with his girl friend, Hanna . . .

There was a rally in Friedrichshain. The speaker was Dr. Goebbels. There were five thousand people inside the park, another three thousand outside.

And everything was nice and peaceful, only a few small disturbances every so often out on the street.

So far, so good. Goebbels left. The crowd sent him off with shouts of excitement. Outside on the street the police captain, who commanded the barricade, shouted idiotically: "No demonstration while the speaker is leaving. No shouting 'Heil!'" It was one of those stupid orders . . . Did this incompetent, weak-kneed tin god really believe he could stop three thousand people from hailing Dr. Goebbels with a hail of "Heils"?

They heiled and the police immediately lost their nerve and attacked the crowd with truncheons . . . There was shouting and screaming and confusion and pushing . . .

The Berlin police stormed forward.

Cohrs was seized, a cop forced him to the ground with a half nelson. He shouted a word applicable to the cop and the situation.

With millions unemployed, Berliners, in the fall of 1932, watch as a new election poster is being put up. It reads: HITLER IS OUR LAST HOPE. [*Staatsbibliothek, West Berlin*]

It was often hard to tell whether the demonstrators provoked the police or the police provoked the demonstrators. At any rate, there were constant clashes. [*Staatsbibliothek, West Berlin*]

He was arrested.

At the same instant he saw his girl friend, Hanna, surrounded, as she pushed into the police captain.

The captain is six feet tall. Hanna is five and a half feet.

But the captain turned sharply on his heel, his face bright red: "Arrest her! This woman attacked me!"

Two policemen with raised truncheons immediately jumped on the girl.

Schulz also saw all this . . . "I'm a witness," he shouted angrily at a policeman. "I want to make a statement" . . .

"All right, then, come along. You're under arrest" . . .

As they were being booked, Schulz kept protesting . . .

"Don't complain so much," the desk sergeant laughed . . . "You have a choice of cells tonight—with the Communists or the non-politicals. As you wish" . . .

Schulz decided that wolves are better than hyenas . . . And so they were taken into a cell with six criminals . . .[3]

In these fictionalized or at least dramatized accounts by Communist and Nazi writers, the police were always the villains. The sober *Vossische Zeitung* saw it differently. Here, dated August 10, 1931, is one of its accounts about an incident of the kind that occurred continuously, involving either left or right.

The day of the [Prussian state] elections had been quiet. At 9 P.M., there was an attack by Communists at Bülowplatz and three police officers were killed.

Immediately after this attack, an anti-police riot broke out all over the district. It appeared to have been planned. Thousands of people began to attack individual policemen on their beats. Police were shot at from windows and doorways. Police reinforcements rushed to the scene within a few minutes and quickly repressed the riot. About twenty people on the Communist side were injured and one body was found later. Among the wounded were women and children. Order was restored at about 1 A.M.

The attack on the policemen could be reconstructed by independent witnesses. According to their accounts, Police Captains Anlauf and Lenk, as well as Sergeant Willig, were on an inspection patrol, walking from the Karl Liebknecht House [Communist headquarters] to the Babylon cinema . . . As the three policemen approached the theater, two men jumped behind them. Both shot at once. Captain Anlauf was fatally shot in the neck. Captain Lenk, who had heard something move behind him, turned and was shot in the stomach. After the shooting, the assassins pushed past their victims. Sergeant Willig pulled his revolver and blocked their path. Both men ran into the lobby of the movie theater. Captain Lenk, badly wounded, dragged himself toward the theater, and the sergeant, who followed the criminals inside, was shot in the stomach and arm. He collapsed. Captain Lenk died

Most of the street brawls were between Nazis and Communists. Here, Saxony's mounted police attempts to establish order during a 1929 May Day demonstration in Dresden. [*Staatsbibliothek, West Berlin*]

On January 22, 1933, a week before Hitler was appointed Reich Chancellor, Nazi Stormtroopers marched on the Communist headquarters at Berlin's Bülowplatz. The Communists refused to be provoked. The Weimar Republic's police kept watch in armored cars. [*Staatsbibliothek, West Berlin*]

on the stairs. Both killers ran through the theater and vanished out a back door. They must have known the floor plan.

[After several hundred police arrived at the scene] bullets whistled through the streets and across Bülowplatz. The big searchlights of the police vans illuminated the roofs from which shots were fired and rocks were thrown . . .[4]

The noisiest and most vicious agitator was Paul Josef Goebbels, who had received his Ph.D. degree in literature at Heidelberg University. Goebbels' special obsession was anti-Semitism. He shouted to ever-larger rallies:

The Jew is the real demon of destruction. When he smells rot and garbage, he appears out of the hidden depths and begins to undermine everything. He wears the mask of those he wishes to exploit, plays the good friend of his victims, and his innocent victims note, only too late, that he has broken their necks . . .

"But there are also good Jews," you say. There are surely plenty of rotten specimens among our own people who use unethical means to exploit their fellow Germans. But why do you say "good Jews"? When you say that, you show that you, too, believe that a Jew is basically something low and despic-

able. Just as we do. Why do you ask us why we are enemies of the Jews when you, without even knowing it, are also his enemy? . . . We are the enemies of Jews because we identify ourselves as Germans. The Jew is our greatest curse.

But this will change, as surely as we are Germans.[5]

Actually, Berlin had only 215,000 Jews among its 4.3 million inhabitants at the time. Many of them no longer listing "Hebrew" as their religion considered themselves as German as their Christian neighbors. There was no ghetto or Jewish district. Berlin's Jewish community responded to this anti-Semitic irrationality with traditional German-Jewish rationality. It had long ago adopted the philosophy of cultural assimilation advocated by Moses Mendelssohn in the eighteenth century. Most Berlin Jews therefore shrugged at Goebbels' tirades as a political excess that would pass, just as the anti-Semitic waves of the late nineteenth century seemed to have passed.

Starting in March 1930, Chancellor Brüning, a conservative liberal, earnestly but ineptly attempted to cope with the crisis with constitutionally questionable "emergency powers," largely ignoring the Reichstag. The Weimar Republic ceased to function as a democracy. The Nazis kept gaining strength, although when there were free elections, they never got more than 44 per cent of the vote.

On June 1, 1932, Hindenburg, persuaded by his Prussian Junker friends, suddenly dropped Brüning and appointed a new chancellor, Franz von Papen. Politically unknown—"not bad, not really malevolent, but irresponsible, vain, scheming and pitifully superficial," is how Golo Mann describes him—Von Papen was the puppet of the "old boys' club," as it was called, a clique of the reactionary military establishment and the industralists who wanted to be rid of what was left of all this Weimar nonsense, but without the plebeian Hitler if possible. "Oh, no! No my poor little Franz," Frau von Papen was said to have exclaimed, when she heard of her husband's appointment.

Poor little Franz, indeed. He really thought he could "tame" the Nazis.

The kaleidoscope of political faces and events now started revolving at dizzying speed. On January 30, 1933, Goebbels wrote in his diary:

At noon we sat in the Kaiserhof [Hotel] and waited. The Führer was in the President's office . . . Our hearts were torn between doubt and hope, between happiness and despair. We had been too often disappointed to believe in this miracle . . .

Torturous hours of waiting. Finally a car rounded the corner of the building. The masses began to shout. They seemed to sense that a great change was imminent or had already occurred.

The Führer was coming!

A few minutes later he was in the room. He did not say anything. We did not say anything. His eyes were full of tears.

It had come to pass.

The Führer had been appointed Chancellor. He had just taken the oath of office before the President. The great decision was made. Germany's destiny was about to take a historic turn.[6]

Less than a month later, the Reichstag, by now the hollow symbol of a dead Republic, went up in flames.

Though the Nazis themselves, it later turned out, instigated the fire, they blamed it on the Communists. This served them as an excuse to fill prisons and concentration camps with their political enemies.

A month after that, the novelist Hermann Kesten wrote to the poet Ernst Toller:

I lived six weeks in the Third Reich, but that was a sufficient lesson for a novelist, an instructive purgatory. We have seen enough since 1914. But this silent transition from law to lawlessness. Neighbors who suddenly become murderers. The police, in league with the murderers, persecuting the innocent.

I keep thinking each collapse, each revolution, is staged by the few for the few. Most people don't understand, neither supporting nor condemning. A change in the weather affects them more than changes in government. Don't the German people

Leaders of the Nazi party at a rally in 1932. From left to right, Count Wolf von Helldorf, Adolf Hitler, City Councilman Engel, Josef Goebbels, and S. A. Commander Wilhelm Brückner, [*Staatsbibliothek, West Berlin*]

comprehend that this new government will be Germany's gravedigger?[7]

Those who, for those fabulous dozen years, had made Berlin what it was artistically and intellectually, did understand. They understood that this new government was not only Germany's gravedigger but also ready to throw them, the most outstanding exponents of German culture, into mass graves and gas ovens. Those who could, fled. They fled to every point of the compass and some fled again and again.

Bert Brecht escaped from Berlin on February 28, 1933, to Prague and from there went around the world in search of a Berlin which he found again in 1949.

In December 1933 he paused in Copenhagen. He reflected:

Homer had no home
And Dante was forced to leave.
Li Po and Tu Fu wandered through
A civil war which destroyed thirty million
people.
Euripides was threatened with prosecution
And they held closed the dying
Shakespeare's mouth.
François Villon was sought not only by
the muse
But also by the police.
Called "the beloved,"
Lucretius went into exile.
So did Heine, and so
Under the straw roofs of Denmark fled
Brecht.[8]

"Most people don't understand . . ." [*Landesbildstelle, West Berlin*]

NOTES

CHAPTER 1 Revolution

1. Alfred Niemann, *Kaiser und Revolution: Die entscheidenden Ereignisse im Grossen Hauptquartier im Herbst 1918* (Berlin: Verlag für Kulturpolitik, 1928), pp. 138–39.

2. Artur Iger, *Spartakustage: Aus Berlins Bolschewistenzeit* (Berlin: Verlag Heimatschutz, 1919), pp. 37–39.

3. Phillip Scheidemann, *Memoiren eines Sozialdemokraten*, II, (Dresden: Reissner, 1928), pp. 310–14.

4. From *Die junge Garde*, January 17, 1919.

5. From *Illustrierte Geschichte der deutschen Revolution* (Berlin: Internationaler Arbeiterverlag, 1929), p. 272.

6. Count Harry Kessler, *In the Twenties: The Diaries of Harry Kessler*, trans. Charles Kessler (New York: Holt, Rinehart and Winston, 1971) pp. 52–53, 56–57.

7. Iger, op. cit., pp. 100–4.

8. From *Der Prolet*, no. 5, 1920.

9. From Brecht's poem *To Posterity* (also quoted at the beginning of this chapter). Bertolt Brecht, *Gesammelte Werke*, IX: *Gedichte* (Frankfurt am Main: Suhrkamp, 1967) pp. 722–23. Translation by Erich von Kahler (hitherto unpublished).

CHAPTER 2 Inflation

1. Hans Ostwald, *Sittengeschichte der Inflation* (Berlin: Neufeld & Henius, 1931), pp. 74–75.

2. Friedrich A. C. Lange, *Gross-Berlin Tagebuch 1920–1933* (Berlin: Erich Borkenhagen, 1951).

3. "*Die Kinderhölle in Berlin*," special issue, *Die deutsche Nation*, II, 1920, pp. 1–6.

4. Harry Domela, *Der falsche Prinz* (Berlin: Malik, 1927), pp. 73–75.

5. Ostwald, op. cit., p. 128.

6. Erik Jan Hanussen, *Meine Lebenslinie* (Berlin: Universitas, 1930), pp. 242–44.

CHAPTER 3 After Hours

1. Eugen Szatmari, *Das Buch von Berlin* (Berlin: Piper Verlag, 1927), pp. 140 ff.

2. Heinrich Mann, "Varieté im Norden," *Essays* (Berlin: Aufbau, 1954), pp. 301–2.

3. Erich Kästner, *Fabian*, in *Gesammelte Schriften für Erwachsene*, II (Munich: Droemer-Knauer, 1969), pp. 59–61.

4. Hellmuth Krüger, "Lieber Gott," *Uhu*, no. 11, 1929.

5. Pick Nick, "Berliner Ballbericht," *Die Ente*, no. 1, 1932.

6. Szatmari, op. cit., pp. 146–47.

CHAPTER 4 The Underworld

1. Paul Zech, *Vor Cressy an der Marne* (Laon: Revillon, 1918), pp. 14–15.

2. Leo Heller, *So siehste aus—Berlin* (Munich: Parais, 1927), pp. 75–77.

3. Weka [Willi Pröger] *Stätten der Berliner Prostitution* (Berlin: Auffenberg, 1930), pp. 41–44.

4. Ibid., pp. 46–47.

5. Gottfried Benn, *Frühe Lyrik und Dramen* (Wiesbaden: Limes, 1952), p. 17.

6. Bertolt Brecht, *Gesammelte Werke*, VIII: *Gedichte* (Frankfurt am Main: Suhrkamp, 1967), pp. 271–73.

7. Szatmari, *Das Buch von Berlin*, pp. 157–58.

8. Heller, op. cit., pp. 72–73.

9. Alfred Döblin, *Berlin—Alexanderplatz* (Olten: Walther, 1961), pp. 349–50.

CHAPTER 5 The Intellectuals

1. Josef Kastein, "Romanisches Kaffee," *Das Stachelschwein*, no. 2, 1925.

2. Rumpelstilzchen [Adolf Stein], *Berliner Funken* (Berlin: Brunnen, 1927), pp. 70–71.

3. Carl von Ossietzky, in *Die Weltbühne*, December 15, 1931.

CHAPTER 6 Newspapers and Radio

1. Alfred Hugenberg, in *Deutsche Allgemeine Zeitung*, December 3, 1931.

2. Willi Münzenberg, *Solidarität: Zehn Jahre Internationale Arbeiterhilfe* (Berlin: Neuer Deutscher Verlag, 1931), p. 7.

3. *Völkischer Beobachter*, June 28, 1922.

4. *Die Rote Fahne*, June 24, 1922.

5. *Vossische Zeitung*, June 24, 1922.

6. *Berliner Tageblatt*, June 24, 1922.

7. Hans Bredow, *Vier Jahre deutscher Rundfunk* (Berlin: Reichsdruckerei, 1927), p. 11.

8. E. Kurt Fischer, ed., *Dokumente zur Geschichte des deutschen Rundfunks und Fernsehens* (Göttingen: Musterschmidt, 1957), pp. 201–2.

CHAPTER 7 Art

1. Paul Westheim, "Berlin, die Stadt der Künstler," in Herbert Günther, ed., *Heir schreibt Berlin* (Berlin: Internationale Bibliothek, 1929), pp. 317–18.

2. Johannes Molzahn, in *Der Sturm*, no. 6, 1919.

3. Otto Dix, in *Berliner Nachtausgabe*, December 3, 1927.

4. *Der Sturm*, no. 4/6, 1923.

5. Excerpt from a manifesto cited in Bernard S. Myers, *The German Expressionists: A Generation in Revolt* (New York, Praeger, 1966), p. 220.

6. Ibid., p. 222.

7. Heinrich Zille, unpublished manuscript, Academy of Art, West Berlin.

8. Käthe Kollwitz, *Tagebuchblätter und Briefe*, ed. Hans Kollwitz (Berlin: Mann, 1948), pp. 87–88.

9. *Tagebuch*, no. 9, 1928.

10. *Völkischer Beobachter*, July 18, 1937.

CHAPTER 8 Theater

1. Franz Hadamowsky, ed., *Max Reinhardt: Ausgewählte Briefe, Reden, Schriften und Szenen aus Regiebuchern* (Vienna: Georg Prachner, 1963), pp. 89–90.

2. Franz Ferdinand Baumgarten, *Zirkus Reinhardt* (Potsdam: Hans Heinrich Tillgner, 1920), pp. 45–46.

3. Felix Ziege, *Leopold Jessner und das Zeit-Theater* (Berlin: Eigenbrödler, 1928).

4. Erwin Piscator, *Das politische Theater* (Berlin: Adalbert Schultz, 1929), pp. 129–32.

5. Max Lenz, "Piscator auf der Probe," *Das Theater*, no. 8, 1927.

6. Alfred Muhr, *Kulturbankrott des Bürgertums* (Dresden and Berlin: Sibyllen, 1928), pp. 78–79.

7. Julius Bab, *Albert Bassermann: Weg und Werk* (Leipzig: Erich Weibezahl, 1929), pp. 318–19.

8. Arthur Eloesser, *Elisabeth Bergner* (Charlottenburg: Williams, 1928), pp. 63–64.

9. Wolfgang Heine, ed., *Der Kampf um den Reigen* (Berlin: Rowohlt, 1922), pp. 150–51, 219–20.

10. *Berliner Börsen-Courier*, September 1, 1928.

11. Bertolt Brecht, *Gesammelte Werke*, V: *Theoretische Schriften* (Frankfurt am Main: Suhrkamp, 1967), p. 126.

12. Alfred Kerr, *Die Welt im Drama* (Köln: Kiepenheuer & Witsch, 1964), pp. 267–68.

13. Brecht, op. cit., p. 129.

CHAPTER 9 Film

1. Jakob von Hoddis, "Varieté," *Der Sturm*, no. 21, 1911.

2. F. W. Koebner, "Film," in Lothar Brieger and Hanns Steiner, eds., *Zirkus Berlin* (Berlin: Almanach, 1919), pp. 112–16.

3. Curt Moreck, *Sittengeschichte des Kinos* (Dresden: Paul Aretz, 1926), p. 177.

4. Rudolf Kurtz, *Expressionismus und Film* (Berlin: Verlag der Lichtbühne, 1926), pp. 62–64.

5. Luis Trenker, *Meine Berge* (Berlin: Neufeld & Henius, 1931), p. 124.

6. Munkepunke [Alfred Richard Meyer], *1000% Jannings* (Berlin: Prismen, 1930), pp. 148–53.

7. Bert Brecht, in *Blick in die Welt*, no. 20, 1931.

CHAPTER 10 Music and Dance

1. Alban Berg, *Briefe an seine Frau* (Munich: Langen-Müller, 1965), pp. 551–52.

2. Kurt Singer, "'Wozzeck'—die Oper des Grausens," *Vorwärts*, December 15, 1925.

3. R. Wr., "Uraufführung der Oper 'Wozzeck' von Alban Berg," *Kreuz-Zeitung*, December 15, 1925.

4. Leopold Schmidt, "Wozzeck," *Berliner Tageblatt*, December 15, 1925.

5. Edmund Kuhn, "'Wozzeck' von Alban Berg," *Germania*, December 16, 1925.

6. Ernst Krenek, *Prosa, Dramen, Verse* (Munich: Lagen-Müller, 1965), pp. 98–99.

7. L. Moholy-Nagy, "Neue Gestaltung in der Musik," *Der Sturm*, no. 14, 1923.

8. Mary Wigman, in *Die Musik*, no. 35, December 1932.

CHAPTER 11 Architecture

1. Marcel Franciscono, *Walter Gropius and the Creation of the Bauhaus in Weimar: The Ideals and Artistic Theories of Its Founding Years* (Urbana: University of Illinois Press, 1971), Appendix E, p. 281.

2. Bruno Taut, *Alpine Architecture*, ed. Dennis Sharp, tr. Shirley Palmer (New York, Praeger, 1972), pp. 122–23.

3. Hans M. Wingler, *The Bauhaus, Weimar, Dessau, Berlin, Chicago* (Cambridge, Mass.: MIT Press, 1969), p. 31.

4. Ibid, p. 36.

5. Paul Scheerbart, *Glass Architecture*, ed. Dennis Sharp, tr. James Palmes (New York: Praeger, 1972), p. 41.

6. Ulrich Conrads, *Programs and Manifestoes on 20th Century Architecture* (Cambridge, Mass.: MIT Press, 1962), p. 55.

7. Ibid., p. 57.

8. Ibid., p. 123.

CHAPTER 12 Sports

1. Fritz Wildung, *Arbeitersport* (Berlin: Der Bücherkreis, 1929), pp. 149–50.

2. Adolf Koch, ed., *Körperbildung—Nacktkultur* (Leipzg: Oldenburg, 1924), p. 205.

3. Ibid., p. 172.

4. Adolf Koch, *Wir sind nackt und nennen uns Du!* (Leipzig: Oldenburg, 1932), pp. 62–64.

5. Walter Mehring, *Gedichte, Chansons, Lieder* (Berlin: Fischer, 1928), pp. 34–35.

6. *Die Literarische Welt*, February 4, 1927.

7. Bertolt Brecht, *Gesammelte Werke*, I: *Prosa* (Frankfurt am Main: Suhrkamp, 1965), pp. 132–34.

CHAPTER 13 Youth

1. Werner Hensel, ed., *Der singende Quell* (Kassel: Bärenreiter, 1933), p. 5.

2. Kurt Gauger, "Alle die um einen Altar schreiten," *Weisser Ritter*, VI, 1926, p. 273.

3. Georg Götsch, "Wandervögel und Bühne," in Ludwig Pallat und Hans Lebede, eds., *Jugend und Bühne* (Breslau: Hirt, 1924), pp. 155–56.

4. Franz Lepinski, *Die jungsozialistische Bewegung, ihre Geschichte und ihre Aufgaben* (Berlin: E. Laub, 1927).

5. Wilhelm Stahlin, *Die völkische Bewegung und unsere Verantwortung* (Sollstedt: Buchverlag des Bundes Deutscher Jugendvereine, 1924).

6. Baldur von Schirach, *Die Hitler-Jugend: Idee und Gestalt* [Berlin: Zeitgeschichte, 1934), pp. 183–84.

7. "tusk" [Eberhard Köbel], *Gesammelte Schriften und Dichtungen*, ed. Werner Helwig (Heidenheim an der Brenz: Südmark Fritsch, 1962), p. 42.

CHAPTER 14 Collapse

1. Carl Wehner, "Arbeitslos," in Robert Seitz and Heinz Zucker, eds., *Um uns die Stadt* (Berlin: Sieben Stäbe, 1931), pp. 80–81.

2. Klaus Neukrantz, *Barrikaden am Wedding* (Berlin: Internationaler Arbeiter Verlag, 1931), pp. 109–12.

3. Wilfrid Bade, *Die SA erobert Berlin* (Munich: Knorr & Hirth, 1933), pp. 210–17.

4. *Vossische Zeitung*, August 10, 1931.

5. *Der Angriff*, July 30, 1928, quoted in Josef Goebbels, *Der Angriff: Aufsätze aus der Kampfzeit* (Munich: Zentralverlag der NSDAP, 1935), pp. 329–30.

6. Josef Goebbels, *Vom Kaiserhof zur Reichskanzlei* (Munich: Zentralverlag der NSDAP, 1935), pp. 251–52.

7. Hermann Kesten, *Deutsche Literatur im Exil* (Basel: Kurt Desch, 1964), pp. 28–29.

8. Bertolt Brecht, *Gesammelte Werke*, IX: *Gedichte* (Frankfurt am Main: Suhrkamp, 1967), p. 495.

BIBLIOGRAPHY

(This selected bibliography is limited to studies available in English.)

ANGRESS, WERNER T., *Stillborn Revolution: The Communist Bid for Power in Germany, 1921–1923* (Princeton: Princeton University Press, 1963).

AUSTIN, WILLIAM W., *Music in the Twentieth Century* (New York: Norton, 1966).

BERTAUX, FÉLIX, *A Panorama of German Literature, from 1871–1931*, tr. John J. Trounstine (New York: McGraw-Hill, 1935).

BRECHT, ARNOLD, *Prelude to Silence: The End of the German Republic* (New York: Oxford University Press, 1944; New York: Fertig, 1968).

CARTER, HUNTLY, *The Theater of Max Reinhardt* (New York: Kennerley, 1914).

CLARK, ROBERT T., *The Fall of the German Republic* (London: Allen & Unwin, 1935).

CONRADS, ULRICH, ed. *Programs and Manifestoes on 20th-Century Architecture*, tr. Michael Bullock (Cambridge, Mass.: MIT Press, 1970).

COPER, RUDOLF, *Failure of a Revolution: Germany in 1918–1919* (London: Cambridge University Press, 1955).

EISNER, LOTTE H., *The Haunted Screen: Expressionism in the German Cinema and the Influence of Max Reinhardt*, tr. Roger Greaves (Berkeley: University of California Press, 1969).

ESSLIN, MARTIN, *Brecht: The Man and His Work* (Garden City, N.Y.: Doubleday, 1971).

EWEN, FREDERIC, *Bertolt Brecht: His Life, His Art, and His Times* (New York: Citadel, 1967).

FRANCKE, KUNO, *German After-War Problems* (Cambridge, Mass.: Harvard University Press 1927).

FRIEDRICH, OTTO, *Before the Deluge: A Portrait of Berlin in the 1920's* (New York: Harper & Row, 1972).

FUEGI, JOHN, *The Essential Brecht* (Los Angeles: Hennessey & Ingalls, 1972).

GAY, PETER, *Weimar Culture: The Outsider as Insider* (New York: Harper & Row, 1968).

HAFTMANN, WERNER, et al., *German Art in the Twentieth Century* (New York: Simon and Schuster, 1957).

INNES, C. D., *Erwin Piscator's Political Theater* (London: Cambridge University Press, 1972).

KESSLER, HARRY, COUNT, *The Diaries of a Cosmopolitan: 1918–1937*, tr. and ed. Charles Kessler (London: Weidenfeld & Nicolson, 1971).

KRACAUER, SIEGFRIED, *From Caligari to Hitler: A Psychological History of the German Film* (Princeton: Princeton University Press, 1947).

KRISPYN, EGBERT, *Style and Society in German Literary Expressionism* (Gainesville: University of Florida Press, 1964).

LANGE, VICTOR, *Modern German Literature, 1870–1940* (Ithaca, N.Y.: Cornell University Press, 1945).

LEBOVICS, HERMAN, *Social Conservatism and the Middle Class in Germany, 1914–1933* (Princeton: Princeton University Press, 1969).

LEY-PISCATOR, MARIA, *The Piscator Experiment: The Political Theatre* (New York: James H. Heineman, 1967).

McKenzie, John R. P., *Weimar Germany, 1918–1933* (Totowa, N.J.: Rowman & Littlefield, 1971).

Mander, John, *Berlin: The Eagle and the Bear* (London: Barrie & Rockliff, 1959).

Mann, Golo, *The History of Germany Since 1789*, tr. Marian Jackson (New York: Praeger, 1968).

Masur, Gerhard, *Imperial Berlin* (New York: Basic Books, 1971).

Mendelsohn, Erich, *Letters of an Architect*, ed. Oskar Beyer, intro. by Nikolaus Pevsner (London: Abelard-Schuman, 1967).

Pehnt, Wolfgang, *Expressionist Architecture*, tr. J. A. Underwood and Edith Kuntner (New York: Praeger, 1973).

Roh, Franz, *German Art in the Twentieth Century*, tr. Catherine Hutter (Greenwich, Conn.: New York Graphic Society, 1968).

Samuel, Richard, and R. Hinton Thomas, *Expressionism in German Life, Literature and the Theatre (1910–1924)* (Cambridge, Eng.: Heffer, 1939).

Scheerbart, Paul, *Glass Architecture*, ed. Dennis Sharp, tr. James Palmes (New York: Praeger, 1972).

Snyder, Louis L., *The Weimar Republic* (Princeton: Van Nostrand, 1966).

Sokel, Walter, *The Writer in Extremis: Expressionism in Twentieth-Century German Literature* (Stanford: Stanford University Press, 1959).

Spalter, Max, *Brecht's Tradition* (Baltimore: Johns Hopkins University Press, 1967).

Stern, Fritz, *The Failure of Illiberalism: Essays in the Political Culture of Modern Germany* (New York: Knopf, 1972).

Stern, Guy, *War, Weimar and Literature: The Story of the Neue Merkur, 1914–1925* (University Park, Pa.: Pennsylvania State University Press, 1971).

Taut, Bruno, *Alpine Architecture*, ed. Dennis Sharp, tr. Shirley Palmer (New York: Praeger, 1972).

Taylor, A. J. P., *The Course of German History* (London: Hamish Hamilton, 1945).

Van Abbe, Derek, *Image of a People: The Germans and their Creative Writing Under and Since Bismarck* (New York: Barnes & Noble, 1964).

Waite, Robert G. L., *Vanguard of Nazism: The Free Corps Movement in Postwar Germany, 1918–1923* (Cambridge Mass.: Harvard University Press, 1952).

Waldmann, Eric, *The Spartacist Uprising of 1919 and the Crisis of the German Socialist Movement* (Milwaukee: Marquette University Press, 1958).

Watt, Richard M., *The Kings Depart: The Tragedy of Germany: Versailles and the German Revolution* (New York: Simon and Schuster, 1969).

Willett, John, *The Theater of Bertolt Brecht* (London: Methuen, 1967).

Wollenberg, Hans H., *Fifty Years of German Film*, tr. Ernst Sigler (London: Falcon, 1948).

INDEX

Abortions, 119
Abraham, Karl, 42
Academy of Arts, 62, 72
Academy of Fine Arts, 107, 108
Academy of Music, 107–8
Adenauer, Konrad, 1
Admiral Girls, 29
Admirals-Palast, 23, 29, 79
Aeschylus, 81
Air Force Academy Chapel, 125
Albers, Anni, 122
Albers, Hans, 83, 104
Albers, Josef, 122
Alexander, Franz, 42
Alexanderplatz, xvii, 37
Alexandrinerstrasse, 34
All-Berlin Relay, 131
Allgemeine Elektrizitäts Gesellschaft, 52
All Quiet on the Western Front, 47
Alpine architecture, 120–21
Alt-Bayern (cabaret), 25
America, 115 (*see also* New York); movies made in, 93
American Relief Administration, Hoover Commission, 15, 18
Amerongen, Holland, 3
Ammer, K. L., 88
Arbeiter Illustrierte Zeitung, 50–52
Arbeiterjugend, 143
Arbeitersport, 129–30, 133
Arbeitstrat für die Kunst, 68, 119–20
Archipenke, Alexander, 65
Architecture, 117–27
Arnold, Karl, 82
Arp, Hans, 65
Art, 61–76
Aschinger's (restaurant), 11, 30
Atrium (theater), 103
Aufklärungsfilm, 43
Autobahnen, 133
Auto races, 133–34, 135
Autumn Salon, 65
Avus race track, 133–34, 135
Baal, 88
Baden, Prince Max von, 2, 3
Bahn, Roma, 89
Baird, John Logie, 59
Baker, Josephine, 28, 134, 135
Balls, 27–30
Barcelona, 124–25
Barlach, Ernst, 64, 73
Barnowsky, Victor, 84
Bassermann, Albert, 81, 84, 85
Battleship Potemkin, 92, 93
Bauhaus, the, 63, 66, 68, 112, 121–22, 123, 126, 144
Baumgarten, Franz Ferdinand, 79–81
Bayer, Herbert, 122
Beckmann, Max, xviii, 64, 70
"Beda," 115
Beggar's Opera, 88
Behrens, Peter, 118
Bell, Alexander, 57
Benjamin, Walter, 88
Benn, Gottfried, 35–36
Berg, Alban, 108–11
Bergner, Elisabeth, 84, 85, 86
Berlin-Alexanderplatz, 39
Berliner Börsen-Courier, 87–88
Berliner Illustrirte, 49
Berliner Tageblatt, 49, 53, 58, 81, 88, 125
Berliner Theater, 79
Berlin-Potsdam track race, 130
Bernhard, Georg, 55
Bicycle racing, 134–36
Bismarck, Prince Otto von, 118
Bismarckjugend, 143
Black Friday, 149
Blatt der Hausfrau, Das, 47
Blaue Engel, Der (*The Blue Angel*), 100, 115
"Blaue Reiter" group, 66
Bliven, Bruce, xviii
Blue Angel, The, 100, 115
"Blue-White" organization, 142
Boccioni, Umberto, 65
Books, book publishing, 43–47
Bötticher, Hans, 47
Boxing, 136–37
Boy Scouts, 139
Brancusi, Constantin, 65
Brandenburg Gate, 2, 118, 129, 133
Brandenburg woods, 4
Brecht, Arnold, xviii
Brecht, Eugen Bertolt, xiv, xviii, 11, 15, 36–37, 68, 76, 79, 82, 87–88, 90, 103, 104; and boxing, 136–37; contemplates bust, 48; in Denmark, 155; and poetry contest, 135; in Romanische Café, 42
Bredow, Hans, 57, 59
Breitenstrater, Hans, 137
Breuer, Marcel, xviii, 122, 126, 127
Briand, Aristide, 147
British (English) movies, 93, 104
Broadway (show), 87
Brückner, Wilhelm, 154
Brüning, Heinrich, xviii, 147, 153
Büchner, Georg, 108, 109, 110
Bülow, Hans von, 111
Bülow, Marie von, 111
Bülowbogen, 35
Bülowplatz, 151, 152
Buried Alive, 30
Burri, Emil, 137
Büschingplatz, 35

Cabaret, 24–27
Cabinet of Dr. Caligari, The, 95, 99
Cafés, 41–42
Campfires, 140, 142
Catholic Center party, 143
Cassirer, Paul, 62, 125
Chagall, Marc, 47, 65
Chansons, 115–16
Charlie's Aunt, 88
Chocolate Kiddies, 111
Christophe Colomb, 107
City Opera (municipal opera), 107, 112
Clair, René, 97
"Club dada," 67
Cocaine, 37

College for Gymnastics, 130
Colm, Gerhard, xviii
Cologne, 1; Exhibition (1914), 120
Columbus House, 125
Communists, Communism, 50ff., 147, 149ff. *See also* Revolution; specific persons
"Composition ZUIII" (Moholy-Nagy), 68
Constructivism, 63, 67, 68, 82–84, 144
Copenhagen, 155
Curtius, Julius, 147

Dadaism, 67, 115
Dagover, Lil, 95, 138
Dalcroze School, 113
Dame, Die, 47
Dance, 112–13; Folk, 140
Danton's Death, 109
Delaunay, Robert, 65
Denmark, 155
Depression, 147–55
Dessau. *See* Bauhaus, the
Deutsche Freischar, 143, 144
Deutsches Theater, 77, 79, 87
Deutsche Tageszeitung, 56
Deutsche Werkbund, 122
Diem, Carl, 130
Diener, Franz, 137, 138
Dietrich, Marlene, xviii, 87, 100, 103, 115–16
Dix, Otto, 67, 72
"d.j.1.11," 144, 145
Döblin, Alfred, 40
Doehring, D., 50
Dolchstosslegende, 147
Domela, Harry, 15–17
Dreigroschenoper, Die. *See Threepenny Opera, The*
Dresden, 151
Drugs, 36–37
Drums in the Night, 89
Duchamp, Marcel, 67
Dudow, Slatan, 103, 105
Dulles International Airport, 125
Duncan, Isadora, 112–13

Ebert, Friedrich, 3ff., 10, 20, 147
Eckardt, Hans von (author's father), xiii–xiv
Eckardt, Marianne von, xiv
"Eichelborn" (Feininger), 71
Eichhorn, Emil, 7
Einstein, Albert, xviii, 43, 57, 58, 119
Einstein Tower, 121
Eisenhower, Dwight D., 134
Eisenstein, Sergei, 92
Eisler, Hanns, 103, 105
Eldorado, 31
Ellington, Duke, 111–12, 114, 115
Engel (City Councilman), 154
Engel, Erich, 87, 88
Engels, Fritz, 81
England (Britain) and movies, 93, 104
Ernst, Max, 65
Erzberger, Matthias, 52, 54
Eternal Road, The, xviii
Eurythmics, 113
Everyman, 77
Expressionism, 66–67, 72 (*see also* Architecture; Theater); in dance, 113; in films, 95, 99
Expressionist Architecture, 119
Eysold, Gertrud, 86

Fabian, 24–25
"Falling in Love Again," 115
False Prince, The, 15–17
Feininger, Lyonel, 64, 68, 71, 122
Femina (night club), xiv
Fenichel, Otto, 42
Feuchtwanger, Lion, 137
Feuilletons, 41
Fichte, Johann Gottlieb, 129
Film, 91–105; pornographic, 43
Finck, Werner, 27
Fischer, Samuel, 42, 43, 111
Flechtheim, Alfred, 47, 68
Flötenkonzert von Sanssouci, Das, 96
Folk music, dancing, 140
Frankfurter Zeitung, 47
Frau Luna, 115
Frederick. *See* Friedrich
Freikörperkultur (FKK), 130–33
Freikorps, the, 7, 10, 11, 52
French, the, 129; movies, 93
French Huguenots, 22
Freud, Sigmund, 42–43, 85–86
Frey, Hermann, 115
Fridericus, 71–72
Friedrich II (Frederick the Great), 96
Friedrichstrasse, xvii, 24, 25, 36, 124
Friedrich Wilhelm IV, 117
Friends of Nature, 139
Fritsch, Willy, 97
Froelich, Carl, 96
Fürtwangler, Wilhelm, 106, 107, 109
Futurists, 62–63, 65

Gallery of Twentieth-Century Art, 125
Gangsters, 37–39
Gay, John, 88
Gay, Peter, 143
Gebühr, Otto, 96
George, Heinrich, 84–85
George, Stefan, xvi, 45
German Association of Architects, 118
Germania (paper), 111
Gewitter über Gottland, 84
Giedion, Sigfried, 121
Gilman, Sander, xix
Glasarchitektur (glass architecture), 123–24
Gloria Palast, 97
Goebbels, Paul Josef, 149, 152–53, 154
Good Soldier Schweik, The, 76, 82
Graetz, Paul, 26
Gramophone disks, 112
Gröner, General Wilhelm, 1–2
Gropius, Walter, xviii, 68, 118ff., 123, 126, 127
Grössenwahn (café), 25, 26, 66
Grosses Schauspielhaus, 24, 77, 79–81, 121
Grosz, George, xviii, 41, 61, 67, 70, 73–76
Grunewald race track, 133
Gulbransson, Olaf, 106
Gymnastics. *See* Sports

Haas, Willi, 135
Haftmann, Werner, 63
Hamsun, Knut, 43
Hanish, and Mazdaznan, 65
Hanussen, Erik Jan, 18–20
Happy End, 88
Hardenberg, Friedrich von, 139
Harnack, Adolf von, 43

Harvey, Lilian, 92, 97
Hašek, Jaroslav, 82
Hasenheide, 129
Hauptmann, Carl, 95
Hauptmann, Gerhart, 42, 43
Heckel, Erich, 64
Hegemann, Werner, 119
Heidelberg, xiv
Heilige Berg, Der, 99
Helfferich, Karl, 54
Helldorf, Count Wolf von, 154
Heller, Leo, 38–39
Hellerau, 113
Hellmer, Arthur, 84
Henie, Sonja, 137
Henschke, Alfred, 43–47
Hertz, Heinrich, 57
Hindemith, Paul, xviii, 68, 107, 108
Hindenburg, Paul von, 2, 30, 143, 147, 153
Hirschfeld, Magnus, 43, 131
Hitler, Adolf, xiv, xviii, 11, 59, 133, 147, 153, 154; and art, 76; and *Battleship Potemkin*, 92–93; and Jesse Owens, 138; and music, 107; and youth, 143, 144, 145
Hitler Youth, xv, 143, 144
Hoffman-Fölkersamb, Hermann, 139
Hohenzollerns, the, 62, 96
Hölderlin, Friedrich, 139
Holländer, Friedrich, 115
"Homform," 66
Homolka, Oskar, 83
Homosexuality, Wandervögel and, 142
Hoover, Herbert, 15, 18
Hoppegarten race track, 133
Horney, Karen, xviii, 42
Horse racing, 133, 134
Hostels, youth, 140
Housing. *See* Architecture
Huber, Fritz, 43
Hugenberg, Alfred, 49–50, 92, 96, 100
Hülsenbeck, Richard, 67
Hundekeller, 17

Igel, xvii
Iger, Artur, 10
Ihering, Herbert, 88
Im Dickicht der Städte, 87, 137
Impressionism. *See* Art; Theater
Im Westen Nichts Neues, 47
Inflation, 12–20
Institute for Sexual Science, 43
Intellectuals, 41–48
Internationale, Die, 3
International Style, 126. *See also* specific proponents
In the Thickets of the City. *See Im Dickicht der Städte*
Invalidenstrasse, 3–4
Isherwood, Christopher, 42
Italy, Italians, 62, 65

Jacobsohn, Siegfried, 47, 81
Jannings, Emil, 100, 102
Janowitz, Hans, 99
Jawlensky, Alexei von, 64
Jazz, 112, 114
Jena, 129
Jessner, Leopold, 77, 81, 84
"Jessner stairs," 81–82
Jews, 132, 147, 152–53 (*see also* specific persons); Wandervögel and, 142
Joachim, Joseph, 107
Johanson, Sigrid, 109
"Johnny," 115–16
Johnson, Alvin, xviii
Jonny Spielt Auf, 112, 114
Journals. *See* Magazines
Jungfrau von Orleans, Die, 91
Jungenschaft, xv

Kabinett des Dr. Caligari, Das (*Cabinet of Dr. Caligari*), 95, 99
Kaiser, Georg, 87, 112
Kaiser Wilhelm Gedächtniskirche, xvii
Kaiser-Wilhelm-Gesellschaft, 43
Kammerspiele, 77
Kampf um den Berg, Der, 99
Kandinsky, Wassily, xviii, 63, 64, 66, 122
Kapital, Das, 88
Kapp (Wolfgang) putsch, 11
Karlshorst race track, 133
Kästner, Erich, 24, 45
Katacombe, (cabaret), 27
Kerr, Alfred, 52, 88, 89
Kessler, Count Harry, 7–10
Kesten, Hermann, 153–55
Kestenberg, Leo, 107
Keusche Susanne, Die, 92
Kiel, 1
Kirchner, Ernst Ludwig, 64, 71
Klabund, 26, 43–47
Klee, Paul, xviii, 64, 70, 122
Kleiber, Erich, 108, 109, 110, 111
Klein, Arthur, Family, 25
Klein, Melanie, 42
Kleines Schauspielhaus, 86
Klemperer, Otto, xviii, 109
"Knock-Out Punch, The," 137–38
Köbel, Eberhard ("tusk"), xv, 144, 145
Koch, Adolf, 131–33
Kokoschka, Oskar, 64, 65–66
Kolbe, Georg, 68
Kollwitz, Käthe, 62, 70, 72–73, 74
Kongress Tanzt, Der, 97
Koralle, Die, 47
Korsch, Karl, 88
Kortner, Fritz, 83
Krauss, Werner, 95
Kreiser, Walter, 47
Kreisler, Fritz, 107
Krenek, Ernst, 112, 114
Kreutzberg, Harald, 113
Kreuz-Zeitung, 88, 109–11
Krüger, Hellmuth, 25
Kuhle Wampe, or Who Owns the World?, 103, 105
Kuka (café), 26
Künstler-Café, 26
Kuppers, Hannes, 135–36
Kurfürstendamm, 24, 25, 35, 36, 42
Kurtz, Rudolf, 99

Laban, Rudolf von, 113
Lagerfeuer, Das, 144
Lamberty, Friedrich, 140
Lambertz-Paulsen (actor), 37–38
Landsberg, Otto, 3
Langemarck, 139
Lapland, 144
Lasker-Schüler, Else, 42
League of Nations, 147
Lebens Eduards des Zweiten von England, 87

Lechter, Melchior, xvi
Lederer, Emil, xviii
Lederer, Mrs. Emil (author's mother), xvii, xviii
Lehrter Bahnhof, 69
Leipziger Platz, xiv
Leipziger Strasse, 8–10
Lenin, Nikolai, 1, 7, 53
Lenya, Lotte, xviii, 89
Lenz, Max, 82–84
Lewis, Sinclair, 42
Lieben, Robert von, 57
Liebermann, Max, 62, 65, 72, 73, 76
Liebknecht, Karl, 4ff., 52, 54, 124
Life of Edward II of England, 87
Lincke, Paul, 115
Lissitzky, El, 63, 67
Literarische Welt, Die, 135
Litfassäulen, 33
Lohmann, Commander, 92
Lohner, Fritz, 115
Lokalanzeiger, 49
Lorre, Peter, 83
Lubitsch, Ernst, 94
Ludendorff, Erich, 92
Lumière brothers, 91
Lunacharski, A. V., 92
Luxemburg, Rosa, 10, 11, 52, 54, 124

Macke, August, 64
Madame du Barry, 94
Mädchen in Uniform, 96, 103
Magazines, 47–48, 51
Major Barbara, 15
Malevich, Kasimir, 63
"Manifesto of Extreme Expressionism," 66–67
Mann, Golo, 10, 17, 153
Mann, Heinrich, 42, 43, 100
Mann, Thomas, xviii, 43
Mann ist Mann (*Man Is Man*), 88
Marc, Franz, 64
Marcks, Gerhard, 68, 122
Mariendorf, 104
Marx, Karl, 88
Marx, Wilhelm, 147
Masolle, and sound pictures, 104
Maxwell, James Clerk, 57
May Day, 151
Mayer, Carl, 99
Mazdaznan, 65
Medicine balls, tossing, 131
Mehring, Walter, 26
Meitner, Lise, 43
Mendelsohn, Erich, 68, 118, 121, 122, 125
Mendelssohn, Moses, 153
Messter, Oskar, 91, 93
Metal Workers Union, 125
Metropol (theater), 23
Meyer, Alfred Richard, 100–3
Meyerhold, Vsevolod, 82
Mihaly, Denes von, 59
Mies van der Rohe, Ludwig, xviii, 117, 118, 121, 122, 124–25, 126–27
Milhaud, Darius, 107
"Miss Nobody," 25
Moholy-Nagy, Laszlo, xviii, 14, 63–64, 68, 112, 122
Moholy-Nagy, Sibyl, 69
Molzahn, Johannes, 66–67
Mondrian, Piet, 63, 65
Money, 149. *See also* Inflation
"Moon Play" (Klee), 70
Morris, William, 122
Moscow, xvi. *See also* Communism; Communists
Mosse, House of, 49, 56. *See also* specific publications
Mosse, Rudolf, 49
Mountain-climbing films, 98, 99, 100
Movies, 91–105; pornographic, 43
Müller, Otto, 64, 68, 70
Munch, Edvard, 10, 62, 63
Munich, 145
Municipal Opera (City Opera), 107, 112
Munkepunke, 100–3
Münzenberg, Willi, 49, 50–52
Münzstrasse, 24
"Muscular Dynamism" (Boccioni), 65
Music, 106–22; folk, 140
Muthesius, Hermann, 122
"My Parrot Won't Eat No Hard Boiled Eggs," 115

Nacht gehört uns, Die, 104
Napoleon, 129
National Socialists. *See* Nazis
Nazis (National Socialists), xiv, xv, 27, 48, 50, 53–54, 147ff. (*See also* specific persons); and architecture, 127; and Olympics, 138; and youth, 144–45
Negri, Pola, 94
Neher, Carola, 88
Neher, Caspar, 11, 87, 90
Nernst, Walter, 43
New Republic, The, xviii
New School for Social Research, xviii
Newspapers, 49–56
New York, xviii, 67; stock market, 149
Niemann, Alfred, 1–2
Night life, 21–31. *See also* Underworld, The
Nipkow, Paul, 59
Nipkow wheel, 59
Nobel Prize, 48, 147
Nolde, Emil, 64, 68
Nollendorfplatz, 35, 36; Theater am, 79, 82
Norddeutsche Allgemeine Zeitung, 3
Norway, 62
Noske, Gustav, 3
Novalis, 139
Novembergruppe, 68–69, 119
Nudism, 130–133

Oersted, Hans, 57
"Olive Orchard, The" (Van Gogh), 64
Olympics (1936), 59, 130, 138
Ondra, Anny, 137
Opel, Fritz von, 134, 135
Opera. *See* Music
Oranienburg, xv
Oresteia (Aeschylus), 81
Organization Consul, 52
Orlik, Emil, 41–42, 69
Orpheum (ballroom), 70–71
Ossietzky, Carl von, 47–48
Ostrich races, 134, 135
Ottwalt, Ernst, 103
Owens, Jesse, 138

Palestrina, 107
Pallenberg, Max, 83
Papen, Franz von, and Frau von, 153
Paris, 67
Paris Mannequins, 29
Pass & Garleb, xiv, xv
Paulsen, Harald, 89
Pechstein, Max, 68

Pehnt, Wolfgang, 119
Pfitzner, Hans, 107
Philharmonic: Berlin, 107; Vienna, 110
Phoebus Film Company, 92
Photograph and Film Office, 92
"Pick Nick," 27–29
Peirrot Lunaire, 108
"Pillars of Society, The" (Grosz), 61
Piscator, Erwin, xviii, 77, 126
Planck, Max, 43
Planck, Max, Institute for the Advancement of Science, 43
Poelzig, Hans, 79, 80, 118, 119
Police, 39
Popular music, 113–16
Pornography, 94–99
Porten, Henny, 93
Post Office, 57, 59
Potsdam, 143
Potsdamer Strasse, xvii, 65
Prentzel, Curt, 137
"Primitive Man" (Munch), 63
Prostitution, 34–36
Psychoanalysis, 42–43

Quakers, 15
Querschnitt, Der, 47

Race tracks, 133–34
Radek, Karl, 53
Radio, 56–59
Rado, Sandor, 42
Raffkes, 17–18
Rapallo, Treaty of, 52, 53–54
Rathenau, Walther, 52–56, 62
"Reading Monks," 73
Reden an die deutsche Nation, 129
Reich, Charles, 139
Reich, Wilhelm, 42
Reich Film Act, 99
Reichstag, 94; fire, 88, 153
Reigen, 86–87
Reinhardt, Max, xviii, 24, 26, 77–79, 81, 84, 86, 94
Reis, Johann, 57
Reiss, Erich, 43–44
Remarque, Erich Maria, 44, 47
Renaissance Theater, 79, 84
Rentenmark, 20
Residenzkasino (Resi), 26, 31
Revolution, 1–11, 118–19
Revues, 23–24
Richard III, 81
Riefenstahl, Leni, 99, 100
Rilke, Rainer Maria, 139
Ringelnatz, Joachim, 26, 47
Rise and Fall of the City of Mahagonny, 88
Romanische Café, xvi, 41–42
Romeo and Juliet, 82, 86, 87
Rote Fahne, Die, 53, 54, 55
Roth, Joseph, 42
Rück, Fritz, 7
"Rumpelstilzchen," 42
Ruskin, John, 122
Russia(ns) (Soviet Union), 6, 7, 63, 82, 144; films, 92–93; Treaty of Rapallo, 53, 54
Rutherford, Ernest, 63

Sachs, Hanns, 42
Sackett, Frederic, 103
Sacre du Printemps, Le, 108
Sagan, Leontine, 96, 103
Saint Joan, 85, 86
Saint Joan of the Stockyards, 15, 88
Saltenburg, Heinz, 84
Salvation Army, 15, 18
Salzburg Festival, 77
Samson-Körner, Paul, 137–38
Savings Club "German Oak," 37
Saxe-Weimar-Eisenach, 121
Scala (theater), 23, 25, 26
Schacht, Horace Greeley, 20
Schall und Rauch (cabaret), 26, 77
Scharoun, Hans, 118, 126
Schaubühne, Die, 47
Scheerbart, Paul, 122, 123
Scheidemann, Philipp, 3, 5–6, 52, 54
Scherl, August, 49
Scherl papers, 49
Schiffbauerdamm. *See* Theater am Schiffbauerdamm
Schiller, J. C. F. von, 81, 85
Schiller Theater, 79
Schlemmer, Oskar, 122
Schlusnus, Heinrich, 107
Schmeling, Max, 137, 138
Schmidt-Rottluff, Karl, 64
Schnabel, Arthur, 107, 109, 111
Schnitzler, Arthur, 85–87
Schönberg, Arnold, 107ff., 111
Schrebergärten, 130
Schreker, Franz, 107
Schützendorf, Leo, 109
Schwarze Kater (cabaret), 25
Schwitters, Kurt, 67–68
Science, 43
"Seated Couple" (Müller), 70
Sebastian, Georg, 112
Sex, 43
Shaw, George Bernard, 15, 85, 86
Siemenstadt, 126, 127
Sights of New York, 104
Six-Day Bicycle Race, 134–36
Ski Wunder, 99
Skladanowsky, Emil, 91, 92
Skladanowsky, Max, 91, 92
Sladek, Maximilian, 86
Slevogt, Max, 42
Social clubs, criminal, 37–39
Social Democrats, 4ff., 94, 109. *See also* specific persons
Socialists, 147; and youth, 143
Songs. *See* Music
Soviet Union. *See* Russia(ns)
Space, Time and Architecture, 121
Spartacists, 4ff.
Speer, Albert, 127
Sports, 129–38
Sportspalast (Sports Palace), 134, 136, 137
Sprechgesang, 109
Staatliches Schauspielhaus, 81
Staatstheater, 87
Stadtbaukunst alter und neuer Zeit (periodical), 126
Stahlhelm, 50
Stam, Mart, 127
Staudinger, Hans, xviii
Steglitz High School, 139
Stehr, Hermann, 42
Stein, Adolf, 42
Steiner, Rudolf, 113
Sternberg, Josef von, 100, 102
Stijl, de, 63
Stinnes, Hugo, 16, 18
Strauss, Richard, 111, 134
Stravinsky, Igor 108

Stresemann, Gustav, 147
Stuckenschmidt, Hans Heinz, 107
Sturm, Der, 47, 64, 66–67, 69
Sturm Publishing House, 47, 123
Suprematists, 63
Szatmari, Eugen, 22–23, 31, 37–38, 107
Szeny, Martini, 30

Tagger, Theodor, 84
Tägliche Rundschau, 56
Tairov, Alexander, 82
Taliesin (Taliesin West), xvi, 121
Tauber, Richard, 107
Taut, Bruno, 118ff., 125–26
Taverne, the, xvi–xvii
Technical Manifesto of Futurist Painting, 62–63
Telegraphen Union, 49
Television, 59
Tempelhof airport, 129, 130
Tempo, 49
Teutonia sports club, 129
Thalia (theater), 79
Thälmann, Ernst, 147
Theater, 77–89. *See also* Architecture; Night life
Theater am Nollendorfplatz, 79, 82
Theater am Schiffbauerdamm, xix, 79, 88, 112
Theater des Westens, 79
Thompson, Dorothy, 42
Threepenny Opera, xiii–xiv, xvii, xix, 79, 88, 89, 90, 112; film, 103, 104
Tiller Girls, 26, 29, 30
Tillich, Paul, xviii
Toller, Ernst, 153
Touters, 34
Trenker, Luis, 98, 99, 100
Trianon (theater), 79
"Tri-Ergon," 104
Trommeln in der Nacht, 87
Tschudi, Hugo von, 62
Tucholsky, Kurt, 26, 47
Turnverein, 129
Twardowski, Hans Heinrich von, 26
Tzara, Tristan, 67

Ucicky, Gustav, 96
Uhu, 47
Ullstein, Leopold, Ullstein company, 47, 49, 55
Underworld, the, 33–39
Undset, Sigrid, 43
Unemployment, 147–49
United Theaters, 84
Universum Film A.G. (UFA), 49, 92, 97, 100; movie palace, 125
Unter den Linden, 11, 24
Urania lecture hall, 57

Valetti, Rosa, 26, 89
Valentin, Kurt, xv, xviii
Valentiner, Wilhelm, 68
Van Gogh, Vincent, 62 ,64
Varieté (vaudeville), 23, 25
Variety shows, 29
Vaudeville, 23, 25
Veidt, Conrad, 95, 97, 138
Versailles Treaty, 119, 147
Vienna, Congress of, 97
Vienna Philharmonic, 110
Villon, François, 88
Vogt, and sound pictures, 104
Völkischer Beobachter, 53–54
Volksbühne, 79, 82
Volkshaus, 120
Vorwärts, 94–99, 109
Vossische Zeitung, 49, 53, 151

Wagner, Cosima, 111
Walden, Herwarth, 47, 64–65, 66, 69
Walking race, 131
Wallenstein, 85
Walter, Bruno, 107, 109
"Wandering St. Peter," 115
Wandervögel, 130, 132, 139–43
Wannsee beach, xiv
Wartburg Festival, 129
Watergate Apartments, 125
Wauer, William, 69
Weber, Die, 81
Wedding (workers' district), 149
Wedding, outdoor, 140
Wedekind, Frank, 87
Wege zur Kraft und Schönheit, 94
Weill, Kurt, xiv, xviii, xix, 68, 88, 109, 112
Weimar Culture, 143
Weinert, Erich, 26
Weisse Hölle von Pitz Palu, Die, 98, 99
Weisse Maus (cabaret), 26
Weisse mit Schuss, 22
Weissenhof, 126–27
Welk, Ehm, 84
Weltbühne, Die, 47–48
Werfel, Franz, 44
Westens, Café des, 25
Westheim, Paul, 62
What Baedeker Won't Tell You. *See* Szatmari, Eugen
Whiteman, Paul, 112
Whither Germany?, 103, 105
Wichmannstrasse, xix
Wieck, Dorothea, 103
Wienes, Robert, 95, 99
Wigman, Mary, 113
Wilder, Billy, 42
Wildung, Fritz, 129–30, 133
Wilhelm II, Kaiser, 1ff., 62, 119
Wilhelm Tell, 81
Windhorstbunde, 143
Wintergarten (theater), 23, 25, 191
Wissell, Rudolf, 3
Wolfe, Thomas, 42
Wolff, Louise, 111
Wolff, Theodor, 56
Wolff's Telegraph Bureau, 2
"Women's Bath" (Beckman), 70
Wozzeck, 108–11
Wrestling clubs, 38, 39
Wright, Frank Lloyd, xvi, 122
Writers. *See* Intellectuals; Newspapers
Wunderlich, Frieda, xviii

Youth, 130, 132, 139–45

Zech, Paul, 33–34
Zickel, Martin, 84
Ziege, Felix, 81
Zielka, Café, 25
Zille, Heinrich, 70–72, 74, 130
Zirkus Schumann, 79
Zucker, Paul, xvi, 68
Zuckmayer, Carl, 42, 45, 87
Zuntz, Café, xvi
Zupfgeigenhansel, Der, 140
Zurich, 67
Zweig, Stefan, 43, 44
Zworykin, V. K., 59

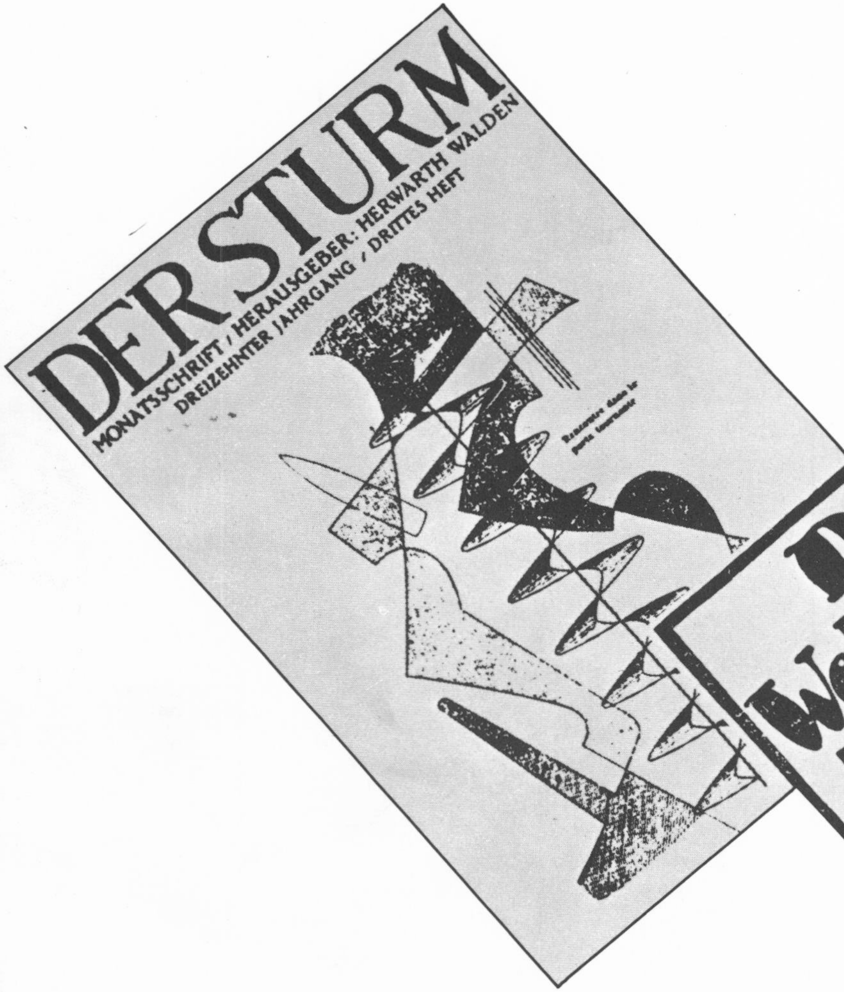

DER STURM
MONATSSCHRIFT / HERAUSGEBER: HERWARTH WALDEN
DREIZEHNTER JAHRGANG / DRITTES HEFT

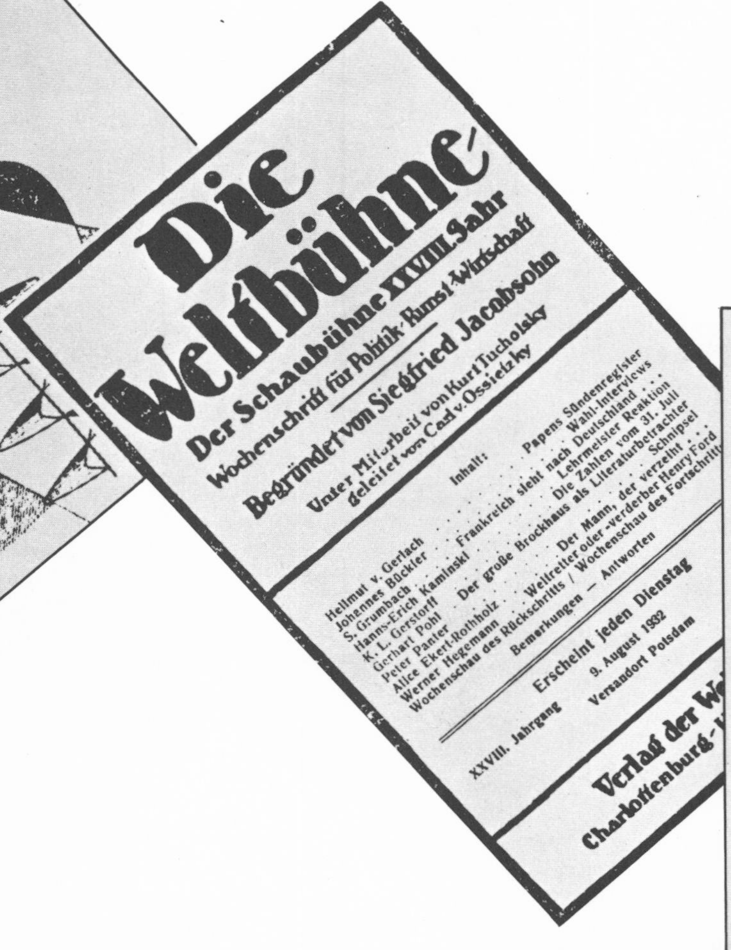

Die Weltbühne
Der Schaubühne XXVIII. Jahr
Wochenschrift für Politik · Kunst · Wirtschaft
Begründet von Siegfried Jacobsohn
Unter Mitarbeit von Kurt Tucholsky
geleitet von Carl v. Ossietzky
Inhalt:
Hellmut v. Gerlach . . . . Papens Sündenregister
Johannes Bückler . . . . . Wahl-Interviews
S. Grumbach . . . Frankreich sieht nach Deutschland . . .
Hanns-Erich Kaminski . . . . Lehrmeister Reaktion
K. L. Gerstorff . . . . . . Die Zahlen vom 31. Juli
Gerhart Pohl . . Der große Brockhaus als Literaturbetrachter
Peter Panter . . . . Schnipsel
Alice Ekert-Rothholz . . . . Der Mann, der verzeiht . . .
Werner Hegemann . . . Weltretter oder -verderber Henry Ford
Wochenschau des Rückschritts / Wochenschau des Fortschritts
Bemerkungen — Antworten
Erscheint jeden Dienstag
XXVIII. Jahrgang 9. August 1932 Versandort Potsdam
Verlag der We
Charlottenburg-

Direktion r. hausmann
Steglitz zimmermann
strasse 34
DER dada
50 Pfg.
dadadegie
hausmann · baader
3/ 3333/3333
5,0
Ach
3,14159
כשר
Jahr 1 des Weltfriedens. Avis dada
Hirsch Kupfer schwächer. Wird Deutschland verhungern? Dann muß es unterzeichnen. Fesche junge Dame, zweiundvierziger Figur für Hermann Loeb. Wenn Deutschland nicht unterzeichnet, so wird es wahrscheinlich unterzeichnen. Am Markt der Einheitswerte überwiegen die Kursrückgänge. Wenn aber Deutschland unterzeichnet, so ist es wahrscheinlich, daß es unterzeichnet um nicht zu unterzeichnen. Amorsäle. Achtuhrabendblattmitbrausendeshimmels. Von Viktorhahn. Loyd George meint, daß es möglich wäre, daß Clémenceau der Ansicht ist, daß Wilson glaubt, Deutschland müsse unterzeichnen, weil es nicht unterzeichnen nicht wird können. Infolgedessen erklärt der club dada sich für die absolute Preßfreiheit, da die Presse das Kulturinstrument ist, ohne das man nie erfahren würde, daß Deutschland endgültig nicht unterzeichnet, blos um zu unterzeichnen. (Club dada. Abt. für Preßfreiheit, soweit die guten Sitten es erlauben.)
Die neue Zeit beginnt mit dem Todesjahr des Oberdada
A d 1
Mitwirkende: Baader, Hausmann, Huelsenbeck, Tristan Tzara.

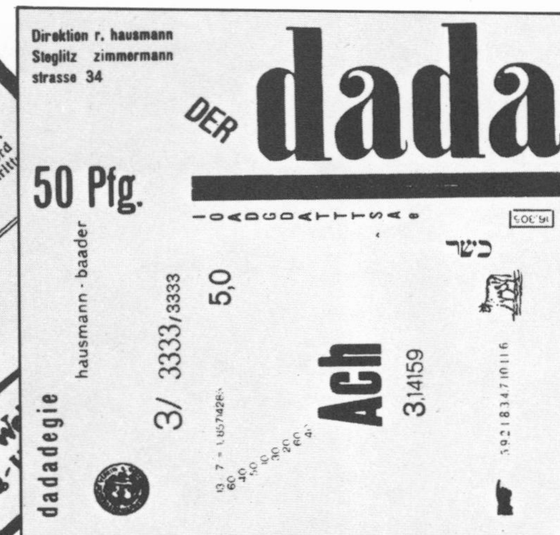

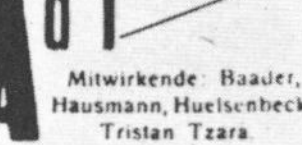